THE GIANTS OF SUMO

Angela Patmore has been a sportswriter for some thirteen years. She has written on a wide variety of subjects, and has a special interest in sports psychology. She is the author of a book on pressure in top-class sport, *Sportsmen Under Stress*, and her other books include *Leading From the Front* with Mike Gatting and *Murder in the Squash Court* with Jonah Barrington.

THE GIANTS OF SUMO

ANGELA PATMORE

Macdonald
Queen Anne Press

A QUEEN ANNE PRESS BOOK

© Angela Patmore 1990

First published in Great Britain in 1990 by
Queen Anne Press, a division of
Macdonald & Co (Publishers) Ltd
Orbit House
1 New Fetter Lane
London EC4A 1AR

A member of Maxwell Macmillan Pergamon Publishing Corporation

Jacket design – Peter Champion
Book design – Peter Champion and Ann Samuel
Cover photographs – Allsport

British Library Cataloguing in Publication Data
Patmore, Angela, *1946-*
    Giants of Sumo.
    1. Sumo
    I. Title
    796.8125

    ISBN 0-356-18120-0

Typeset by Angel Graphics, London
Printed and bound in Great Britain by The Bath Press, Bath, Avon

CONTENTS

INTRODUCTION 7

PART 1   THE FOREGROUND

RING RITES   11
RANKING THE CHAMPIONS   19
RULES AND TECHNIQUES   25

PART 2   THE PROFILES

THE GREATEST
CHIYONOFUJI   35
HOKUTOUMI   45
ONOKUNI   51

THE LARGEST
KONISHIKI   57

THE BIG FAVOURITES
AKINOSHIMA   65
ASAHIFUJI   69
HOKUTENYU   74
KOTOGAUME   79
MITOIZUMI   82
SAKAHOKO   87
TERAO   91

THE HEAVY SET: OTHER FIRST DIVISION CONTENDERS
DAIJUYAMA   97
ENAZAKURA   99
FUJINOSHIN   99
HANANOKUNI   100
HANANOUMI   101
ITAI   101
JINGAKU   104

KASUGAFUJI   104
KINOARASHI   106
KIRISHIMA   106
KITAKACHIDOKI   109
KOBOYAMA   109
KOTOFUJI   111
KOTOINAZUMA   111
KOTONISHIKI   113
KUSHIMAUMI   113
KYOKUDOZAN   116
MASURAO   116
MISUGISATO   119
OZUTSU   119
RYOGOKU   121
SASSHUNADA   121
TAGARYU   123
TAKAMISUGI   123
TAKANOFUJI   125
TAKANOHAMA   125
TOCHINOWAKA   127
TOCHITSUKASA   130
WAKASEGAWA   130

PART 3   THE BACKGROUND

THE SPORT OF GODS   133
STABLE LIFE   139
SCHEDULES AND SALARIES   147
ZEN IN THE ART OF MACHISMO MAINTENANCE   151

SUMO GLOSSARY   157
FURTHER READING   159

INTRODUCTION

In thirteen years of writing about international sport and sports psychology, sumo is the most important thing I've seen. Important, because behind each simple bout there lies a huge invisible world of spiritual powers and self-mastery.

The giants of sumo are no ordinary sportsmen. They aren't egotistical or vain. They don't cheat. They don't throw tantrums when they lose, or vaunt when they win. They are rigorously trained to behave impeccably at all times, living rather like monks in harsh stables where they are brought on by a lot of well-intentioned cruelty. Those who rise to the top of the rankings have been greatly hurt and greatly hit with a split bamboo cane called the *shinai*. The same cane is used in kendo to represent the sword. The trainees who learn by it are not only unbelievably large, but capable of strength beyond their own physical limits.

In a way, quite apart from their strange physical appearance, they are not of this world. They belong in a Buddhist temple or at a Shinto shrine. Consequently you will not find the word 'fat' anywhere in this book. Big, yes. Fat, no. To become acquainted with these men is to respect them greatly, and find them splendid and attractive in their own right. If by the time you've read their profiles you don't feel affection for sumo's giants, I've gone wrong somewhere.

It was impossible to keep you entirely up to date because while I'm writing, they're fighting, and form and rankings change very rapidly. The statistical facts are accurate at the time of going to press, with as many last-minute changes as my publishers could reasonably bear. The book could not possibly have been written without the help of my researchers and contacts in Japan. I should like to thank the following profusely:

Mr Syd Hoare, President of the British Sumo
    Association
Mr A. Shiraishi
Mr Malcolm Dennes and MD Associates, Japan
    Consultants
Mr A. Kochi, of the Japan Sumo Association
Mr A. Minehata

I should also like to acknowledge a debt to *Sumo World* magazine, with all its interview material and up-to-the-minute data on the sport, and I recommend any Western fan of sumo to take out a subscription (write to Andy Adams, Editor and Publisher, Yurakucho Denki Building, 20th floor, 1-7-1, Yuraku-cho, Chiyoda-ku, Tokyo 100). And finally, thanks to Channel 4, without whose television coverage I should never have clapped eyes on sumo in the first place. Their brave experiment in beaming the *basho* into our living rooms inspired Briton Nathan Strange, after some tuition from Syd Hoare, to become, albeit briefly, the first ranked European *rikishi* in history. May he not be the last.

Angela Patmore
Christmas 1989

PART 1

THE FOREGROUND

RING RITES

For sumo, though centuries have passed, in many ways time stands still. Some of its pageantry harks back a thousand years to a time of imperial palaces and gold-brocaded splendour, and no other sport on earth can boast such bizarre and beautiful ceremonies. The wrestlers who take part in this ancient assay of manliness, near naked and self-effacing though they are, trail clouds of glory from the gods for whom their battles were originally performed. Their sacred rites or *gishiki* cannot easily be translated into English or explained as to their 'meaning'. They refer to a harmony in the universe and a kind of human dignity (*kanroku*) of which the Japanese are very fond, and some Westerners, having once witnessed these things, become hopelessly addicted to sumo for the rest of their lives, even taking up residence in Japan so that they can continue to feast their eyes on this strange lost world.

Sumo does everything with grandeur. Even its *gyoji*, or referees, are ablaze with colour and totally respected by the combatants, unlike their counterparts in 'mortal' sports. They act as Shinto priests to purify the stadium and the *dohyo* (the fighting ring) before a tournament, and have many other solemn duties to perform, befitting men who dedicate their lives to their profession from the age of 13 or 14 (officiating in minor bouts very early in the morning). They all belong to one of two ancient houses, called Kimura and Shikimori, with slightly different flourishes of their wooden war fans or *gumbai uchiwa*. The chief referee, whatever his own name may be, is always called Kimura Shonosuke, and his second in command is always known as Shikimori Inosuke.

They have a rigid ranking system and are allocated bouts, according to their station, between fighters of equivalent seniority.

Though they are all decked out in gorgeous, heavy silk *hitatare* like those a Samurai warrior would have worn at court (complete with black court headpiece or *eboshi*), their wrist tassels and rosettes show the colours of their rank. These range from lowliest black, green and green-and-white for the junior men, up through red-and-white to vermilion for the more senior gyoji, and for the referees at the top, tassels come in purple-and-white. The head gyoji himself, who always officiates in the final bout of the day, is the only one who is allowed to wear tassels of imperial purple, and like his underlings, his gumbai is strung with the matching colour. Only the senior referees wear socks and sandals. The rest go barefoot.

There is much ceremonial attached to the gyoji's job. The head man or *tate-gyoji* is required to paint the *shikona* or fighting names of the leading combatants on big sheets of paper and flourish these to the crowds as he warbles the names in a stylized, Kabuki theatre voice. During a bout, the referee is expected to yell shrill, set cries. 'Nokotta!' means 'You're still in the ring!' 'Hakkeyoi!' means 'Keep going!' The proceedings are all directed with the aid of the war fan, which is used to signal the winner by pointing to his corner (east or west). The referee's decision is accepted unblinkingly by the wrestlers, even if it is wildly wrong. No Gatting–Shakoor Rana rows here! But the decision *may* be called in question by one of the five ringside judges, who raises his hand to call a *mono-ii* or judges' conflab on the dohyo. If

The dohyo *— a sacred place amid the crowds.*

this happens the five black-robed elders step into the ring whilst the wrestlers, and the unfortunate gyoji, await the outcome.

Since March 1969, the senior judge has had the help of a small earphone connecting him to another official watching a video replay. This is because all sumo remembers a disastrous day during that March basho when the great Taiho was 'robbed' by a wrongful decision and lost the chance of continuing his 45-bout *rensho* or winning streak. Had it not been for this blunder, he might have gone on to break the all-time record of Futabayama, which stands today (at 69). When the judges have deliberated, they announce their decision. They may either uphold the 'direction of the fan', or over-rule it, or sometimes they may call for a re-match – always popular with the audience. The poor gyoji is permitted the odd mistake, but several will prompt his demotion – or even his retirement – and the *sanyaku gyoji's* finery includes a little ceremonial sword, should he wish to disembowel himself.

The performers on the dohyo need no reminding that they have set foot in a sacred place. They know that it has been blessed in a sort of 'harvest festival' dedication ceremony, anointed with *saké* (rice wine) as a libation to the gods, and sprinkled with a lot of purifying salt. Should there ever be blood accidentally spilled on the dohyo, the combatants must immediately retire while the clay is carefully scraped and cleaned and inspected. Above the ring hangs a huge canopy built to resemble the roof of a Shinto shrine. It was once supported by four pillars decorated with bunting to represent the four seasons, but these have now been replaced, to permit a better all-round view of the platform, by four enormous tassels suspended from the canopy and coloured green for spring, red for summer, white for autumn and black for winter. Beneath the red and white tassels, on the surface of the dohyo, are baskets of salt which play an important part in one of sumo's famous rituals, the *shikiri naoshi*, discussed later. There are also cedar buckets of water standing in their own small niches at the sides of the platform, for rinsing the wrestlers' mouths.

When all is ready, around late afternoon, and the lower-rankers have completed their bouts and been bundled on and off with very little ado, an announcer or *yobidashi* in strange trousers steps onto the dohyo and knocks together a pair of traditional wooden clappers. The ring is swept with more than usual care, and all eyes turn towards the *hanamichi* – the so-called 'flower paths' leading down from the great east and west dressing rooms. The aisles still bear the name because once upon a time, when the wrestlers fought in two opposing teams ('east' and 'west' are now only nominal), they would file out with flowers in their hair: calabash blossoms on one side and hollyhock blooms on the other. The Japanese see nothing effeminate about flowers, and winning wrestlers are often festooned with bouquets.

Amid a growing hubbub in the auditorium, the first half of the top division personnel come down the hanamichi and step up on to the dohyo one by one to face the audience. (The Second Division have a similar *dohyo-iri* or ring-entering ceremony, but theirs is obviously less exciting than the procession of these *Makunouchi* or First Division men.) They are not wearing their fighting belts but brilliantly coloured, gorgeously embroidered ankle-length aprons called *kesho-mawashi*, donated by patrons and sponsors, and fringed with heavy gold braid. Some of these aprons, like one belonging to Grand Champion Chiyonofuji which is covered with pearls, are worth a small fortune and the leading fighters have a large wardrobeful to choose from.

When all the first team are on the platform, they turn towards the centre, clap their hands, raise their right arms, hitch their aprons, raise both arms, and then turn and file out the way they came. Foreign onlookers are reminded disrespectfully of the hokey-kokey, though the ritual is probably a much-truncated version of an earlier dohyo-iri intended to show that they had no concealed weapons and that they were calling the attention of the gods to their purity of body and spirit. When they have disappeared, they are replaced on the dohyo by the second half of the Makunouchi men, who go through the same strange little sequence. They then withdraw.

There is now an expectant buzz, followed by whispers, followed by thunderous clapping and cheering. Down the hanamichi comes an announcer banging his sticks, followed by a gyoji in his court finery. Behind them comes the *tsuyu harai*, a 'dewsweeper' or herald, himself a high-ranking wrestler in splendid apron, and behind him, magnificently weighed down by the 30-lb white rope belt or *tsuna* from which he derives his title, is the *Yokozuna* – the Grand Champion – himself. He is an awesome sight as he marches solemnly towards the ring. The sacred belt of his office has been plaited to drum beats by his *ichimon* stable-mates wearing white gloves so as not to besmirch its purity – it is the symbol not only of his rank, but of his connection with all things *kami* or venerated. The same rope hangs at Shinto shrines, and around the Grand Champion it is tied in accordance with strict tradition, finishing either in a huge bow or a stiff loop at the back. Beneath his tsuna the great man wears one of his own rich collection of aprons, and on top of that, dangling from the copper-cored belt, are the white lightning flashes or *gohei*, made out of paper and equally holy. The Yokozuna ascends the dohyo, followed by his *tachi-mochi* or sword-bearer, another fighter of high rank, with the Grand Champion's long ceremonial Samurai sword upright in its scabbard, a reminder of his lethal status as a martial artist.

Once in the ring, the Yokozuna squats down between his retainers, and begins a long and moving ceremony. First he slowly swings his arms above his head to describe a circle (perhaps the empty 'O' of Zen contemplation?) and then he brings his arms round and down in a great resounding clap.

He is calling the gods of Shinto to witness his purity, and to symbolize this cleanliness he rubs his palms together at arm's length, like the Samurai warrior wiping his hands with grass before a death battle. Repeating the pattern, he extends his arms outwards, showing his hands are empty and that he conceals no weapon. Then he gets up and goes to the centre of the circle, where he claps, cleans his hands again, and displays his open palms. He then spreads his feet wide, and with his left hand under his heart, he extends his right arm, flicking his right palm outwards with a graceful flourish. He repeats the gesture the other way round and then, in a movement that signifies driving evil spirits out of the dust, he raises one leg impossibly high in the air and stamps down with an almighty thud that you can hear at the back of the stadium. A tremendous roar of approval goes up, as the Grand Champion inches himself slowly upright by

wriggling his toes and heels together, his eyes fixed in a deadly gaze. The enormous *shiko* 'strong leg' stamp is repeated, to deafening applause, with alternate legs, pushing down each time on the knee with his hand, and the ritual is rounded off with a hitch of his ceremonial apron. Returning to his retainers, he then squats again, goes through his original sequence, and finally rises, bows, and goes back up the aisle with his retinue, the gyoji following behind.

The whole ceremony is difficult to 'explain', and the Japanese get very bored with Westerners seeking to give an account of what cannot be put into words. But it invokes harmony, serenity and the old laws of purity and dedication among warriors, and is almost certainly intended as a prayer to the gods to grant good fortune, good crops and good weather (sumo used to be per-formed out of doors). The Yokozuna performs the rite when he is newly appointed at the Meiji shrine, so we may assume its strong religious overtones. There are slight variations on the ritual, depen-ding on whether the Grand Champion has adopted the *Unryu* style or the *Shiranui* tradition (which is a little more emphatic). Both styles honour great fighters of the Edo period, though they probably emerged later than that. The most striking feature of both is undoubtedly the mighty shiko stamp, which requires long hours of practice and a special knowledge of balance. To the onlooker it has a strange, non-human quality, putting one in mind of an enormous heavy object tipped up on its side and then righting itself with a great crash to re-establish order. Each Grand Champion performs the ceremony in turn, and it is given the special name of the *yokozuna dohyo-iri*.

The shiko stamps are also a feature of that other strange affair, the pre-fight posturing, not normally seen in full on British television but considered vital by the Japanese in deciding the outcome of the physical fighting. The bouts of the lower-rankers have fewer symbolic refinements, but the higher the wrestler ascends up the *banzuke*, or list of rankings, the longer is his shikiri naoshi, or preliminary face-off. *Juryo* (Second Division) fighters get three minutes, and the men of the top division are permitted a full four minutes by Japanese television, with the audiences glued to every move. (Four minutes is nothing, by the way. The wrestlers were once

The gyoji *(referee) directs proceedings with a war fan.*

allowed unlimited time.) The shikiri naoshi provides the electrical storm, the psychic-charged movements and the lightning flash looks. The actual fighting is merely the thunderclap after the event.

Following some high stamping and flexing, the combatants dip into their salt baskets and fling a handful in their various styles. Then they stride (or waddle according to size) to the centre of the ring, where they squat down behind white lines, hands on knees. Orchestrated by the gyoji with his war fan, they touch their fists down on the clay and bend forward, glaring directly into each other's eyes in a way that triggers fights in the animal kingdom. They rise, still keeping a beady eye on

each other, turn, and strut back to their corners, with the occasional contemptuous slap on their belly bands. More salt is thrown, and 'power water' (*chikara-mizu*) is ladled out of a cedar bucket to rinse out their mouths. There is also 'power paper' (*chikara-gami*) for patting the lips and wiping under the armpits, though some, like Chiyonofuji and Hokutenyu, make a point of bringing their own flannels for a good rub down. Everything for cleanliness. The fighters then return to their marks to go through more crouching (*shikiri*) and staring (*niramiai*), and this is repeated anything up to five times, with feelings of tremendous affront and aggression hopefully growing at each gesture and baleful stare.

At last, the time-keeping judge sitting under the huge red tassel signals to yobidashi and gyoji that four minutes are up, and the referee calls the fighters to synchronize themselves for the release. They then fly out at each other in the *tachi-ai*, or jump-off. To appreciate the full significance of the pre-fight battle, we have only to compare these animal-like, threatening, rude and bare-faced proceedings with the strict etiquette governing every other aspect of sumo, where the gladiators are expected to keep their behaviour and feelings entirely in check. They must hide their personal emotions with mask-like efficiency. It is considered proper not only to help one's vanquished foe up off the clay, but to bow to him and avoid rubbing in one's victory by the smallest look or deed. *Sumotori* really *do* treat triumph and disaster just the same, and woe betide any man displaying pride or temper about the outcome. Bear in mind, too, that the shikiri naoshi must appear all the ruder to a Japanese, whose whole life is conducted according to strict laws of propriety and to whom even the routine behaviour of Western sportsmen must seem unthinkably obscene.

Etiquette permeates all aspects of sumo, including the presentation of prizes. The winner is signalled by the referee pointing his fan at the appropriate corner. To point at the wrestler himself would be too direct and unseemly. During the rather embarrassing handing over of cash prize money, both winner and referee crouch on their haunches. The filthy lucre is discreetly hidden in an envelope, presented not by hand, but on the back of the gyoji's fan. In return for such courtesy, the winning *rikishi* (wrestler) makes a chopping movement with the side of his hand over the envelope, signalling thanks to heaven, earth and man for their generosity. The winner of the *yusho* or tournament is presented, if not with a gift from the gods, at least with a gift from one of them: the Emperor's Cup or *Tennoshihai*, commissioned by the late Emperor Hirohito himself and made of solid silver. It comes with the grand banner of the Sumo Association, and later a life-sized portrait to hang in the roof of the Kokugikan Stadium, all amid much bowing and singing of the national anthem.

But perhaps the most moving and poignant of sumo's pageants occurs at the end of each day's programme, when a low-ranking fighter, decked out for the occasion in gingko-leaf topknot and kesho-mawashi, steps up on to the clay to perform the *yumitori-shiki* — the Ceremony of the Bow. As punters edge discreetly towards the exits, this lone wrestler in all his finery performs a display of swinging and twirling the Japanese longbow to commemorate a time when the tournament winner received such a weapon for his pains, along with 2,500 bushels of rice. The proud recipient of the original is thought to have been the fighter Ganzaemon, who was honoured at a castle basho by the warlord Oda Nobunaga. For centuries afterwards, so the story goes, the highest ranking wrestler (an *ozeki* in those days before the rank of yokozuna was officially created) received a bow, the *sekiwake* (Junior Champion) was presented with a bowstring, and the *komusubi* (Junior Champion, second grade) was given an arrow. And the ozeki in question was so pleased with his gift that he performed this little ceremony of gratitude. It may all have happened hundreds of years ago, but then sumo time is measured in thousands of years. The bottom line of the banzuke, displayed outside at every tournament, has an inscription which, roughly translated, means, 'May people flock to sumo for another thousand years, and another ten thousand years'. 'Chiyonofuji', the shikona of the principal Grand Champion, means 'Fuji of a thousand generations'. The whole sport is steeped in eternity.

RANKING THE CHAMPIONS

There are literally hundreds of wrestlers on the sumo mountain, and only those who have reached the summit are seen on Britain's television coverage. Spare a thought for the likes of Herne Bay's Nathan Strange, who battled courageously to get into the Fifth Division to join the 270-odd already there – he has now given up the sport. There are six official divisions (*Maezumo* is not a division, but simply refers to all those struggling to get on to the foothills). The sumo mountain looks like this:

THE DIVISIONS

← MAEZUMO →

The First and Second Divisions are quite separate from the others. The wrestlers in these two top echelons are known as *sekitori* – a term of respect – and they fight each day of every 15-day *basho*, or tournament. (The lower ranks only compete on seven days.) Sekitori do not do chores around the *heya* or sumo stable. They have personal servants dancing attendance on them from the lower ranks, and wear magnificent kesho-mawashi or brocaded aprons for their ring-entering formalities; these aprons are stored in special lacquered trunks, each with its owner's name on. The colourful silk mawashi you see on Channel 4's fight coverage are another little privilege of the sekitori. Lowlier ranks wear a coarse black woven belly band for their fights. There is even a different hairstyle. Whereas the meaner ranks sport a simple topknot, sekitori have their hair dressed in the famous gingko-leaf style for all formal occasions, including their bouts in a tournament. And there's another difference as well. Sekitori actually earn a living from sumo, getting a regular monthly salary. (The rest get pocket money if they're lucky.)

The Second Division, consisting of 26 fighters, is called *Juryo*, meaning 'ten coins', because that is what they used to earn. The wrestlers at this rank are also referred to as 'contenders', because they are contending to get into the top division – where they will earn considerably more. Juryo men are not quite as well off in the servants department as the top division, but they are certainly looked after. Their only task is to supervise the practice bouts of the junior ranks.

The line separating the 'haves' and 'have-nots' of sumo is called *maku*, or the curtain, which is why the Third Division is known as *Makushita*, below the curtain. There was once apparently a custom to have the high-rankers curtained off at a court tournament, though the idea of barriers in sumo is in any case prevalent. Getting from one side of this particular barrier to the other is very hard indeed. Wrestlers who do make the transition find that their lives change completely. They are suddenly addressed appreciatively as So-and-so-*zeki* – roughly the equivalent of 'sir' – instead of 'Oi you!' which is what they had grown used to in the lower ranks. They are paid, they are waited upon, and they are treated like men who have made it, instead of lads who have lagged it.

The lower-rankers beneath their dignity are an extremely courageous lot. The Third, Fourth, Fifth and Sixth Divisions face conditions rather worse than the Marines and public school fagging put together. In Makushita, the Third Division, there are about 120 wrestlers, some of them old hands on the way down, or who never quite made it through the 'curtain'. These men are apt to be very harsh indeed with the youngsters, and tales of woe include terrible good hidings and being woken at all hours to attend to seniors arriving back late from a night on the town. Beneath these Makushita men come the 200 fellows in *Sandanme*, who have less authority in the pecking order, and rather more in the way of chores, and then down we go to the real agony columns of *Jonidan*, which consists of about 280 topknotted youngsters, sweating and struggling in the practice ring, scrubbing pots and scrubbing the backs of those higher up the ladder. But even these are better off than the 70-odd poor devils in *Jonokuchi*, like Britain's Nathan Strange, who every day of their lives feel the weight of the sumo mountain on top of them. They have very little on their minds, in this lowliest division, other than 'let me out of here'.

All the wrestlers of whatever rank are divided at tournaments into 'east' and 'west', to commemorate the time when they fought as teams. 'East' is considered somewhat higher than 'west', though to judge by the pairings for each bout, nobody takes much notice which side you were originally listed on.

The First Division

Top of the heap, of course, are the familiar figures we see on our television coverage. The 38 men at present on sumo's summit are collectively known either as Maku-uchi or Makunouchi – they are *inside* the curtain (or maku). In order of importance, they are:

Yokozuna   Grand Champion

Ozeki   Great Barrier
Sekiwake   Junior Champion
Komusubi   Junior Champion, 2nd Grade
Maegashira   Senior

The three champion ranks of ozeki, sekiwake and komusubi are often referred to collectively as *sanyaku*, or 'three ranks' – usually when an assessment is being made of somebody's prospects (as in 'he can be expected to make sanyaku in the next couple of years').

To begin at the bottom, with the *maegashira*: there are between 24 and 28 of these 'seniors', divided between 'east' and 'west' and numbered maegashira 1, maegashira 2, etc. (down to maegashira 13 and maegashira 14). The quota changes, to take account of quotas further up the top-division list.

Next up on to the dohyo come the komusubi, of whom there are always two, one 'east' and one 'west'. This is a tough spot for any wrestler to maintain, because the komusubi is expected to fight one of the big names on the opening day of the tournament – an often demoralizing experience. If he can avoid going all to pieces in the rest of his bouts as well, he may eventually earn promotion to the next rank up – sekiwake, or ozeki attendant (*wake* actually means 'young'). Again, there are always two of these, and in recent years one of them always seems to have been an Izutsu stable fighting brother – either Terao or Sakahoko. The requirements for promotion are hereabouts becoming extremely exacting. To move up again, to ozeki, a wrestler would need to hold the sekiwake rank for three consecutive basho with scores of 11 wins or better, which few do.

Ozeki is very special. It used to be the highest rank of all, in the days before 'yokozuna' was officially recognized, and it means 'Great Barrier', from *seki* meaning barrier and *o-* meaning big or great. Most who reach this Great Barrier rank never break through to become yokozuna. They either continue on the second rung for the rest of their careers, or gradually slide back down again. They are protected to a certain extent from the latter. Because the post requires three good consecutive scores at sekiwake to attain it, it can only be lost if the fighter turns in two successive miserable scores of 7–8 or worse. This keeps the important Great Barrier men fairly stable on the

A yokozuna *cannot be demoted. Chiyonofuji symbolizes perfection in his sport.*

ranking list. There may be six active at one time, though this is not considered desirable. Equally, if no one were good enough to qualify, there might be no ozeki at all.

But the biggest jump of all is the one between ozeki and yokozuna. Technically it requires two consecutive yusho or tournament wins at the ozeki rank. Since the war only a handful of fighters have met this qualification. The alternative is to show what the elders consider 'equivalent success', and this has varied from time to time according to the richness of the available talent. At all events the rank of Grand Champion carries a heavy 'character' qualification because it implies great moral and spiritual rectitude.

The yokozuna is not, as we in the West understand it, a sports champion. He stands on the summit of the sumo mountain above the level of worldly clouds, and because he has conquered himself in order to achieve this dignity, he is no longer a struggling fighter like other fighters. He is not, in the strictest sense, a mere 'man' at all, for the gods have shown their approval of him by his success. He cannot therefore be demoted back to the rank and file of ordinary sumo wrestlers. If he does badly in a tournament, he must bow out gracefully, making some excuse, and return to the dohyo next time, when he is 'better'. If he keeps losing, he must retire. A losing yokozuna cannot be tolerated, because he offends not only the rank, but all that it signifies in terms of spiritual development. He cannot lose, for the same reason that a Japanese soldier cannot surrender.

The number of active yokozuna varies, like the number of ozeki, because it depends on the richness of the field. Very briefly there have been five, though there may equally be none, and in lean times men have been promoted who afterwards proved unworthy of the rank.

Apart from the yokozuna, all the wrestlers move up and down the ranks according to merit as perceived by the elders of the Japan Sumo Association, and they base their decisions on win–loss records in the tournaments. A majority of wins over losses (i.e. 8–7 or better for a sekitori in a 15-day basho) is know as kachi-koshi, and puts a fighter in line for promotion. A majority of losses over wins (7–8 or worse) is called make-koshi, and makes a wrestler liable for demotion. The higher you go, the tougher your competition, and the more demanding the requirements for

another move up the ladder. If you are, say, a middle-ranking senior and you finish a basho with a brilliant score, you may jump several rungs all at once, whereas if you are a yokozuna and do as much, you merely meet the requirements of your rank. The ideal is zensho-yusho, or 15–0, a 'perfect score'. Even the tournament winner is generally unable to manage this, though Chiyonofuji does it as often as he can.

The elders deliberate on each wrestler's performance in a tournament, and issue their new ranking list on a large board known as the banzuke, which is a thing of beauty written out in extraordinary traditional calligraphy with the high-rankers in big, bold characters and the lowlier ones writ rather smaller. The bottom fellows in the Sixth Division are in characters so tiddly that they are known as mushi-megane, 'needing a magnifying glass'. The list is photographed and published 13 days before the next tournament, and includes referees, judges and elders all similarly painted in according to rank. A banzuke appears on the page opposite and if you don't understand it you will nevertheless appreciate it as a work of art.

Of course, though it gives a wrestler's family a tremendous thrill to see their boy's name 'growing' up the billboard, they do not usually bathe in his reflected glory for long. When he gets among the higher ranks, he is generally expected to adopt a shikona or strong fighting name if he has not already done so, though a few fighters have been known to hang on to their own names regardless. Ex-Yokozuna Wajima kept his name throughout his career and ex-Yokozuna Futa-haguro ('Two Mountains') wanted to do likewise but was put under pressure to change 'Kitao' to something more poetic when he became a Grand Champion. Sekiwake Terao retains his mother's maiden name, though he too may soon come under scrutiny by the Sumo Association if he rises any higher in rank.

Often there are traditions at individual stables about naming their fighters, and some have famous shikona to confer from former champions. 'Asashio' or 'Morning Tide' is traditionally given to a promising wrestler at Takasago heya. Kasugano stable use the prefix 'Tochi-' for their men out of respect for their eighth Oyakata Tochigiyama; Sadogatake heya give their lads 'Koto-', and so on. Foreigners, of course, are all

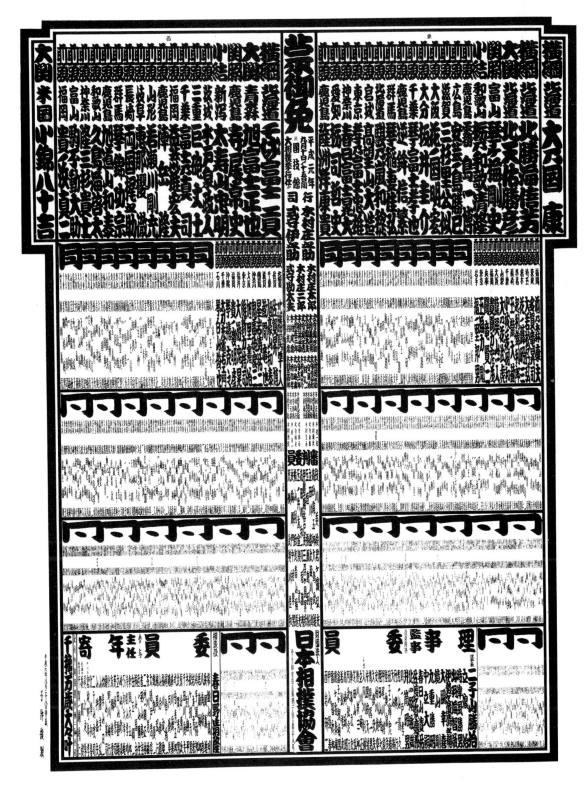

The banzuke – *a thing of beauty displays the rankings of all those taking part in a tournament. The lower the rank, the smaller the name.*

given Japanese-sounding names before they start fighting. Jesse Kuhaulua became 'Takamiyama' after a great sumo reformer, and Salevaa Atisanoe was given the name 'Konishiki', meaning 'little brocade'. Wrestlers may also change their names if they have a run of bad luck. Mitoizumi was once 'Koizumi', and Hananoumi changed his shikona several times. In any case, fighting names aren't permanent. When a wrestler retires he generally reverts to his own name or, if he becomes a stable boss, adopts a different name altogether. Pity the sumo historian trying to sort through this lot!

The following are some of the favourite choices, in case you should ever do what Nathan Strange (Hidenokuni Hajime = England's First) has done and need a shikona of your own. Separate words can be combined in different ways to produce some marvellous appellations.

gawa	river	**hana**	flower
hama	beach	**hikari**	light

inazuma	lightning	**shio**	tide
kaze	wind	**tama**	jewel, treasure
koto	lute	**tochi**	horse chestnut
mitsu	three	**umi**	sea
miya	shrine	**waka**	young
O-	great	**yama**	mountain
ryu	dragon		

And so on. The habit of using these aliases apparently came about when masterless Samurai wrestlers fought on street corners and wanted to conceal their identity, but today a fighter's shikona is sung out in a shrill voice by a yobidashi flourishing a fan, and anything less than dignified would cause amusement in the audience. For obvious reasons, Japanese place names are very popular, and ancestry is always kept in mind, but most of the names have an elemental or natural reference, linking the fighter to forces beyond his physical strength. These are no ordinary antagonists.

RULES AND TECHNIQUES

Sumo wrestlers do battle in a ring, in their case a genuine circle, delineated not by high boundary ropes but by a set of straw bales, sunk in a clay platform with just their tops sticking out like a ridge. The hard clay platform measures 18 feet square and is raised two feet above the ground, and the strange straw circle on top of it is 15 feet in diameter, with gaps to denote the compass points north, south, east and west. This arena, sacred and symbolic, is called the *dohyo*. If I as a woman were to climb up on it, the whole structure would have to be dug up and rebuilt, because women are considered to defile the battleground. (There used to be women sumo wrestlers in the bad old days, but best not to mention those if you're on a polite day out at the Kokugikan Stadium.) The dohyo is blessed in a religious ceremony before each tournament by referees dressed as Shinto priests. As far as human beings can make it, it is a 'pure' place, and salt is continually cast on its surface to reinforce this purity.

The fighters who enter this sacred arena are naked except for a ten-yard silk sash wrapped under the crotch and round and round the waist like a tyre. This is called the *mawashi*. It is decorated with starched silk tassels or *sagari*, attached to a string, which fall off during combat but which are a reminder of similar tassels hanging at Shinto shrines. The white rope belt and white paper zigzags worn by a Grand Champion during his ring-entering ceremony are similar reminders, for these men are no ordinary sportsmen. The fact that their physical battle is often over in a matter of seconds, whilst their preparations and preliminaries seemingly go on forever, shows how heavily loaded with meaning

their fights are intended to be. They are *not* just about physical strength and brutality. If the fighters are worn out by their efforts, the referees may call a *mizu-iri*, or break, to let them get their breath back. Something more is at stake than their brute force.

The basic object for each wrestler is to beat his opponent by sending him either down inside the sacred circle, or out of it altogether. If any part of his body other than the soles of his feet touches the clay, he has lost, and he can be unbalanced by pushing, pulling, twisting, smacking, tripping, throwing or ramming — in fact by any means which does not involve clenched fists (these are strictly forbidden), eye-gouging, finger-bending, throat-grabbing or interfering deliberately with his top-knot or crotch-band. Fouls are called *hansoku*, and you will see very few of them because these fighters are impeccably behaved.

Basically that's all there is to it, and there are only a couple of small exceptions to the 'touching the clay' rule, both of them probably intended to protect the losing wrestler from unnecessary injury. One is this: if you choose to carry your victim over the edge of the circle to deposit him outside, you are permitted to plant a foot over the straw ridge in so doing. The other exception occurs when you're inside the ring and you execute a move that unbalances you both. In this case you are allowed to break your fall with your hand to prevent yourself landing on top of the victim like a sack of coal. If you happen to weigh over 28 stone, like a few of the top division men, this is only fair.

Once the long preliminaries of the *shikiri naoshi* or face-off are over, the *gyoji* (referee)

Tsuppari. *Konishiki under attack from The Typhoon himself.*

signals with his fan facing the front and the two crouching combatants fly out at each other in what is known as the *tachi-ai*. The rhythm and timing of this clash is very important and the fighters must meet at the exact midpoint of the space between them. If one of them blunders, either accidentally or on purpose, this is called a *matta*, and they must start the jump-off again. Sumo is always painstaking in its fairness because it is both a sport and a sacrament, and the gods are among those watching the outcome.

The Japan Sumo Association compiles an official list of permitted winning techniques or *kimarite*, but as this list is very long, and as most of the techniques are rarely seen, it is generally sufficient to know the most common methods. (There are also various manoeuvres, not in themselves winning techniques, which are used to soften up an opponent before administering the *coup de grâce*.) Provided you know the ones below, you will enjoy sumo thoroughly and be able to work out what's going on.

There are two basic battle plans: *oshi-zumo* and *yotsu-zumo*. Oshi-zumo involves setting about your opponent by pushing and shoving. Yotsu-zumo requires that you grab hold of his person and his belt and then wrestle him out or down by means of throws, trips, driving force or any other legal method. Of course, the obvious thing to grab hold of is his silk tyre or mawashi. Many purists consider yotsu-zumo to be the 'real' sumo, and they point to Chiyonofuji as a shining exponent of the art. But it's not everyone's cup of tea, and many modern spectators like to turn on their television sets and see lightning-fast shoving and slapping attacks of the kind that have made Terao famous. When you are a young *deshi* (apprentice) in a stable, you learn pushing and shoving first, before you're allowed to graduate to the science of belt-grappling, and some wrestlers, like Konishiki and Kotogaume, can't seem to be bothered with it even later on. It's a question of taste, but Konishiki and Kotogaume have won one basho between them, and Chiyonofuji has won 29. Make of this what you will.

Oshi-zumo

Let's start like the apprentices with oshi-zumo. There are two basic methods of shoving your opponent to kingdom come. One is *oshi* itself, or pushing, and the other, more severe, way is *tsuki*, or thrusting. Thrusting and slapping are done at terrible speed, using open-handed blows to the face, chest and armpits, and this attack is called *tsuppari*. Open-handed blows to the neck (you mustn't throttle him) can be quite devastating and this is called *nodowa* or *nodowazeme*. Yokozuna Hokutoumi has a lethal line in throat thrusts, and all of these shoving attacks are designed to drive the opponent backwards. If you do this by shoving him under his armpits the attack is known as *hazu-oshi*. Hananoumi is very good at this armpit pushing.

The following are some of the more common kimarite using pushing, shoving and thrusting. All require a low centre of gravity to bring them off successfully, with great strength in the legs and hips (*ashi* and *koshi*) to drive forward whilst keeping well anchored. To withstand such an attack, a wrestler must have solidity and depth (*futokoro-ga fukai*) to make him as immovable an object as possible.

oshi-dashi

The push-out. One of the most popular of all the winning techniques. The opponent is pushed backwards until he steps out of the ring.

oshi-taoshi

The pushdown. The same as oshi-dashi only worse. The opponent is pushed out and down until he topples over backwards.

abise-taoshi

The chest lunge. Instead of using the arms to push, this technique uses the chest and body-weight to knock the victim over. Used to advantage by Asahifuji on Akinoshima on day three of the UK-televised Aki basho 1989.

tsuki-dashi

The thrust-out. Driving the opponent out of the ring using rapid open-handed smacks and thrusts.

tsuki-otoshi

The side thrust-down, or twist-down. Used to counter-attack a fighter with an inside hold. A fierce shove at his side, accompanied by a wrenching twist of your body, will often send him spinning and staggering.

tsuki-taoshi

The thrust-down. Using ferocious smacks and shoves to knock the blighter over, in or out of the ring.

hataki-komi

The dodge and slap-down. The sumo equivalent of the air shot in golf is falling victim to this, demonstrated for Channel 4 viewers by Hanano-kuni at the expense of Nankairyu. The dodger senses someone coming at him a bit too wildly and low out of the tachi-ai, steps aside and smacks him to the clay. Sometimes the victim falls forward on his face with scarcely any help at all, which is very satisfying.

okuri-dashi

The push-out from behind. Usually accomplished by dodging suddenly aside as an opponent pushes forward towards the edge. A quick shove from behind gives him a suitable send-off. (Sometimes confusingly referred to on the tele-vision commentary as the 'carry-out'.)

okuri-taoshi

The push down from behind. The same as the last one, but done in the ring. (Wrongly referred to as the 'carry-down'.)

okuri ashi

Not a winning technique and nothing to do with the push out from behind, this simply refers to a leg-over! It happens when a wrestler is in the process of winning by a lift-out (*tsuri-dashi*) and puts his leg over the straw ridge in setting down his victim. It's legal to get your leg over in this way.

Yotsu-zumo

So much for pushing and thrusting. Now we come on to the nitty-gritty of the actual wrestling techniques: holding or *yotsu-zumo*, which makes possible all sorts of throws, trips and other winning manoeuvres. Yotsu means 'four' and refers to the four-hands-on and four-leg stance. If you have a left hand inside on his mawashi, this is called *hidari-yotsu*, and if you have a right hand grip inside on his sash, it is called *migi-yotsu*. Different wrestlers have different preferences. Some, like Sakahoko, are miraculously clever at getting the most advantageous grip of all – both hands inside on the belt, or *moro-zashi*. Alternatively, you may prefer to work from an outside grip, reaching over your opponent's arm or even over his shoulder to seize his belt in *uwate-zumo*. With this *uwate* grip you might then like to execute an overarm throw (*uwate-nage*). Many of Chiyonofuji's victims fall to an outer arm throw like this. Whichever grip on the belt you choose – and what often happens is that both wrestlers get squared off with one hand inside on the belt and the other outside – you must then

use all your power and ingenuity to manoeuvre your foe by ramming, pushing, pulling, twisting, driving, throwing or tripping him until he goes out or down. As with pushing and thrusting, the impulse power is likely to come from the hips and legs rather than simply from muscular arms and shoulders, which is why sumo wrestlers look like no other fighters on earth. They have so little time to exert their strength in such a small space that they cannot afford to be top-heavy. Balance is fundamentally important: to unbalance a man is almost certainly to beat him at this game. The following are some of the most popular grappling techniques.

yori-kiri

The force-out. This is the sumo wrestler's bread-and-butter technique. Statistically most wins are by yori-kiri. Using a good belt-hold and clenching the victim firmly, the attacker drives forward and backs him out of the circle.

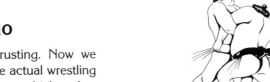

yori taoshi

The force out and down, or crush-out. Like yori-kiri but done with a more ramming style against an opponent who has lost his anchorage. The victim is sent crashing over backwards outside the ring.

uwate-nage

The outer or overarm throw. Uwate-nage uses an outer arm grip on the belt, followed by a twist of the upper body and a forward lean to send the victim sprawling.

shitate dashi nage

The same as the previous one, except that it's accomplished by means of an inside belt grip instead of an outer arm hold.

shitate-nage

The inner or underarm throw. The same idea, but using an inside-handed grip on the belt.

sukui nage

The scoop throw. This requires an inner arm grip, not on the opponent's belt, but on his body under his shoulder blade.

uwate dashi nage

The outer arm flick down, also called the pulling outer arm throw. Like uwate-nage, but using a pulling flick from the side, rather than close-quarter bending and swinging. The wrestler intending to 'pull' this off steps back with one foot, 'opening' his body out, and pulls the opponent forward. He often works his head against his victim's shoulder to turn him sideways on, for more convenient flicking.

kote-nage

The forearm throw. The outer arm version of sukui nage, achieved by pressure against the opponent's lower arm and using a twist of the upper body and a forward bend to fling him over. Sometimes called the arm-lock throw.

kubi nage

The neck throw. What you do when you're in a jam and none of the above are feasible. The opponent's head and neck are grabbed in the joint of the elbow and used to chuck him to the clay.

tottari

The arm twist. Koboyama lists this as one of his favourites. The victim's arm is seized with both hands, one on the wrist, the other round the elbow, and then pressed forward, round and down.

ashi-tori

An uncommon one, but fun. The attacker gets hold of his opponent's leg with both hands and pulls him about until he falls over. Terao used this technique to surprise Hokutenyu recently, though he finished him off by a force-out. Hananokuni also enjoys it.

tsuri-dashi

The lift-out. With a strong two-handed grip on the opponent's sash, the attacker hoists him up in the air and carries him over the straw ridge. It is considered bad form, by the way, to have your mawashi done up so loosely that when your opponent grips it, he gets hold of a pathetic little strand. In the ensuing struggle to lift you up by it, he may be seriously hampered.

tsuri-otoshi

The lift and smash down. If the victim kicks up a fuss about being carried out, he may be suddenly smashed down onto his knees instead, using the same double-handed belt grip.

hikkake

The arm grab pull-down. Used against a slapper, the counter-attacker grabs one arm and pulls the opponent off balance.

hiki-otoshi

The front pull-down. Similar to hataki-komi, except that the attacker pulls the opponent straight down without sidestepping first.

soto-gake

The outer leg trip. The attacker hooks his leg round the outside of his victim's to unbalance him.

uchi-gake

The inner leg trip. Toppling an opponent by winding one leg inside and round the back of his.

keta-guri

The leg-block and pull. Used at the tachi-ai. The attacker blocks one of his charging opponent's legs from the side and then heaves him over by his shoulder or arm.

kekaeshi

The ankle or knee kick. Similar to the above, but with a definite kick to the lower leg.

utchari

The backward arch and pivot throw, or spin throw. The most stunning of them all. When all is apparently lost, the man with his heels against the straw ridge suddenly arches backwards and twists with all his might, heaving his assailant out with him and ensuring that he either keeps one of his own feet in bounds or else touches down fractionally after his foe. Further information obtainable from Kirishima, c/o Izutsu stable, as he practically owns the patent.

1. A giant trophy for a giant triumph. Konishiki becomes only the second non-Japanese ever to win the Emperor's Cup.

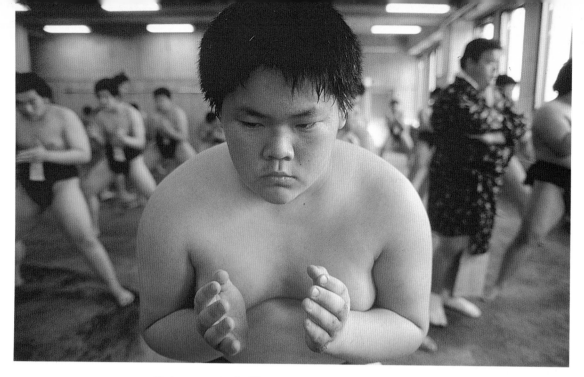

2. A new recruit. Sixty per cent do not last a year.

3. A lone wrestler performs the yumitori-shiki, *the Ceremony of the Bow.*

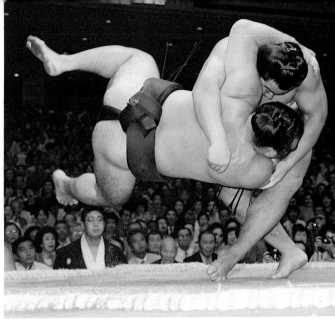

4. ABOVE Sumo is not about lard. The power and grace of Chiyonofuji dispatching an underling.

5. LEFT Terao pitching a baseball in his tinted specs. They said The Typhoon was too light to shine at sumo.

6. Top division men go through their colourful ring-entering ceremony.

7. The Wolf demonstrates one of his favourite throws: uwate-nage.

8. LEFT The mark of a star. Mitoizumi signing a handprint – The Salt Shaker hasn't always had it so good.

9. OPPOSITE Sumo is full of sacred rites. Hokutoumi casts a shower of salt.

10. ABOVE The Sea Slug having a laugh before his tragic time on the brink of promotion.

11. LEFT Destined for the summit. Little Akinoshima practising his high stamps looks set to trample some giants into the dust.

12. OPPOSITE Gentle giant Onokuni. This losing yokozuna has been in grave danger of losing his locks in the dreaded hair-cutting ceremony.

13. The Bulldog's style is to come crashing out of the tachi-ai to shove and slam. This is oshi-zumo at its best.

14. The shikiri naoshi. *The spiritual battle precedes the physical one and often determines the outcome.*

PART 2

THE PROFILES

THE GREATEST

CHIYONOFUJI

Rank: Yokozuna
Stable: Kokonoe
Weight: 125 kg (19 st 10 lb)
Height: 183 cm (6 ft)

Try a little experiment on your friends. Next time sumo is on television, ask them to take a look at Chiyonofuji as he goes through his pre-fight preliminaries and see if they notice anything peculiar. You needn't tell them who Chiyonofuji is, or that he is the second most successful yokozuna in sumo's 2,000-year history, with 29 yusho to his credit. Just say he's a Japanese sportsman, and see what they make of his shikiri naoshi (pre-fight face-off). The chances are that they will detect something rather odd, which they may not readily be able to put into words. For a start, Chiyo's face is utterly serene and composed. Sportsmen's faces do not normally look like this before they perform. Their features are contorted with tension and concern about the coming battle. Ah well, your friends may say, but then the Japanese are an inscrutable people: they never show their feelings on their faces. But if you look at the faces in the audience, or at the other rikishi trying to affect the same composure as 'The Wolf', you can see that indeed they do. They all express something, and one or two even grimace as they go through their ring rites, and express quite a lot. Not Chiyonofuji. His face is a blank, like a Noh theatre mask. One does not often see this expression, other than on meditating Buddhists,

or exotic martial artists like the monks who perform Shorinji Kempo. It is the empty 'O', the void upon which much of Zen is centred, and to Western eyes it is very strange.

Then there's another funny thing. Chiyonofuji goes through his dohyo rituals in carbon-copy fashion, never varying his routine. If you video-record a few of his bouts and play back the pre-liminaries, they are all identical. Not just similar, but precisely the same. They make up a collection of timeless ceremonies on the tape which could be spliced in and out before various bouts without anyone being able to spot the difference. The performer could almost be a hologram. His salt-flicking is always done with precisely the same flourish of his right wrist, at precisely the same height and in precisely the same direction. With a hollow slap on his mawashi or belt-band he signals his cornermen to hand up his flannel, with which he wipes his face, underarms and belly, always in that order. His high shiko stamps are always identical; his crouches are the same, with an empty glance at his opponent, like the dead-eyed look of a shark before it strikes. It is devoid of malice and yet malevolent. There is something uncanny in its degree of detachment which we sense as dangerous. The Japanese have an expression, 'ki', which is hard to translate but which means something like 'total force from total harmony'. This force is visible in the face of Chiyonofuji before he fights, and however else he may succeed, by strength, speed, skill or experience, it lies at the heart of his enduring greatness as a yokozuna, like a powerful sponsor coming to his aid. Westerners may not be able to understand sumo as well as the Japanese would like, but from

Utter serenity: Chiyonofuji before battle.

watching The Wolf we get a glimpse of the invisible world behind it, and a notion that something important is going on, which we would like to keep an eye on. At all events, sumo is evidently more than just a 'sport'.

Chiyonofuji was born Akimoto Mitsugu on 1 June 1955, the son of a fisherman, on Hokkaido, Japan's most northerly island. As a small, skinny schoolboy he was fit as a flea, and won various athletic events. He held the school record for high jump and triple jump, and was also remarkably good at the shot put and 100-metre sprint. He is no slouch on the racetrack, even now. At a sumo athletic contest a few years ago he did the 100-metre dash in 11 seconds. When you see him shoot out at the tachi-ai, you might bear this in mind.

He joined Kokonoe stable at 15, after being scouted by former Yokozuna Chiyonoyama, then master of Kokonoe. What the venerable old man thought when he looked upon weedy Akimoto's 11-stone frame is anyone's guess: the boy had his father's angular build, and in early photos you can almost make out his ribcage. But Old Chiyo undertook to train the boy, and he found him miraculously quick. So quick, in fact, that at times he almost seemed to fly. If you watch Chiyonofuji's fights carefully you will notice that he still has tremendous speed through the air. Some of his attacks are actually airborne, launching himself at an opponent with one foot off the ground and sometimes no visible means of support at all. It is as though he has unattenuated power, with no push-off point. This lightning velocity enabled him, slight as he was, to exert tremendous force against opponents twice his size, and shift them in any direction with spiteful violence. And because he was very quick mentally as well, and worked like a fanatic, he learned fast. He made his début in the Aki basho in 1970, having put on five stone in weight – most of it muscle – and having, as he says, picked things up gradually as he went along from bout to bout. He broke into the top division, Makunouchi, exactly five years later, in September 1975.

It was while Chiyo was flexing his growing biceps in the lower reaches of Makunouchi that a strong chain was forged at Kokonoe heya which was to affect him for the rest of his life. In 1977, old Chiyonoyama died. He had been the first of the great Hokkaido yokozuna; in years to come

there would be others, including Taiho, the greatest of them all, and Kitanoumi, a giant of young Chiyo's early years on the dohyo. After Old Chiyo's death, his stable had a new master, also from Hokkaido, and also a former yokozuna – Kitanofuji. His reign as Grand Champion had lasted four years, while Chiyonofuji was learning the ropes, and now he took over at Kokonoe heya, merging it with his own newly formed Izutsu stable and calling them both simply 'Kokonoe'. (The name Izutsu came to be used by another elder.) The new Kokonoe Oyakata and his young apprentice Chiyonofuji had a lot in common. Kita as a fighter had had the same build as Chiyo has now, being just one stone heavier, and accustomed to mastering a huge weight disadvantage. Both were singularly determined and quick, mentally and physically. Both were young and handsome, with just 15 years' difference between master and apprentice; both came from the same region of Japan, used to the same customs, food and dialect. And both had been introduced to sumo by old Chiyonoyama, who taught them strength of character as well as technique. (When old Chiyo had left Dewanoumi heya to set up his own stable, 'Kitanofuji' had gone with him.) Not surprisingly, a bond was formed between young Chiyo and his new oyakata which perpetuated the Hokkaido dynasty.

Also around this time, a young fellow by the name of Hoshi was discovered in Hokkaido, and taken in as a recruit. He was puggish and bashful, and very keen to learn. Chiyonofuji, now a seasoned apprentice of over eight years' experience, observed that this Hoshi worked like the dickens on the practice dohyo, even harder than he was told to work (which was very hard indeed), and recognized a kindred spirit. They became firm sparring partners, doing hour-long *sanban-geiko*, or extended shoving and struggling sessions, with the sweat pouring off them and sand in their hair. Young Hoshi admired Chiyo greatly, and if Chiyo said that he was good, he knew he must be, and would hurl himself at Chiyo even harder than before. When Hoshi eventually became Yokozuna Hokutoumi, no one was prouder or more delighted than Chiyo himself. Westerners might find this rather strange: you'd think that two rival yokozuna from the same stable would be surreptitiously out to upset one another, but Japanese society is more harmonious than this, with a very strong respect for the master-apprentice system, and a long tradition, especially in the martial arts, of knowledge handed down from spiritual father to spiritual son. It is against this background that we have to understand Hoshi's grooming at Kokonoe stable, and that all along he was intended not just as a stable-mate, but a successor to Chiyonofuji. And so the chain would continue unbroken: Chiyonoyama, Kitano-fuji, Chiyonofuji, Hokutoumi, with a Hokkaido heritage between them.

By now it was becoming apparent to Japanese sumo fans that Chiyonofuji was special, and not just because large numbers of women had started flocking after him and sending him articles of underwear through the post. He was a little like Muhammad Ali on the other side of the planet, with unfathomable strength and speed. Like Ali, he defied the usual physical laws of his sport, succeeding against burly opponents who ought on paper to have been able to demolish him easily. Like Ali, he moved effortlessly, with an almost balletic grace and balance, as though Nature herself were manoeuvring him this way and that. Asked about his genius, Ali once explained his hidden power like this:

Nature is a mysterious thing. It is just like me. Sometimes I wonder, when a big fist comes crashing by and at the last moment I just move my head the smallest bit and the punch comes so close I can feel the wind, but it misses me. How do I know at the last minute to move just enough? How do I know which way to move?

Chiyonofuji knew how to move enough, and which way to move. In January 1981, in the Hatsu basho in Tokyo, he moved into a play-off for his first yusho.

He was a lowly *sekiwake* in a sky-blue mawashi. He looked very small and very young. His enormous opponent, Kitanoumi, was a yokozuna, built like a Sherman tank and with 20 titles already to his credit. At the tachi-ai Chiyo flew out and latched hold of the front of the giant's belt with his vice-like left hand. Kitanoumi arched his back and, pulling The Wolf's arm upwards, unhooked himself free. There was a brief stand-off, with both men holding each other's arms, fishing for a better grip on the sash. Kitanoumi, with a left engaged, began to drive forward. Chiyo,

securing an outside right, now completed his circuit with an inside left, turning Kitanoumi, whose face now showed signs of alarm. Suddenly launching himself off the ground, The Wolf now stamped down and bent his knees, Kitanoumi's right hand still questing uselessly, his left wing firmly encased beneath Chiyo's right. The Wolf ducked low, pulled with his brawny right arm, and heaved Kitanoumi forward, sending him crashing down on all fours by uwate nage (an outer arm throw). Watching with his family on a television monitor, his father threw his arms in the air in triumph, venting all his son's emotions for him as Chiyo bowed quietly and took his prize money.

Tumult in Tokyo, tumult in Hokkaido. Chiyo's first Emperor's Cup; promotion to ozeki, the second-highest rank. Silver troughs of saké, van-loads of sponsors' prizes, a motorcade in the snow to his parents' home in Fukushima, Hokkaido, with Kokonoe Oyakata at his side, a filmed reunion on the doorstep of Chiyo's parents, their son grinning modestly with snow-flakes in his eyebrows. Stupid journalists thronging round him asking if the Cup felt heavier than the yokozuna he had thrown; questions about his size, his future plans, his past performances. Chiyo bore it all politely and got back to his work at the stable, throwing Hoshi about. The Wolf hadn't finished yet, by a long chalk.

In the Nagoya basho in July, he was again in contention for the Emperor's Cup. Waiting for him across the dohyo was Kitanoumi, older and wiser than before. This time there was more at stake even than the yusho. Chiyo's results as an ozeki justified promotion here, if he could beat the great man again. He was now 26, with 11 years' experience of stepping onto the clay against an average weight disadvantage of 55 pounds, or 25 kilograms. He was faster than ever, formidably strong, and balanced like a cat. But the battle would be harder than before, because Kitanoumi would not be surprised this time at the impact of his powers. The yokozuna now knew that he had to pull out all the stops, that he was fighting to hold off not just a challenger, but a usurper. And he would call on all his famous resources to crush the young man back down again.

At the tachi-ai, all Kitanoumi's experience counted for nothing as The Wolf once again dived in and seized the front of his sash with his left fist, like a wild dog chomping on a leg of lamb.

Kitanoumi struggled to prevent further damage. Chiyonofuji would not be stopped, pulling the huge foe towards him to try to complete the circuit of left and right grips. Despite Kitanoumi pushing with all his might to prevent it, Chiyo succeeded, bowed forward and spread his feet wide. This was very ominous; Kitanoumi strained and writhed, and managed to undo the right contact. The Wolf's arm was now loose, and Kitanoumi seized the opportunity to try to hurl him down, using his own inner left grip. It was no use. Chiyonofuji's weight distribution was still harmonious: he corrected his balance as quickly as if he had a spirit level in his brain.

A change of direction: now Kitanoumi's massive arms were under Chiyo's armpits, trying forcibly to undo the left grip as well, arching his own waist out of the young ozeki's reach. But The Wolf had by now manoeuvred his prey so close to the rope that Kitanoumi's right heel hovered dangerously over the edge, within inches of disaster. What followed took the yokozuna completely by surprise. Regaining a right outer arm grip, The Wolf now pulled his left cleanly away. He was not going for the force-out, but a throw. He yanked Kitanoumi sharply. The giant did not go down, but went racing forward, unable to stop his momentum, his left arm hooked inoffensively round Chiyo's shoulder for support, his face full of horror as The Wolf forced him sideways over the rope. Kitanoumi went jumping down into the audience. Chiyonofuji had not just beaten but supplanted him.

With his second yusho, Chiyonofuji went hurtling through the Great Barrier without having much time to think about it. (This is always just as well.) He was promoted to yokozuna from sekiwake in a single year. As he processed to the Meiji shrine with his attendants to perform his sacred dohyo-iri, or ring-entering ceremony, 'experts' were already predicting that he was much too lightweight for the job. One of the lightest yokozuna in history, they said, would not last long. But amid the excited crowds around the shrine stood Chiyo's father, his head bowed in prayer. He was asking the gods to make his son a worthy Grand Champion, as indeed they did.

However, it wasn't going to be easy. In September, though Chiyo's spirit was strong, his fitness gave out. His Achilles' heel had always been injury: he was vulnerable because of the strain on his whole physique of grappling with monstrous opponents, and a weak left shoulder was to plague him for the rest of his career. Under continual stress from throwing down giants by uwate nage in particular, this shoulder would come out of its socket, sometimes for long periods, causing great pain every time he moved. In the autumn of 1981, just as he was starting out as a yokozuna, Chiyo was hurt. It couldn't have happened at a worse time, because now the experts would say, 'You see – the tsuna belt was too heavy for the little fellow, just as we said. He's not going to make it.' Chiyo simply couldn't afford this lapse from grace so soon after his promotion. The rank of Grand Champion is supposed to transform a man, so that he fights not just for himself or his stable but for higher things. The yokozuna's white rope belt gives him responsibilities far beyond the calling of a Western champion, to win consistently, to honour the gods, to set an example, to excel himself. He wasn't allowed to be humanly fallible.

Chiyo shut himself away at Kokonoe heya. He bench-pressed, he grappled with hefty stable-mates, fighting to overcome his own physical pain before he could fight anybody else. He made up his mind that nobody was going to cut off his topknot for many a long year to come. The result of all this was quite startling. Far from laying Chiyonofuji low, the injury seemed to drive him to strengthen himself even further. It put him in a very clear frame of mind, and in his 'comeback' basho, the Kyushu in November, he demonstrated his fitness by taking the Emperor's Cup for the third time in a year. As he told Channel 4 some time afterwards, 'My second basho as a yokozuna, making a comeback after an injury, I won the yusho. That victory was the foundation on which I built all these years as a yokozuna.' Not only this, but he was to make the Kyushu his regular 'lucky' tournament until 1989, winning there time and again.

For a while, there was no stopping him. He seized the Cup no less than four times in 1982, winning the November basho as a sort of testimonial. He had close friends in Kyushu and stayed whenever he could, regarding the place as his home from home. The following year he married a Kyushu model, Kumiko, taking his ninth yusho at the tournament there to celebrate. Behind the smiles of success, though, Chiyo was once again nursing his weak shoulder, trying to knock it into shape by fearsome practice routines. The pain of his various injuries began to seep out on to the dohyo and affect his form, and he went into a mental and physical slump. He was paying a very high price for being a yokozuna, higher than his contemporaries. One of these was Yokozuna Takanosato, promoted in 1983, who had worked out a strategem to keep Chiyo from getting his left hand on the belt. It turned out at the time that The Wolf was severely hindered by this ruse, and Takanosato began to beat him with surprising regularity. Not only that: other opponents were beginning to sniff the air and smell blood belonging to their pack leader. He was losing his invincibility. Journalists, always keen for a change of scenery, were suggesting politely that Chiyo had had a good run, but was now pushing 30. Best that he should do the decent thing and retire, like Jesse Kuhaulua (Takamiyama), who was just then having his topknot removed after a great career. There were plenty of strapping young oxen ready to take over: one of these was Konishiki. Another was Onokuni. The fashion for vast rikishi was back with a vengeance, if it had ever been away. The little fellow had been a very good Grand Champion, but you can't turn back the clock, or argue with nature. By the November tournament of 1984, he hadn't won a single basho. He was finished, and that was that.

Kokonoe Oyakata did not think so. He had begun to wear gold-rimmed spectacles to correct his short-sightedness, and watched Chiyo studiously with his bottom lip sticking out, deliberating. Under his guidance, The Wolf's sumo had evolved from an array of inspired winning throws to a more methodical, forward-forcing style, making ground before bringing the throws off. It left him more room to manoeuvre and more margin for error. Then there was Chiyo's number one sparring partner, Hoshi, now a sekiwake, keen to get back to their sanban-geiko, his face permanently crumpled from the strain. Hoshi knew beyond doubt that Chiyo wasn't finished. Indeed, from the way The Wolf still flung him against the walls, he suspected that he had only just started. Nobody at Kokonoe heya was surprised to see Chiyo win 'his' Kyushu basho at the end of 1984, after five tournaments away. They looked forward to his second coming in

1985, and to the sound of pressmen eating their hats. Besides, as Chiyo says, 'I hate losing.'

Chiyonofuji's strength and weight had been upgraded out of all recognition by weight-training. He was one of the new generation of iron-pumping rikishi who had gone beyond bulking up at the chanko stew pot and relied on muscle and speed rather than pear-shaped poundage. His appearance around this time is described by American photographer Joel Sackett, whose pictures were assembled in a fascinating book called Rikishi, published in the US and Japan. Sackett was introduced to Chiyo in a coffee shop in Osaka. The Wolf hardly looked up from his game of 'Space Invaders', but the photographer noted: 'Chiyonofuji was wearing a loose yukata. From a few feet away I could see the definition of his arms, chest and legs. I recall observing that even his toes looked carved from stone.' In 1985 this man of stone was once again in prime condition. By September his oyakata was telling reporters that he was in better shape than he had ever been in his whole career. He was now around 122 kilograms (a little over 19 stone). His midriff had filled out, his weight distribution was perfect for his calling, his strength and force (not quite the same thing) were at full throttle. He was once again as fit as a flea, and began to fly through the air at people as he had done in 1981. He had learned from his clashes with Takanosato, and sealed small chinks in his yotsu-zumo armour.

There have been many analyses of Chiyo's style of belt sumo (he isn't a great tsuppari fan, not needing to resort to hitting people). In the early 1980s he earned a reputation for seizing the front of his opponent's sash with his left hand and stuffing him out by yori-kiri. Sumotori hardly had time to wonder about his abilities. He was equally renowned for a left outer arm grip from which to launch one of his attacks. He liked uwate nage — the outer arm throw — and a variation of this, with a left outside grip swiftly followed by a right wrench behind the opponent's neck, sending him stumbling forward. Crucial to Chiyo's style, the experts have said, is the left hand grip — referred to on the Channel 4 commentary as his 'death grip'. But with the years Chiyo has polished and honed his attack like a Samurai sword until he can kill with both edges. He no longer relies so heavily on his left wing, or even on his famous blitzing. Many of his victories these days are by finesse and timing as much as by force, though uwate nage still features heavily in his repertoire. Technical generalizations are only as good as the people who make them, and all that can be safely said of Chiyonofuji is that he can adapt himself immediately to any physical proposition set to him on the dohyo, and respond with a closing move. His force is on both wings, down or up, forward or backward. He can win with his left arm, his right arm, or both together, inside or outside or in any combination, by force-outs, push-outs, belt throws, beltless throws, and trips. He can leap, lunge or lift, carrying huge rivals calmly across the ring and depositing them in the audience or toppling them over backwards by flying in their faces. He wins by tsuki-otoshi against an opponent who happens to have an inner arm grip, twisting and thrusting downwards, and he is mighty at pulling an opponent in against him by an outside grip and then wrenching him off balance and down. But simply watch his bouts on film, or replay them over and over, and the individual techniques become blurred into irrelevance. What we see is a spectacle of predatory power. Like a shark thrashing in the water, there are very few physical moves he cannot make to subdue his prey and gobble it down with dead-eyed indifference. To analyse them individually is rather quaint, a hobby for the technically minded, like collecting statistics and demonstrating that they prove something or other. Chiyonofuji does whatever is technically necessary to beat people, and if he does not know on the dohyo what it is, he will go away and work something out. Everything else is beside the point.

The new Kokugikan Stadium opened for the January basho in 1985, and The Wolf won it. He was to keep up this habit of winning all the basho at the new sumo centre until January 1987, adding substantially to his haul of yusho. He won there again in May, and again in September, where at the Aki basho he took his 13th title with his third perfect score or zensho-yusho, 15–0. His latest challengers, Onokuni, Kitao and Konishiki, were 'shucked' aside and Chiyo was now heading fairly fast up the list of all-time winners, tying Wajima in third place for the highest number of yusho, on 14, with a back-to-back victory at the Kyushu in November and then surging ahead in 1986 to take his 15th. Not that he couldn't be beaten.

Hokutenyu reserved his best performances for Chiyo and was always a problem; Hananoumi could upset him, and so could assorted others. But before they could begin preening themselves, Chiyonofuji would come at them from a different angle, heave them over and reassert his dominance. No one held a winning record against him except Takanosato, and he retired in 1986.

When The Wolf was injured, as he was in March 1986, he had an assistant willing to 'deputize' for him: Hoshi, now vying for a place on sumo's second-highest rank, and taking the Haru basho himself. Otherwise Chiyo could manage nicely, dispensing with Kitao (promoted to yokozuna that year on the strength of two runner-up performances) to take the May basho 13–2, and storming through the rest of the year with the Emperor's Cup permanently in a two-handed grip. By the autumn, Chiyo had become the monarch of the dohyo and an international celebrity. Under the supervision of Dewanoumi Oyakata the sumo bandwagon rolled out to Europe in the autumn, with The Wolf performing his ring-entering ceremony in front of Premier Chirac at Paris City Hall, and winning a token basho before roaring French fans. He was now beyond question the most popular star in sumo, dominating his sport as only the greatest champions of history have done. He rounded off the year by winning as usual in Kyushu and looked set to continue his reign in 1987 without too many disturbances.

But fate has a way of balancing extremes, and although Chiyo began by taking the Hatsu basho in January (his 20th yusho), there followed another bleak period of injury and exhaustion. Hoshi took over the stable's yusho-winning responsibility in March, and was promoted to yokozuna after a runner-up performance in the May basho against Onokuni. Kokonoe heya now had two Grand Champions, with young Hoshi now known as Hokutoumi, and Chiyonofuji, despite a painful shoulder, showed him how to perform the dohyo-iri and rejoiced louder than anyone else at his friend's achievement. But once again a cloud had descended over The Wolf's future. Once again comments were made that he was in decline and that, great as he was, he couldn't go on forever. Some said that perhaps he was conserving his energies to let his stable-mate shine; others that at the ripe old age of 32 he didn't appear to have much energy left. At that time of life, most sumotori were thinking about a coaching position or owning a chanko parlour. The Wolf responded as he always had, by a crushing display of his dominance. In the Nagoya basho in July he hoisted the new 6 ft 6 in Yokozuna Futahaguro (formerly Kitao) high in the air, as though giving a child a 'flying angel', and dumped him over the rope for yet another yusho.

In September, as seen on British television, Chiyo's right-hand man Hokutoumi had to deputize for him again and take the Cup; The Wolf had put his back out throwing down Asahifuji on day ten and had to withdraw. But it didn't stop him taking his 22nd yusho at Kyushu two months later, with his fourth perfect score of 15–0. By now Chiyo was used to challengers who were going to knock him off his perch, including Konishiki, who had given him a buffeting. They didn't bother him particularly, except for one sly and slippery fellow from Oshima heya who seemed mighty determined to get hold of him. Asahifuji emerged in 1988 as Chiyo's most dangerous foe. He was beginning to shadow Chiyo at tournaments, keeping pace with his scoreline and often ending up in contention for the title. The fact that 'The Slug' was an ozeki, tipped for imminent promotion, and that he was particularly tough and crafty, gave The Wolf something to think about. In January 1988, in the Hatsu basho in Tokyo, Chiyo lost to him on *senshuraku* (the final day) to finish tied third on 12–3. This was not a small loss like the others, a mere blemish on his win–loss record that could easily be wiped away. It was a real and visible thrashing, for Chiyo had been muscled out under protest by an adversary he simply couldn't get a grip on.

The Wolf did not win the March basho either, sitting it out with a strained shoulder. Onokuni, now a yokozuna, hugged the trophy to his massive belly as Chiyonofuji was forced to rest up and survey his past achievements. He was coming up to his 33rd birthday, his eighth year as a yokozuna, his 18th on the dohyo, all of them fighting out from underneath massive and ever-growing giants. Nowadays there were other things he liked to do, apart from punishing himself with weights and gruelling *keiko* (training). He was now a family man and naturally wanted to spend time watching his children grow up, like other fathers. They only grow up once, and then you've

missed it, and Chiyo is passionately fond of his children. He likes to be quiet and private, away from the hurly-burly, playing Mah-Jong, or reading. He has a large number of books for a rikishi, and enjoys poetry, among other things. The noise level at a basho rises to almost pathological screaming and yelling by the last day's bouts, and Chiyo can only stand so much of this racket before he feels inclined to get out on a golf course somewhere and follow a small white warty ball. On such occasions he can relax and unbend slightly, wearing Western clothes and having a laugh. In the early part of 1988 he was tired and his shoulder was painful. His successor on the dohyo, Hokutoumi, had established himself. Perhaps the time had come to bow out.

Chiyo thought about his career, his collection of 22 yusho, his cups and awards and prizes; his wardrobe of kesho-mawashi, including a priceless one covered in pearls; his sponsors' presents and free supplies of everything from petrol to mushrooms; his trophies hanging on the wall, the snarling stuffed wolf's head someone had presented him with (he had been given his nickname after watching a 'Lone Wolf' film and he rather liked it); and of course the old bank balance was fitter than he was, with plenty of noughts on the end. It wasn't bad for a life's work. But it was strange to consider that in spite of all his titles and trophies, he hadn't one single all-time record of his own; not one. Taiho and Kitanoumi had won more yusho; Taiho and Futabayama and others had won far more consecutive bouts; Oshio, who wasn't even a yokozuna, held the record for most career bout victories. Chiyo simply wasn't up there on the rolls of honour at all, except that he had equalled the achievement of Taiho and Kitanoumi in winning five out of the six basho in a single year (in 1986). There was nothing that he alone had done, nothing to go down in history as a demonstration of his efforts as a yokozuna and his thousands of hours of pushing himself beyond his physical limits. Not that it mattered really; he is not a man who likes setting himself impossible targets. He takes each bout as it comes, and each opponent on his merits. But there it was all the same: not one miserable record to his name.

It was while Chiyonofuji was contemplating these things that the Natsu basho got under way in Tokyo. Chiyo started out healthily enough, but his opponent on day six was one of these young challengers, an inoffensive-looking lad called Kotogaume ('The Plum'), who could normally be relied upon to fall forward onto the clay if you shoved the back of his neck. However on day six this harmless dumpling, this push-over, suddenly reared up at The Wolf and dumped him for his first loss. It seemed The Wolf was now to be beaten by young 'Plums'. Where would it all end? Kotogaume a serious threat, Asahifuji outwrestling him, Hokutenyu outfacing him, Onokuni and Konishiki waddling to glory: this would not do. If The Wolf did not reassert himself now, he was about to go down under a pack ravenous to take over the leadership, and he would not get up again.

Chiyonofuji did not lose another bout in the 1988 May basho. He seized the rest of his opponents one by one and forced or flung them out of his sight. Asahifuji was wrestled to the edge and then leapt at, full force, in one of Chiyo's special flying attacks. 'The Slug' could not have been more nonplussed if a kamikaze pilot had suddenly swooped at him out of the blue. Chiyo went on to take his 23rd yusho with a 14–1 scoreline and set out on a winning bender the likes of which sumo has rarely seen. Besides, he now had another spur to motivate him: his faithful friend Hokutoumi lay seriously injured in hospital after a training accident before his final bout.

The Wolf swept through the Nagoya basho in July without a single loss, beating The Plum after a disputed call, and over-powering Asahifuji, for his fifth zensho-yusho. The Aki basho in September may have been covered by Channel 4, but it was blanketed by Chiyonofuji. Over went Mitoizumi with a dismissive inner arm flick (shitate-nage). Out went Ryogoku, Tochinowaka and Enazakura by yori-kiri. The Plum perished in seconds by uwate dashi nage (pulling outer arm throw). Akinoshima, in his first fight with The Wolf, was seen off by another inner arm throw. Sakahoko, a clever adversary quite capable of beating The Wolf, put him to the trouble of a soto gake (leg trip), to give Chiyo his 31st win in a row.

He was now running amok. Asashio (now retired from sumo) was dismantled by uwate-nage and Kirishima outmuscled by a force-out, to bring The Wolf the third-longest bout-winning streak of the Showa era (post 1926), with more to come. Could he catch the legendary Taiho on 45?

Or perhaps even Futabayama's 69? His day ten opponent, Hananoumi, gave Chiyo an irksome time and he was glad to get rid of him by a force-out. Then Konishiki, lame in one knee, smacked The Wolf about the face but succumbed to the same fate. Chiyonofuji was now on 35 straight wins, which was very exciting for everybody. The cameras turned towards The Wolf as he waited to step up for his next bout: his expression was as deadpan as ever. Putting a spoke in Terao's tsuppari attack with a left clench on the belt, Chiyo emptied him on the clay by uwate-nage. After 12 days he stood unbeaten, possibly unbeatable, with 36 straight victories. Hokutenyu, after a silly mistake, provided victim number 37. Now only two men could prevent another Wolf whistle through the Aki basho: the first being Asahifuji.

The Slug could stop him, certainly. He was still in with a chance of taking the title and he looked extremely keen to hand The Wolf another good hiding like the one in January 1988. Chiyonofuji got off his ringside cushion with great nonchalance as though about to have a cup of tea. Unable to secure his left-handed 'death grip', so crucial to his style according to earlier commentators, The Wolf simply flipped Asahifuji over by sukui nage – the beltless scoop throw – to clinch his 25th yusho a day early, and in so doing pass Kitanoumi's tally of 24 titles to stand in second place behind Taiho on the all-time Cup-winners' list. Another victory over Onokuni on the final day would bring his *rensho*, or bout-winning streak, to 39 as well, just six short of Taiho's second-place modern record there. Suddenly Chiyonofuji was up among the historic figures. And sure enough, he forced out 'The Giant Panda' on senshuraku to give him yet another 15–0 clean sweep, his second zensho-yusho in a row and his sixth altogether.

It was an astonishing achievement for a man of 33 – the oldest fighter in the top division and, apart from Terao and Kyokudozan, the lightest. He had proved a lot of people wrong and obliged them to revise their theories of success on the dohyo, and in the final tournament of the year, the Kyushu, he went on to extend his domination of that basho and his rensho, or winning streak, to 53 consecutive bouts. It was enough to overtake Taiho's 45 and stand second only to Futabayama on the modern record list and fifth in all of sumo's history. But then suddenly, having clinched his

26th title on day 14, he collapsed against Onokuni and fizzled out of contention for the January 1989 yusho (which was won by the recuperating Hokutoumi). Had he beaten The Panda on senshuraku in November, he would have been within striking distance of Futabayama's 69 consecutive wins. It was the first time Chiyo had ever run out of steam approaching an invisible barrier, and he looked unsettled. Interviewed later by Channel 4, he seemed fairly cheerful about his run having ended at Kyushu. If it had continued into the next basho, 'Imagine the pressure,' he said, grinning with relief. In the Hatsu basho in January he was beaten by Hokutenyu and Asahifuji and up-ended altogether by Terao and Akinoshima (who now looks a fairly formidable challenger).

The Old Man was finished again. By what miracle he managed to power his way to yusho number 27 in the Haru basho in March, standing undefeated on day 14, nobody knew, least of all his opponent Onokuni. But whatever it was it deserted him that day, because in flinging down the 33-stone Panda he heard an ominous crack. His left shoulder, which he had worked so hard to strengthen for so many years, had come out of its socket again (for the 11th time) and as Chiyo stood up there was a searing pain across his back and down his arm. Anyone unfamiliar with sumo's rigid laws of decorum would have been slightly shocked at the spectacle, on senshuraku, of Chiyonofuji as winner of the yusho being presented to a seemingly endless sequence of sponsors and dignitaries, bowing politely but with his left arm taped across his chest, in mortal agony. Pressmen eager to hear about the damage asked if this meant retirement. With incredible self-mastery the Grand Champion told them that no, he would not be retiring just yet, and no, it didn't hurt if he didn't move. He would be back in the thick of things very shortly. Privately he felt that this time they were right: he'd have to retire. His last-day opponent, Asahifuji, had received a walk-over. The Wolf could hardly get into the ring, let alone fight.

The injury was so serious that it put him out of the May basho, kept in the Kokonoe 'family' by Hokutoumi, who was now becoming a yokozuna of some stature in his own right. Then on 12 June, just a few days after Chiyonofuji's 34th birthday, another injury struck, one which hurt him deeply whether he moved or not. The family woke up to find Chiyo's youngest child, Ai, dead in her cot. *Ai* means 'love'. She was just three-and-a-half months old, and her father still dreams about her. He is so fanatically fond of his children that he has defied sumo's strict rules proscribing females near the dohyo or the Tennoshihai (trophy), and has had each of his children, including his daughters, pose with him as he sat holding the Emperor's Cup. Ai had been the last to pose, supported by her father's good arm. A small, private memorial service was held for baby Ai in a Tokyo temple. Chiyo and Kumiko had two little daughters left, and a son.

From this double disaster no one really expected The Wolf to regain his ascendancy very quickly. They were wrong. In the July basho, slightly favouring his healthy shoulder and looking far from his usual harmonious self, Chiyo managed a 12–3 scoreline, good enough in this fairly dreary tournament to qualify for a play-off with Hokutoumi. The Wolf had been upset by Mitoizumi, by a brilliant display from Akinoshima, and by a defiant and ruthless Hokutenyu on senshuraku, and his play-off bout with his stablemate and fellow yokozuna was the first of its kind in sumo history. From the shikiri naoshi on, Chiyonofuji never looked like losing. Whatever his private feelings about his family, his sparring partner or anything else, Chiyo's mind on the dohyo is like the still point of the turning world. Empty of either friendship or malice, The Wolf took Hokutoumi by an inner left grip on the sash and, forestalling a tsuppari attack, yanked him over by uwate dashi nage – an outer arm pull-down.

It was Chiyo's 28th yusho, and in September he edged his tally nearer to Taiho's all-time best of 32 Cups with his 29th, winning it with his seventh perfect score. 'Where's my opposition?' he wondered aloud (Konishiki was to answer the challenge in the November tournament). No one had really looked like beating him. Misugisato, who had had him on the rope, was simply lifted in the air and shaken backwards and forwards before being severely dealt with back in the middle of the ring. The Sumo Association offered to make Chiyo a one-generation elder (like Taiho and Kitanoumi) in recognition of his achievements. The Wolf thanked them for the honour but declined. He was a bit busy just now to think about becoming an Oyakata.

In the Kyushu basho in November, the tables having been turned on him by Konishiki, Chiyo finished runner-up in the tournament he had owned since 1981. He said afterwards that he had been suffering from a fever, but his 13–2 scoreline brought him within 20 winning bouts of reaching the magic 1,000 career victories. No sumotori in history has ever assembled 1,000: the closest was former Komusubi Oshio's career tally of 964, but Chiyo overtook that figure in September. Whatever happens now, he has at least one all-time record to his credit. By the time you read this, he will probably have overhauled his fellow Grand Champion Taiho to take the tournament-tally record as well, and if he hasn't he will, unless somebody stops him with a Sam missile.

He is now entering his ninth year as a yokozuna and though it is not quite true, as Channel 4's commentary has stated, that he is the longest-serving Grand Champion, he is certainly one of the very greatest. Others have served longer, but done less. Only Taiho, in recent history, who himself reigned for a decade, has packed more successes into the record books, and Chiyo is now closing fast even on him. British audiences, who have been introduced to sumo recently by Channel 4's brave experiment in television sports coverage, are indeed privileged to see one of its all-time leading exponents at the summit of his powers, yet without the affectation, conceit or gamesmanship so commonly associated with success in Western sport. Let us hope he has avoided having his topknot cut off before the Japan Festival of 1991. If it is still attached to his head, we shall be able to see him in action at the Royal Albert Hall, as well as roaming the streets as a Japanese tourist. The great man is looking forward to that.

HOKUTOUMI

Rank: Yokozuna
Stable: Kokonoe
Weight: 145 kg (22 st 10 lb)
Height: 181 cm (5 ft 11 ¼ in)

Hoshi Nobuyoshi – 'Hoshi' became his original shikona – was born under an auspicious star in a town called Hiro on Japan's northernmost island. This island, Hokkaido, has been a sort of sumo greenhouse over the years, producing some of the greatest names in the sport, including Taiho and Kitanoumi. Hoshi came to life in what the Japanese call Showa 33 – 1963. It has proved such a good vintage for modern sumo wrestlers that the '1963 Boys' are known collectively by a special name: *Sanpachi-gumi*. They include Kotogaume, Terao, Konishiki and Takanofuji as well as Hoshi himself, whose own birthday was 22 June.

Also growing up in Hokkaido at the time were two other boys he would later get to grips with: chunky Chiba Katsuhiko and skinny Akimoto Mitsugu. The former, as Ozeki Hokutenyu, would give him a pasting on the dohyo whenever he could; the latter, as Yokozuna Chiyonofuji, would become an inspiration, a mentor and a friend. Eight years Hoshi's senior, Chiyo has known the young 'Bulldog' since he was a bruiser of 14, talented at judo but desperate to get into sumo and too young actually to join the stable that had his name down already, for someone there had spotted his potential. For a year this very dedicated and determined Nobuyoshi boy did chores, finished his schooling and waited with bated breath to get into the practice area and start throwing people about, as he did at judo. He was very serious about it, despite his pug-faced cheeky grin, for he had been signed by one of the top stables, the same as Chiyo's, and he meant to get cracking as soon as possible.

Kokonoe heya was special for all kinds of reasons, and it had strong links with Hoshi's birthplace, Hokkaido. The great old master of Kokonoe, who had scouted Chiyonofuji and trained him initially, was former Yokozuna Chiyonoyama (from whom Chiyo gets his shikona). This Chiyo the elder was himself from

The ferocity of The Bulldog. This is the second most successful fighter in sumo after Chiyonofuji, his stable-mate and ally.

Hokkaido, and just as Hoshi was getting into sumo, old Chiyo died. The man who took over his stable and merged it with his own newly established one was another Hokkaido native, the former Yokozuna Kitanofuji. This new, handsome young Kokonoe Oyakata was an exceptionally gifted and inspiring teacher who was to steer both Hoshi and Chiyonofuji to the rank of yokozuna and become the only stable boss since 1949 to field two reigning Grand Champions. He is often singled out on the NHK television footage used by Channel 4, watching Chiyo and Hoshi's matches, wearing gold-rimmed spectacles and acting as senior *shimpan* (judge) in traditional dress, *haori* and *hakama*. He is a very important man in the sumo world, and expects the best out of his apprentices. Chiyo and Hoshi were to give it to him.

It was into the Hokkaido hothouse of Kokonoe heya that Hoshi plunged in March 1979, when he made his début on the dohyo in the Haru basho. It helped that the key people round him at the stable were from his neck of the woods. Accent, diet and customs vary greatly from one region to another in Japan, and it made Hoshi feel slightly less homesick to hear his native dialect, even if the speaker was hitting him with a bamboo stick or flinging him on the floor. He worked extremely hard, and earned a reputation for having an old head on young shoulders. He was disciplined and dedicated, and did as he was told without the slightest objection in his manner. You couldn't get him off the practice area: he loved it, and always tried his hardest. He was smaller than most of his stable-mates (Chiyo had had the same problem when he started), so he worked out that his best bet was to use a very forceful, thrusting and ramming sort of style against them, rather than try to grapple it out on the belt. Tearing out of the tachi-ai and 'clonking' them in the face and neck, he could bruise it out with rikishi who were technically more versatile – at least until he could enlarge his own repertoire of techniques.

His hardest keiko, or practice bouts, were with this Chiyonofuji character, who would twist and tussle the life out of him for an hour on end. This is called sanban-geiko (repeated complete bouts), and Chiyo and Hoshi have kept up their unremitting routine year in and year out. As Chiyo was eight years older, eight years tougher and more experienced, Hoshi would inevitably get a good hiding. His technical knowledge increased, his muscles got bigger, and his young face grew rugged, scarred and cragged from his efforts to beat this Chiyonofuji. Nothing Hoshi would ever encounter on the dohyo in a basho could ever be as bad as this. The only thing that made it tolerable was that Chiyonofuji was a nice bloke, superbly talented himself and a firm believer in Hoshi's potential. Over the years Chiyo would stick by the young man and insist that he had a Grand Champion inside him waiting to get out, even when other people were rubbishing Hoshi as a fairly ordinary fighter who simply liked a good scrap.

Hoshi battled his way into Juryo (the Second Division) in the Haru basho in March 1983. He was only 20, but looked 35 from all his exertions. It took him another six months of ceaseless toil to get into the top division, Makunouchi, but once he'd done that he seemed to gather momentum and do even more terrific practice sessions. He was promoted to komusubi for the first time in the January basho 1984, did very well there and earned sekiwake status for the Haru tournament in March. A few ups and downs followed; in the Aki basho the following year he was back at komusubi, but beating Yokozuna Takanosato and Ozeki Wakashimazu, and toughing it out with the big names now to get his majority. He had greatly improved his technical versatility and was now growing into a very strong and fairly formidable customer. His yotsu-zumo had been nurtured by his constant practice with Chiyonofuji, though he still liked to force the pace with a bludgeoning attack, using open-handed blows to the face and chest of his opponents or nodowa, the throat push, to soften them up. He was aggressive, resilient and extremely quick, coming out of the tachi-ai with fighting-dog ferocity to force his left hand through his rival's defences and inside on to the belt (hidari-yotsu). If Chiyonofuji was the Wolf of Kokonoe stable, Hoshi was now at least the Shar Pei.

After Hoshi made his presence felt at komusubi and sekiwake, he was seen by his stable as yokozuna material and a possible successor to Chiyonofuji, and as always his greatest advocate in this was Chiyo himself. Ozeki, though, presented a bit of a problem for the young hustler. There were so many of them already that the Sumo Kyokai were concerned about squeezing yet another one into the banzuke with a shoehorn, even if he deserved it. So Hoshi jostled about for a bit at sekiwake, producing good results without getting promoted. After he made his majority in the Hatsu basho in January 1986, all eyes turned towards him when he powered to the yusho in the Haru tournament in March, dropping only two of his bouts to finish with a 13–2 scoreline. He followed this up in May with another strong showing, winning the *Kanto-sho*, or prize for Fighting Spirit, on his way to 11–4. It might easily have been another 13–2, but Asahifuji suddenly got hold of him and dropped him by tsuki-otoshi, and Kitao returned Hoshi's charge with interest to beat him by yori-kiri. The Sumo Kyokai were still not keen on having a sixth ozeki, but when Hoshi produced a 12–3 in the Nagoya tournament in July, he was now clearly an ozeki in all but name. So there was a reshuffle at the top. The none-too-keen-on-practice but large and legitimate-looking Ozeki Kitao was promoted to yokozuna – on fairly thin qualifications, it must be pointed out – and Hoshi, amiable and hardworking, and with a haul of fine results, was elevated to ozeki. Kitao became known as Futahaguro, and young Hoshi, with his step up the banzuke, became Hokutoumi, or 'Northern Victory Sea'.

Hokutoumi was true to his form (which is more than can be said for the new yokozuna). In March, in the 1987 Haru basho, he turned in another of his powerhouse 12–3 performances to take his second yusho, and in the next tournament, the Natsu in Tokyo, he was within a stone's throw of the Emperor's Cup yet again, finishing runner-up. In contrast, Futahaguro seemed to be easing along, and even Chiyonofuji appeared to have gone into some kind of decline – Channel 4 commentator Lyall Watson has suggested that Chiyo may have been 'coasting, to let his stable-mate Hokutoumi get promotion', though he seemed to some observers to be genuinely struggling. Hokutoumi, in contrast, was sprouting yokozuna wings.

The Sumo Kyokai were once again in a quandary, even worse than before. Ozeki Onokuni, who had been in a slump, had won the yusho in May with a clean sweep, 15–0. The man who could have forced him into a play-off, Hokutoumi, failed in the clutch against The Panda on senshuraku and was deeply disappointed with himself. In their crucial bout he had come out of the tachi-ai

'clonking' at Onokuni with both hands, only to have The Panda reach in and seize his belt regardless, and then deposit him in the front seats by yori taoshi. Onokuni's zensho-yusho performance so eclipsed poor Hokutoumi's 13–2 runner-up effort that the young 'Bulldog' wanted to go away and hide in a hole. He told reporters that he was mentally and physically exhausted and had nothing much else to say. He had practised and worked with all his might, had two yusho to his credit, and had all-round ability and devotion to his sport, but he had been worrying about promotion to yokozuna and had got himself into such a state that he was too excited to sleep properly, or perform to the real level of his skill in the crunch match. Like any young man on the Great Barrier, he was living on his nerves. Now he had gone and messed it up.

The Sumo Kyokai deliberated. Did Hokutoumi deserve promotion to the highest rank? Strictly speaking, for yokozuna you need two successive tournament wins or something roughly equivalent. But there were also other considerations. Konishiki, the tremendous Hawaiian, was at present on the rank of sekiwake and he really deserved promotion to ozeki for his recent performances. And if they raised The Dump Truck, the whole ozeki platform would look very precarious once again. The public were already showing signs of distrust in the banzuke. They had seen Kitao promoted to the sacred rank of yokozuna on fairly flimsy qualifications, and as Futahaguro he had yet to win a basho. Then there was this other Grand Champion, Chiyonofuji – well, he was all right, they supposed, for a *little* fellow, but he couldn't be expected to last much longer as he simply didn't have the weight. It was a wonder he had managed to struggle on as long as he had, the poor dear! The public considered all this and began staying away from sumo and getting fed up with the same old faces. There was only one thing to do: promote Konishiki to ozeki, promote Hokutoumi to yokozuna, and give Futahaguro the elbow if he continued on his dreary way. So this what the Sumo Kyokai did.

So far as Hokutoumi was concerned, they forgave him for mucking up his crunch bout with Onokuni, and he meant to justify himself to them for their discernment. When the officials come to your stable to tell you of your promotion to yokozuna, you have to vow, 'I will train hard and endeavour to uphold the rank of Grand Champion', and when Hokutoumi said his vow, his eyes glistened because he meant every word. He may have fumbled a key bout, but he had the heart of a yokozuna, and in the months and years to come, he would prove that he had. So, on 28 May 1987, the white rope belt was plaited round Hokutoumi's ample belly. He may have looked sheepish and he may have felt unworthy, but since then he has won the Emperor's Cup three more times, and been runner-up altogether on five other occasions. He has a haul of awards: four for Fighting Spirit, four for Technical Skill, two for Outstanding Performances, one Gold Star. And he has won over the sceptical fans with his exemplary manners on and off the dohyo, his modesty and puggish grin.

Channel 4 audiences have seen him behind the scenes, playing baseball, which is a hobby of his, pulling a face over his glass of cognac on the sumo tour of Paris, and looking suitably bashful at having his hairstyle filmed to explain what 'all Japanese men used to look like'. They have also seen him winning one of his yusho – the 1987 Aki basho – using his customary fast, bulldozing style. He nearly made it two in a row in the Kyushu that November, had Chiyonofuji and Asashio not got in the way, and he ended up in second place behind his yokozuna stable-mate, tied with soon-to-retire Futahaguro on 13–2. He was driving himself very hard and very fast, and unfortunately in 1988 it caught up with him. After an 11–4 performance that January and running-up to Onokuni in a play-off in March with 13–2, a serious lower back injury while warming up for the last day of the May basho put him out of contention for three successive tournaments. Being immobilized in hospital and hearing calls for his retirement, he not only missed his bouts, but missed his gruelling practice schedule as well, and it wasn't until the end of the year that he was in full training again. By then he was ready to demonstrate that he meant to take up where he left off.

He won the yusho in the New Year basho, bull-dozing Asahifuji out in a play-off at the beginning of 1989, and powered his way to 11–0 in the following tournament in March before coming into collision with Ozeki Konishiki, whose tsuppari attack was even fiercer than his own. This seemed to dispirit him, and he lost next day to Hokutenyu on the belt, and then to Asahifuji, who weathered Hokutoumi's thrusting onslaught politely and then spun him

round and out over the rope. His last bout was with the dreaded Onokuni. He managed to avoid being buried alive, but the pair came to an impasse and their bout was declared a draw. When they restaged their hostilities, Onokuni this time got the better of The Bulldog to drop his score to 11–4. Hokutoumi felt duty-bound to rectify this 'lapse' as quickly as possible. He worked extremely hard, and looked extremely dangerous for the upcoming Natsu basho, in May. He had an added responsibility to Kokonoe Oyakata and to his stable-mates because in throwing down The Giant Panda on senshuraku in the March tournament, Chiyonofuji had dislocated his shoulder and would be sitting this one out. There was honour at stake.

Hokutoumi was everybody's favourite for the Cup, but he had to fight it out with three other on-form sekitori keen to take advantage of the ruler's absence: Onokuni, Asahifuji and Hokutenyu. Clearly, there would be unremitting violence for the next 15 days. Hokutoumi, of course, was very determined, and set about his opponents with the sort of finesse one uses to break down a door with a tree trunk. All Sakahoko's wiles were to no avail; Terao's tsuppari slaps went whistling down the wind; Kasugafuji and Itai and assorted others were bundled about the ring and deposited either down or out with a satisfying thudding noise. Young would-be yokozuna Akinoshima proved a bit of a problem, keeping his balance under almighty wrenching. Irritated only slightly, Hokutoumi pulled out a few stops and sent 'The Killer Whale' crashing down on his leg by an inner arm throw, from which Aki didn't get up very easily. The Bulldog's hackles were now well and truly raised. Having seen off Daijuyama, he unleashed such a barrage of wallops against Mitoizumi that 'The Jolly Green Giant' fell over backwards with surprise and horror. The Plum, Kotogaume, had a go at blasting back at Hokutoumi which did him no good at all, and on the home stretch The Bulldog stood snarling in a three-way fight for the yusho with Asahifuji and Onokuni. Hokutenyu, just behind, waited to pick off anyone who faltered. It was going to be tough.

Things began badly for Hokutoumi: Asahifuji managed to worm his way out from under his battering and caught him unawares from behind. Then 'The Polar Bear' actually forged a worrying iron grip on The Bulldog's belt before a thrusting attack could finally finish him off. So Hokutoumi had to be content with going into the final day in a three-way tie on 12–2 with The Slug and The Panda. His senshuraku bout was with the Mortifying Mound Onokuni, who had given Hokutoumi so many worries in the past. Not here. The Bulldog surged out of the tachi-ai as if he meant to charge through the rear seats and then, cutting his momentum and getting his timing just right, he pulled Onokuni forward, toppling him onto the clay: 13–2. He had finished on the same score as The Slug, who had won his final-day bout with Hokutenyu. So into a play-off went Asahifuji and Hokutoumi for the 1989 Natsu title. Learning from his previous mistake of trying to smash The Slug into submission, The Bulldog flew out and seized him by the sash. Asahifuji was moving forward in a very high gear, no doubt expecting to be rammed across the ring, and although an arm throw failed to do the trick, a shove from behind succeeded in sending him tottering over the rope by okuri-dashi. Hokutoumi had won the Emperor's Cup. It was his fifth yusho, adding suitably to the huge Kokonoe tally, and he knew Chiyo would be pleased.

There was another play-off for the Nagoya basho, and Hokutoumi was involved again. This time, though, the circumstances were quite extraordinary, and history was in the making. The Bulldog had battled his way unblemished through the first six days, come unstuck against Akinoshima, and then dropped bouts to Masurao and Konishiki. A score of 12–3 is a fair working average for a yokozuna but he generally gets his report card marked, 'can do better'. Somebody else who can do better was Hokutoumi's esteemed stable-mate, fellow-Yokozuna Chiyonofuji. Strangely, he had also turned in 12–3, having been upset on senshuraku by an obstinate Hokutenyu. If anything, Hokutoumi had done rather more than Chiyo to make the score: some of his fights had been extremely tough, and he was lucky to meet Asahifuji as his last opponent when The Slug was feeling sleepier than usual, or he might not have got into the elimination bout at all.

Sumo fans had never witnessed a play-off between two yokozuna stable-mates before. It is far from usual for stable-mates to fight each other in earnest at all, let alone for Grand Champions from the same heya to square off. There was a hubbub of excitement during the shikiri naoshi as

the combatants studiously avoided looking into each other's eyes. Chiyonofuji used to give the odd withering glance but is not renowned these days for prolonged staring at anybody: just the sight of him is usually enough to send a shiver up their spines. Hokutoumi, though, who ought to have been giving a few meaningful looks, appeared to feel slightly soppy about the whole proceedings. He went through his ring rites shyly, like a man caught taking part in women's mud-wrestling, and the Japanese audience knew already, as they often do, what the outcome would be.

One could understand Hoku's feelings. Here he was, forced to fight for the Emperor's Cup with the very chap who had been strongly instrumental in getting him to yokozuna in the first place, and who had stoutly defended him against carping critics for umpteen months. How could you look daggers into the soul of such a person, particularly when the man was fighting his way out of a serious injury, and had recently lost one of his children to cot death? Hokutoumi couldn't do it, any more than he could beat Chiyo for the yusho. It was a foregone conclusion. The Wolf came out of the tachi-ai and got his left hand inside on Hoshi's belt rather than outside, as is his custom. The Bulldog looked bewildered and struggled to free himself, but the next thing he knew, he was somersaulting through the air and landing painfully on the clay to huge applause. It was Chiyonofuji's yusho, and Hokutoumi's place in history was as runner-up. So long as Chiyo remains a yokozuna, this is how they are likely to continue, with The Bulldog trotting doggedly behind The Wolf, savaging anything his leader may have missed. One can only guess at Kokonoe Oyakata's feelings of satisfaction as he lets the pair of them off the leash, though a knee injury in the August tour hampered The Bulldog towards the end of 1989 and limited him to two fairly reserved showings in the Aki and Kyushu tournaments.

Hokutoumi's technical armoury is now fairly awesome – one does not often see kata-sukashi (the arm-lock force-down) or abise-taoshi (the chest lunge) featured among the more usual range of hip throws, slap downs, scoop throws, twist downs, and oshi and tsuki techniques – but Hoku is still essentially an oshi-zumo fighter who likes to come crashing out at the tachi-ai to impose his strength — by shoving and slamming alone if he can (he isn't happy winning on the belt). The rest he has mastered by sheer hard work and dedication, to earn him a win–loss rate of 486–245. Chiyonofuji or no Chiyonofuji, this is quite impressive, and Kokonoe estimates that he has another ten yusho in him yet. His shyness will undoubtedly diminish with the years, and marriage (in March 1990) may make him a little less bashful at the basho; he proposed in October to a graduate of Konan Women's University, Kishiko Yamaguchi. Hoku lists his hobbies as baseball, saké and films. He doesn't list 'unremitting practice', but then we know all about that.

ONOKUNI

Rank: Yokozuna
Stable: Hanaregoma
Weight: 195 kg (30 st 10 lb)
Height: 189 cm (6 ft 2¼ in)

Onokuni's fighting name means 'Big Country', but the Japanese know and love him as 'The Giant Panda', with whom he shares the noble bearing of a monster species. To say that Onokuni is large scarcely does him justice. Standing over 6 ft 2 in in his bare flat feet and with a girth that has shrunk slightly since his last appearance on British television, he weighs in at a prodigious 30 stone. This makes him the largest Japanese-born wrestler ever to set foot on the dohyo, second in size only to Konishiki. Of all rikishi in this very spiritual sport, Onokuni is the one who truly looks the part: other-worldly, serene and, even in defeat, unhurried and gentle. He resembles the everlasting Buddha.

The Panda was born Yasushi Aoki on 6 October 1962, in Nemuro, on the northern island of Hokkaido. Aoki is his family's name; Yasushi means 'gentle and kindly'. At 12 the young man was already so enormous compared with his classmates that he was nicknamed 'Zo', or Jumbo. His parents were farming people, and Yasushi was raised among the beet fields and

beef cattle, no doubt benefiting from a lot of steak and protein in his diet. He was good-looking, and attracted the attention of a petite and pretty girl by the name of Noriko, whom he married in 1989. Outside of his schooling and other duties he liked to exert himself at sport. He loved baseball (most Japanese do), as well as swimming, skating, skiing (imagine the sight), and especially judo. Judo was his preferred martial art at school, and it was while he was winning a junior judo championship there that he was first spotted by the Hanaregoma stable boss. Keiketsu saw in the pear-shaped young Yasushi the power and speed of a potential sumotori, and took him back to Tokyo. Yasushi's skill on the belt as an apprentice owed much to his judo knowledge.

He began his sumo career in March 1978. At first he entered Hanakago heya under Keiketsu's tutelage, but when Keiketsu opened his own stable in 1980, becoming Hanaregoma Oyakata, Onokuni was one of the apprentices who went with him. The Panda officially entered the Makunouchi division in March 1983. His early win–loss record was very impressive, with a winning percentage of 0.662. He made sekiwake in just a year, and ozeki in 1985 after an astonishing run in the Nagoya tournament, scoring 12–3 in two consecutive basho. It was at ozeki, however, that Onokuni's problems began to emerge. Ozeki is a very difficult and psychologically testing rank: the young champion is 'on the barrier' ('ozeki' literally means 'great barrier') between ordinary champions and the position of yokozuna, and many able sumotori fail to get through this barrier for reasons which have nothing to do with physical skill or technique. The experience is very nerve-racking, and Onokuni's form began to suffer. On the one hand he could display quite formidable talent, beating even the invincible Chiyonofuji by powering him out on the eighth day of the 1986 Natsu basho. On that occasion he ended up with an 11–4 tally, and was presented, along with Konishiki, to Prince Charles and the Princess of Wales during their official visit to Japan.

On the other hand, Onokuni could go all to pieces. He seemed to choose those very moments when a win would have put him in the reckoning for promotion, which was most exasperating to his fans. Of course there were technical matters needing more attention: he

The Giant Panda under attack. Prone to self-doubt, his huge weight 'advantage' often carries him into the teeth of the gale without spiritual back-up.

needed extra speed at the tachi-ai, and he was unsettled by tsuki and oshi attacks. But the fact was that Onokuni made his mistakes when the pressure was greatest, often getting upset by opponents with less power and skill. A terrible slump began, in which he was overturned on either the first or second days of seven successive basho between March 1986 and March 1987. His sorry collection of scores included four 9–6s and an ignominious 8–7 in the 1986 Aki basho, where he reached 7–1 on day eight and then managed to fumble all the rest of his bouts but one. At last his long-suffering oyakata could stand no more. Onokuni is apt to look lazy and casual whatever his inner emotions, and his Hanaregoma stable boss could be forgiven for thinking Onokuni was

doing it deliberately, and wasting the enormous talent and potential he knew was there. So during practice for the Natsu basho in May 1987, the oyakata let Onokuni have it. The result was quite startling.

He did not lose on the first or second day of the Natsu basho; in fact he did not lose at all. Turning in his first perfect score of 15–0, The Panda bulldozed his way to the Emperor's Cup, and the Yokozuna Promotion Council, who had perhaps got tired of looking at him, once more turned their eyes on Onokuni as a real contender for sumo's highest rank.

The Panda was now challenging for promotion with two other rikishi, Kitao and Hokutenyu — particularly the latter. Hokutoumi, whom he had preceded up the ranks, had swept past him and become a Grand Champion already – a fact no doubt galling to his enormous rival. The Nagoya basho in July put Onokuni in a slightly stronger position with a 12–3 score as The Panda finished runner-up to Chiyonofuji. It was now or never: Onokuni must clinch the matter in the next basho. If he faltered again, the Yokozuna Promotion Council must surely despair of him altogether.

The Aki basho began auspiciously for him. The Panda looked fast and formidable as he crushed his first seven opponents. But then came the old uncertainty on the brink of success: Onokuni faltered against Komusubi Maenoshin and fellow-Ozeki Konishiki to leave himself the unwelcome task of beating all three reigning yokozuna in the closing bouts. Things did not look good. Hanaregoma Oyakata waited ominously in the wings as his protégé lumbered on to the dohyo to face Futahaguro, going through his ring rituals and salt-tossing with his customary unhurried languor. The huge belly seemed almost to touch the ground as The Panda went down into the shikiri crouch. When he stood up, the cherubic face turned slowly this way and that, exhibiting the rosebud mouth and lazy eyes of a gentle fellow about to help with the beet harvest, rather than a prospective Grand Champion. But then, appearances can be deceiving.

Summoning all his strength, Onokuni put Futahaguro out of contention and then, benefiting from Chiyonofuji's withdrawal with an injury, attacked his last yokozuna, Hokutoumi, the man who had overshadowed him in the race for the top. A good tachi-ai sent Onokuni crashing towards the Grand Champion, bullying him towards the edge of the ring. There the wily Hokutoumi stood his ground, broke out of Onokuni's clasp and grabbed The Panda's belt firmly with both hands. It was now Onokuni's turn to be marched backwards to oblivion. With his heels on the straw ridge and his back to the wall, The Panda twisted with all his might, to no avail. Finally deciding attack was his best defence, he went for his favourite move – sticking his tremendous right arm through his rival's armpit and unleashing a scoop throw, sukui nage. Hokutoumi went crashing, and Onokuni strode back to his corner to receive his prize. Panda-monium! It was a tremendous victory and although next day

Hokutoumi won the basho, Onokuni's own victory over Sakahoko gave him the worthy score of 13–2, making him the Promotion Council's choice for the highest honour. It had taken the ozeki 13 basho, but he'd finally come through.

On 2 October 1987 the 62nd Grand Champion stepped up to the Meiji shrine for the traditional tsuna-blessing. He had been instructed in the dohyo-iri by Futagoyama Oyakata as well as Sadogatake Oyakata, and his style was Unryu, like that of Chiyonofuji and Hokutoumi, though performed in a rather more ponderous way. He became the fourth reigning yokozuna, dwarfing the others and outweighing every Grand Champion who ever lived. It had been a rainy, overcast day, but the sun came out at noon for Onokuni's special ceremony. His father had come down from Hokkaido to join in the celebrations.

The year 1987 was a great one for Onokuni, who won an awe-inspiring 40 out of 45 bouts over three basho – a feat only Wakanohana II had equalled in the last 25 years. But after this there was another of his strange slumps. True, he finished runner-up in the 1988 July tournament and won his second title in Osaka in March 1988, flattening The Bulldog in a play-off, but he had pulled out of the January basho after a poor showing, and British viewers who saw him triumphant in 1987 were shown the other side of The Panda in the Aki basho in 1988. Going into that with a 65 per cent success rate, Onokuni floundered about, looking bewildered and fed up to the teeth about losing all three of his first bouts by yori-kiri. Tochinowaka beat him convincingly; Mitoizumi made him look like a beached whale, and then Akinoshima, looking small enough by comparison to be Onokuni's son, buried his head in the great man's chest and refused to be bellied across the ring or intimidated in any way. Worse, the young pretender got a good belt grip himself and marched Onokuni off the dohyo. The Panda simply was not fast enough or aggressive enough. He seemed preoccupied, perhaps with his forthcoming marriage. True, he managed to pull himself together sufficiently to make his majority for the basho (8–7). But few who saw the bout will forget the sight of Onokuni's massive form, on day seven, being twisted past Kirishima's shoulder in the spectacular spin throw – utchari. The Panda had had a weight advantage of some 14 stone (200 lb), and looked to be marching the slender Kirishima over the straw ridge by yori-kiri when the lighter man suddenly planted his heels, bent his knees and, with consummate strength and timing, twisted down, using The Panda's own bulk for momentum. He did it again in the May basho of 1989, again in the Natsu in Tokyo, breaking Onokuni's ten-win streak there with a last-ditch throw on the ridge, and yet again in July – and these defeats illustrate how The Panda is quite capable of falling prey to lighter foe with the speed and skill to use his weight against him, as many a martial art teaches its exponents to do.

Relying on bulk to belly out opponents as much as his old skill on the belt, Onokuni's tachi-ai becomes crucial to his style, and unfortunately there are lots of rivals who are swifter and more explosive at tachi-ai than The Panda with his whacking girth. Slapping attacks (tsuppari), thrusting (tsuki) and pushing (oshi) leave him looking vulnerable. But worse than all this is a general conservatism that has crept into his style: he seems more and more to lack the killer instinct to finish off smaller fry, even on the edge of the ring. So that when he is in a position of greatest advantage, gentle Yasushi tends to beat himself, letting the other man off the hook. Recently this has led to a terrible crisis.

Onokuni's old lack of confidence on the threshold of big wins resurfaced in January 1989. In that New Year tournament he was going strong, but then unaccountably faded to 11–4. In March he was undefeated for 11 days and then lost three of his last four bouts to finish 12–3. His defeats included a very conspicuous one at the hands of Chiyonofuji in which his rival yokozuna badly re-injured his shoulder throwing The Panda's staggering weight. In the Natsu basho in May, Onokuni raced to 10–0 and then went into reverse. Finally, in July, the inevitable happened. The Panda started to come apart at the seams, the result of an unresolved and long-standing psychological crisis. In the Nagoya basho, as his fans looked on in shame and agony, poor Yasushi struggled and blundered his way to one victory in four days and then withdrew from the tournament. The excuse given was a 'bad knee', but nobody really believed there was anything wrong with Onokuni's knee. He was certainly overweight, even for a sumotori, and he now went on a diet, slimming down to a far from svelte 31 stone. Perhaps this would help.

In the Aki basho, The Panda began badly, clawed his way back to 7–4, but then went into a panic. Visibly nervous and lacking in any kind of confidence or self-belief, he blundered his way through the rest of the basho, turning in a score of 7–8. It is difficult for Westerners to appreciate the enormity of what this meant. Here was a symbol of strength and majesty beyond normal human capabilities, one who could not be seen to lose and who could never be demoted back to the rank and file of ordinary wrestlers, turning in a losing score. He had become the first yokozuna since 15-day tournaments began in 1939 *ever* to finish with the unthinkable – make-koshi. Poor Onokuni! He immediately offered to retire, but was told to soldier on, and try to recover his dignity. He sat out the November basho, hoping to make a comeback in 1990. Whether he will or not will depend on his ability to face his own inner crisis, whatever outward solutions may be found.

His fall from grace has been analysed at length in the press, with criticism coming from all sides. Onokuni was accused of being lazy, of neglecting his training, and of being far too cumbersome both on and off the dohyo. In response The Panda's camp replied that he was a sick man, suffering from anoxemia – a shortage of oxygen in his blood – and that this had prevented him from sleeping properly. He certainly looked very tired and played out, but then so he would, were he suffering from nervous exhaustion. Besides, The Panda himself knows the truth of the matter.

In September he was interviewed for Channel 4, looking back to the time when he stopped Chiyonofuji's rensho run in November 1988, and he was asked how this victory came about. The Panda said that there had been 'all this talk' about Chiyo's winning streak, and that he had won by using the style of sumo he has always preferred – going for broke. He explained, 'Before I became a yokozuna, I just went all out to win', but that the responsibilities of his rank had got to him, and his sumo had become 'panicky'. Only intermittently could he manage to produce the style that was the key to his former success: going all out to win. Here lies the key to Onokuni's problems. He went for broke against Chiyo because he was angry. There he was, fighting to keep his reputation as a yokozuna, and here was his rival being lauded and venerated over a winning streak. So Onokuni let fly. Normally he doesn't; normally, and especially since the honour of being a Grand Champion descended upon him from a great height, he keeps some of his power in check. But on this particular occasion, because he had nothing to lose and had suffered all he could stand, Onokuni's inner barriers failed to contain the force within him, and he seized the remarkable and ever-popular Chiyonofuji, and flung the unbeatable and wonderful Chiyonofuji down on his backside. Sick or well, overweight or slim, Onokuni still has this bulldozing power somewhere in his belly. He simply has to find a way to gain access to it again.

Yasushi's favoured techniques are inner and outer arm throws using a migi-yotsu attack, yori-kiri, yori taoshi, oshi-dashi and tsuri-dashi. Smart opponents will avoid getting to grips with him chest-to-chest in the centre of the ring, where The Panda is mightiest. But he is often slow to get down in the clinch – for example against Akinoshima and Asahifuji – allowing the opponent to bury his head in that ample chest and worm one or both arms towards the belt. The Panda likes to thrust his great right meathook under his rival's left arm and to get a good left-handed grip outside on the belt. This is the fulcrum from which he can ram almost anybody backwards out of the ring, and in this he is quite formidable. With a moro-zashi (two inside grips) he can do even better, as he demonstrated at Chiyo's expense in the November 1988 basho. (The Panda finished with a respectable 11–4 there.)

He has to his credit two tournament titles, four Gold Stars, five Outstanding Performance prizes, and one Fighting Spirit prize (think back, Onokuni, to what you felt then). Over 71 basho he has built up a win–loss record of 516 to 294. A married man these days, The Panda lists his hobbies as walking, reading and eating, which may well prove an opponent in itself if he balloons again. A recent dip into the world of advertising – a television commercial showing Onokuni's girth to advantage – was brought to a full stop in a clampdown by the Japan Sumo Association. But he has probably done more to rivet the attention of unsuspecting television audiences in the UK to sumo than even Chiyonofuji's winning ways. People keep tuning in to make sure their eyes didn't deceive them the first time!

THE LARGEST

KONISHIKI

Rank: Ozeki
Stable: Takasago
Weight: 226 kg (35½ st)
Height: 187 cm (6 ft 1½ in)

Konishiki, otherwise known as 'The Dump Truck', is the most successful *gaijin* (foreigner) ever to enter sumo, fighting his way to the second highest rank of ozeki in 1987. His Hawaiian hero and fellow-countryman Jesse Takamiyama, who preceded Konishiki up the ladder, got as far as sekiwake. To reach ozeki is a feat wonderful for any native Japanese, but for an unwelcome intruder from an outside culture it is almost incredible. After his promotion Konishiki received hate mail and threatening phone calls telling him to go back to Hawaii and leave the Japanese national sport for the Japanese. There were long tendentious articles in the newspapers suggesting how and why foreigners should be banned. Konishiki was 'really hurt and really scared'. He thought seriously about giving up sumo altogether because he was so anxious that he hardly slept, and when he did, he had nightmares. He suffered from an abiding worry that some nutcase might walk up and stab him in the street. Promotion to the brink of yokozuna should have made him the happiest fellow in Japan. Instead it made his life a misery.

Even now, although Konishiki has become a familiar star and an accepted public hero, his behaviour is still periodically called in question by members of the press corps for failing to uphold the spirit of sumo on the dohyo, for being insufficiently inscrutable over his wins and losses, for incorrect looks and gestures and for supposedly failing to appreciate the sport's underlying traditions and customs – though Konishiki has tried harder than most to steep himself in sumo's manners and mysteries because he loves the sport so much. In the light of this, his achievement in rising to ozeki is perhaps all the more remarkable, and a measure of his personal courage. Things will never be quite the same for Konishiki as for other wrestlers. He likes to spend much of his time in his room because he considers that there, at least, he doesn't have to watch the way he walks, the way he talks, or the way he looks.

True, he looks rather extraordinary. His naturally frizzy curls are straightened out with tongs to be greased up into the regulation *o-icho-mage* (gingko-leaf hairstyle), though Konishiki's 'fan' is smaller than anybody else's because kinky hair refuses to obey like the smooth locks of the Japanese. His dark skin and friendly Samoan features, betraying his ancestry, single him out and appeal to Japanese women of whom he says 'they react very good'. But his most striking feature – on and off the dohyo – is his staggering bulk. The *Guinness Book of Records* lists Konishiki on two counts: his status as highest-ranking foreigner in sumo, and his position as most massive sumo wrestler of all time. He has to be very careful with the furniture. On one occasion a wooden stool collapsed beneath him, injuring his coccyx, the triangular bone at the base of the spine. He was about to take a bath at

Konishiki preparing to blow somebody away.

the time, and when Konishiki takes a bath, he displaces some water.

In 1988 his weight ballooned to 40 stone, and his skeletal structure refused to put up with it. Injuries to his hips and knees have plagued his career, and now his right knee gave up altogether and put him in hospital where he had intensive therapy on the knee and, on medical advice, shed nearly four stone to relieve the strain on his joints. (He repeated the therapy in January 1989.) He took the weight off in just two weeks in July 1988,

and the combination of starvation and weakness severely affected his form for several basho. Opponents simply leaned on Konishiki's agonizing knee or shoved the listless behemoth out of the ring, capitalizing on his lack of flexibility to turn and fight back in his normal style. It was a period of big bandages, ice-packs and self-recrimination. Everyone had long been on at Konishiki to slim down. Jesse Takamiyama, the man who had originally inspired and helped him to enter sumo, once told a reporter as Konishiki walked away, 'He's going back to his hotel room and eat a whole bag of cookies.' According to Konishiki, although his entire family are big ('and I've been big ever since I was small'), mother, father, nephews and nieces had all suggested he go on a diet. The Dump Truck's attitude had always been that unless his weight adversely affected his form, he would simply carry on eating. Big was beautiful, he thought. Now he's not so sure, but he says injury won't stop him. As long as he can walk, he'll fight.

Konishiki, which means 'little brocade' or 'trophy', was born Salevaa Fuauli Atisanoe in Oahu, Hawaii, on the last day of 1963, of Samoan extraction. Affectionately known as Sally, he became the fifth of eight children, all corpulent and bonny like himself. His dad was a naval arsenal worker, and the family home town is Honolulu. Sally was both intelligent and athletic. At high school he swam, pumped iron and played American football, but he also turned in A grades because he was interested in becoming a university student and then a public prosecutor, 'to fight the evils of the world'.

Jesse Takamiyama, the huge Hawaiian who now runs his own stable (making him 'Azumazeki Oyakata') and who broke down some of the barriers by becoming a respected sumotori himself, had heard about the sizeable Sally back in Honolulu and sent some of his friends to scout him out. They talked to the young man about becoming a wrestler, but Sally wasn't the slightest bit interested. He knew nothing about sumo, apart from the fact that his famous fellow-countryman Jesse had changed his name from Kuhaulua to Takamiyama and been a great success at it, and besides, he had other plans. It was only when Jesse himself turned up in Sally's home town and approached him personally that the junior colossus changed his mind and decided to take the huge gamble.

Delighted to find the odd McDonald's in Tokyo to make him feel slightly less homesick, Sally nevertheless found life in Takasago heya most severe. True, he had stable-mate Jesse there to reassure him, but he himself spoke no Japanese, and the culture shock hit him even harder than his other stable-mates on the practice dohyo. As a 'prospect' and noviciate, the new foreigner was naturally given a good hiding on the ring by everybody, and by his superiors with a stick – this

is quite routine in a sumo stable, and one just has to put up with it. Konishiki says that you can always tell the new recruits in a heya, because they're the ones who are black and blue and in tears, thinking of running away to mother. On one particular occasion his many chores, before sumo school began, included cleaning the toilets on four storeys and all the stairs as well, at four o'clock in the morning, and he'd diligently done all this and gone off to his lessons. When he returned to the stable he was somewhat surprised to receive a whack over the head with a bottle from one of the senior rikishi who said that he had omitted to empty all the rubbish, an additional duty on Sally's list that he had failed to understand. It was at this moment in his budding career that the young Konishiki showed the character that was to see him all the way to ozeki. He bowed to the sekitori and said Gotsu'an' desu – 'thank you'. This deference is expected of all underlings in the strict sumo hierarchy, and those who cannot knuckle under either quit or simply fail to make the grade. Konishiki knuckled under. Unlike many foreign rikishi he quickly immersed himself in the heya atmosphere and set himself the difficult task of learning to speak and write Japanese. He had always been a good student and soon he was showing unusual progress. One of his stable-mates began to joke that Konishiki spoke better Japanese than Mitoizumi, whose sleeping mat was next to The Dump Truck's on the floor. More important, his revered stable-master Takasago was telling people that Sally had learned in a year what it took Jesse Takamiyama ten years to master.

Those who knew Konishiki best helped him. The invaluable Jesse would translate what the stablemaster was telling him in the practice area and advise him on Japanese customs and behaviour in public. Stable boss Takasago told him not even to think about the absurd prejudice and the 'Stop Konishiki Movement' as Sally began to climb up the ladder. His stable-mates, like Asashio (who retired in 1989), Mitoizumi and the Samoan Nankairyu (who fled the sport dramatically in 1988), all boosted his morale and lifted him on their shoulders when he was promoted. And Chiyonofuji, though not of Konishiki's heya, helped him train. Sally says that even watching The Wolf inspires him. When Konishiki first entered sumo he was shocked to see the diminutive Chiyo 'throwing 400-pound people all over the place'. Chiyo practised with him, as did many other senior wrestlers, and gave him technical tips appropriate to his style, for which Konishiki is still grateful. He also struck up a friendship with Mitoizumi, his fellow snorer in the sekitori sleeping quarters and a man, like himself, larger than life. These days they bewail their bad joints together.

Whatever Konishiki's progress at learning Japanese, his talent spoke for him most eloquently, and so did his Samoan fighting spirit. Having joined Takasago heya in July 1982 and entered the ring in the Nagoya basho, Konishiki achieved a very creditable early record of 252 wins against 155 losses, a success rate of 0.619, with his Makunouchi entry coming exactly two years after his début, in the 1984 Nagoya basho. In only his second Makunouchi tournament – the Aki in September 1984 – he scored a remarkable 12–3, upsetting two yokozuna, an ozeki and a sekiwake and running Tagaryu very closely for the title.

Promoted to komusubi he went on in 1985 to produce another 12–3 score, this time in the Natsu (May) basho where he finished runner-up and earned the prize for Fighting Spirit (his second Kanto-sho) and promotion to sekiwake. In 1986 there were two 12–3 scores, in the Haru basho in March and again, after a knee injury in May, in the Aki basho in September. But Konishiki's finest hour thus far came in 1987 in the Natsu tournament. On successive days he upset Futahaguro and Chiyonofuji – his second win over The Wolf in as many basho – and his defeat of the two yokozuna and 12–3 tally won him his fifth Kanto-sho or Fighting Spirit award. It was after this showing, on 27 May, that Konishiki was promoted to ozeki, five years after his initiation into the holy world of Japan's national sport. On behalf of the American community Sally was congratulated on 'this American first' by Mike Mansfield, the US Ambassador to Japan, and hoisted on to the shoulders of his stable-mates. He had won 33 bouts over three basho, a remarkable record, though of course he had yet to win the Emperor's Cup or produce a 15–0 performance (zensho-yusho), which would put him into the reckoning for eventual promotion to yokozuna. His stable boss Takasago, who died suddenly from a stroke in 1988, had predicted that Sally would reach the topmost rank by his

25th birthday. Sadly this was not to be.

Konishiki began 1988 promisingly with a 12–3 runner-up performance in the Hatsu basho in January (his 4th second place) but then he became increasingly crippled by his painful right knee and his gargantuan proportions. His injury began to create what he calls a weak point in his mind. In the subsequent Haru, Natsu and Nagoya tournaments he barely scraped through with his majority (8–7) and in the Aki basho in September, shown on British television, he slumped to absolute disaster with a make-koshi score of 3–12. He had not long come out of hospital and had perhaps been ill-advised in taking part at all, sitting on a record second only to Chiyonofuji with a winning percentage of 66 and being unfit to defend it. It was the nadir of his career. In November 1988 things improved slightly and he hit back with a 10–5. But then in January 1989 he was once again in hospital losing 35 lb and having treatment on his knee. He had dropped out of the Hatsu basho on day twelve having already lost nine bouts, and he was now in grave danger of losing his ozeki rank. Using a barrage of left-right thrusts to his opponents' heads and chests he finished 10–5 in the Osaka basho in March, but in May it was back to 9–6 and in the July tournament, the Nagoya, Sally barely made his majority. He was having trouble with his shoulder as well now, and it pained him to hurry out at the tachi-ai. His famous tsuppari attack, without proper knee support, had come to resemble the charge of the Scots Greys at Waterloo: doomed to failure for all its bravery. Besides, he had been thinking quite seriously about chucking up the whole game. He'd been runner-up five times, but he'd never won a yusho. Perhaps he never would, even with all his dieting and punishing knee-strengthening on the tours. His weight was now down to 35½ stone, and he'd worked his behind off. For what? Things couldn't get much worse.

Yes they could. In the Aki basho 1989, Sally hit rock bottom, turning in an unspeakable 5–10. It began badly, trailed off in the middle, and the less said about the end, the better. Channel 4 fans of The Dump Truck stared at their sets in dismay. He was now what the sumo insiders call kadoban – in imminent danger of demotion – and he had three alternatives. He could accept the fact gracefully and slide down the ranks, retire, or – more unlikely than ever – do something remarkable in the November tournament. He had a lot on his mind. His parents had been injured in a car accident back in Hawaii, and he'd flown home to see how they were. Back in Japan, shortly after the Aki basho, there had been a very sad hair-cutting ceremony on the dohyo, as Sally's fellow-ozeki and stable-mate Asashio had retired. The Dump Truck was among the last to snip the weeping Asashio's topknot, and many a thought crossed his mind as he wielded the brass scissors. Somehow his fighting spirit had got to get him out of this mess.

The result was so surprising that for quite a time even Sally couldn't believe it. He went through the November tournament like Hercules unchained. His knees worked, his shoulder worked, his tachi-ai got infantry support, and he clonked and smashed his way to 11–1, faltering only against Hokutoumi on the belt. Then he set his sights on Chiyonofuji, clumping The Wolf in the face and chest so ferociously that Chiyo hardly had time to breathe in. Overcoming his nervousness and increasing insomnia, and rampaging past The Plum to finish with a career-best 14–1, Sally suddenly realized he'd won the Emperor's Cup! And as he stood on the dohyo for the presentation ceremony, he did what poor old Asashio had done a few weeks before. 'I tried not to cry in the ring,' said Sally, 'but I couldn't help it.' A message of congratulations was read out from George Bush in the White House, to say that Sally had given all Americans something to shout about. He was only the second foreigner ever to win the Cup: his fellow-Hawaiian Takamiyama had done it 17 years before – and Jesse said that he was even happier about Sally's triumph than he'd been about his own. To celebrate, Jesse, Sally, Briton Nathan Strange and a few of the lads went disco dancing, thudding the night away.

Konishiki's main strength as a wrestler is the obvious one – his quite spectacular power. His nickname, The Dump Truck, refers to an ability he has, when not disabled by injury, to roll over an opponent and deposit him in the garbage. He has always relied on power sumo – pushing, thrusting, smacking and bulldozing his rivals out of the ring, and using sheer might and weight to settle the hash of more cagey opponents. His style is typical of Takasago fighters, many of them burly and brutal about their business. (One of the

fiercest shoves ever witnessed on Channel 4 by British sumo fans was the one administered by Mitoizumi to Akinoshima as he clung in defiance to the huge Takasago giant during the Aki basho in 1988, and this bludgeoning format has worked very well for 'The Salt-shaker's' stable-mates too.) On form, Konishiki is unrivalled at it; Asashio beat many a foe in this way, and Nankairyu, before he left the sport, hurled himself at anyone and anything with reckless abandon.

In Konishiki's favour during his storming run to ozeki was the fact that many adversaries were unsettled by the sight of him, let alone his frightening blitzkrieg style. They did not know quite what was hitting them, but they knew it was very large and very painful. Conversely, when they saw him weakened and crippled by a suspect knee, they realized that this monster could be finessed just like anyone else, and beaten on the belt, and made to look foolish. Kirishima saw through Konishiki's defences on a number of occasions, turning his weight against him with consummate skill. Sakahoko exploited Konishiki's weaknesses even more ruthlessly, seizing the behemoth's belt in a moro-zashi and frog-hopping at him until he tottered backwards over the straw ridge. The bigger they come, the heavier they fall, and when his injuries began to interfere with his form, Konishiki fell very heavily and very often, sometimes on his enormous belly, to the unseemly delight of some of the crowd who like their wrestlers Japanese.

The late Takasago Oyakata saw the key to Konishiki's success as the tachi-ai. Before he died in 1988 this is what he was trying to teach the huge young man: speed at the tachi-ai. He considered Konishiki's jump-off to be sub-standard. He wanted him to get down lower more quickly and be more explosive off his mark. Konishiki himself is the first to admit how important the jump-off is to a wrestler's performance. He says that you need a particularly good start to wrestle in his strong-arm style; that the initial charge is 'like seventy per cent of the bout'. And he believes his own tachi-ai needs sharpening up. He needs to stay lower and move his opponent around more. Sally says that the style he has adopted is one of the hardest styles. He told the Foreign Press Club after his promotion to ozeki, 'Even a regular person can go up and grab anyone's belt because most of them have that style of just going up and grabbing someone's belt to try to throw them and try to shove them out. But the best way is to do tsuppari,' – slapping and bludgeoning. He thinks that although this style is harder to learn – perhaps leaving less margin for error – once perfected it wins more bouts than belt grips, and is of course much more spectacular to watch. Whether or not Konishiki is right about tsuppari (traditionally most Japanese wrestlers and connoisseurs seem to have favoured the cleverness of belt grips rather than brute force), the fact remains that, having gained confidence in it and relied on it for his success, he is reluctant to concentrate on anything else, even when he is not quite so successful. One doesn't come all the way from Hawaii to mess about mastering techniques that any puny little son-of-a-gun can do. So although Sally says that 'learning more techniques would help me', his instinct is to use force, and when this does not work, more force again. Unfortunately his opponents have cottoned on, and learnt to adapt. This is Konishiki's dilemma.

Sally sees that his rivals, in the main, are unable to come straight at him chest-on because they know that they will lose. Now, he says, 'they try to trick me'. Konishiki's weapons are tsuki and oshi techniques: the frontal push-out, frontal force-out, thrust-out, thrust-down, frontal push-down and backward force-down. He favours migi-yotsu (right hand inside grip). He also has at his disposal the twist-down and a force-out clamping the rival's elbow. If he gets what he calls 'squared off' against an opponent – shoulders even and chest-to-chest – he is more or less invincible. He talked about this to Channel 4 in the 1988 televised basho, and explained that if he was balanced and square he could use his power easily, but that 'if they come halfway, or go on the side, I'd be always trying to use one hand – that's my weak point, when they try to get me off balance'. He told British viewers that although he does practise belt techniques, when he actually gets in the ring he doesn't have one hundred per cent confidence in them. He can use them in a crisis, but he's more comfortable fighting his own way. At least if he loses on his own terms, he doesn't feel frustrated. If he loses on the belt, it's more upsetting to him.

For all his fabulous strength, Konishiki is intelligent enough to know that a lot depends on mental power rather than physical prowess. This is true of all sports and sumo, with its shikiri naoshi, its animal gestures and staring sessions, is full of spiritual rivalry and 'psyching' techniques. Konishiki says 'You've got to have a strong mind', and part of every rikishi's training concentrates on the head and the heart. The late Takasago Oyakata told a Channel 4 interviewer, 'Konishiki hasn't been here long enough yet to show good *shin* [heart]. That hasn't been fully developed yet. What he has now is more technique than heart.' This is a very telling comment from the man behind Konishiki's training. Sally says he found one of the hardest things to learn in sumo was wrestling people on the ring who were friends, stable-mates and sparring partners. One doesn't generally meet stable-mates during a tournament, but one fights them elsewhere all the time, and one is constantly wrestling and practising with rival rikishi from one's *ichimon* or family of stables, and in this respect sumo is very unusual. Konishiki had to find an artificial way of working up anger towards these people. He psyches himself up by saying 'I hate that guy I wrestle today'. If he sees a wrestler injured – particularly if he has been responsible for it – he finds it very hard to unleash himself and perhaps hurt the man again, because he knows them all and they've been his allies and buddies since he settled in Japan. Unfortunately they are also rivals to be beaten if a wrestler is to climb the slippery pole to yokozuna, and if he is to succeed at the highest level, he must put them away. Perhaps this, as much as the more obvious physical injury, has held Konishiki back from the highest rank, and perhaps this lack of detachment is what Takasago Oyakata was referring to when he observed Sally's lack of 'shin'. Mental supremacy is more than guts or courage – he possesses those in huge proportions.

In repose, Konishiki is a gentle giant: charming, good-humoured and totally lacking in conceit. His humility and naturalness, so refreshing to anyone used to dealing with Western sportsmen nursing swollen egos, have given a favourable impression not only to Japanese women (romance is definitely in the air) but also, rumour has it, to the Princess of Wales when she talked to Konishiki during an official visit to the 1986 summer basho in Tokyo. When world boxing champion Mike Tyson paid a call to Takasago stable to see what sumo wrestlers did for weight-training, Konishiki greeted him in an enormous pink and blue tracksuit like an amiable fan welcoming the visiting hero. He explained to British television viewers, 'I don't really have the feeling that I'm a celebrity. I still have that little kids' stuff in me that if anybody popular comes round, I want to meet them more than they want to meet me. I come from Hawaii – you hardly find any stars coming down to Hawaii!' For a major sports personality, Sally isn't exactly overburdened with self-confidence.

Konishiki may still be only 26, but in the long term one of the disadvantages of his preference for a forceful style on the dohyo is that it places a continual and growing strain on his anatomical structure, already coping with 35½ stone. His renowned fighting spirit – forcing his way back into contention from losing positions – has stretched his physical powers to their limits and got him into what he calls 'danger areas', where injuries occur. Since his right knee gave way, Sally has had to adapt by economizing on fight-backs. Instead he hopes that by improving his tachi-ai and initial attack, he'll be able to avoid the rear-guard actions so stressing to his hips and knees. This calls for a fairly major change of attitude. One of Konishiki's best-loved words in Japanese is *gaman* – which means 'endurance', but which he translates as 'fighting back'. This courage has brought him no less than five *Kanto-sho* or Fighting Spirit prizes. He has also garnered three *Shukun-sho* or Outstanding Performance awards, one *Gino-sho* or Technique award, and two *Kinboshi* or Gold 'merit' Stars (for beating a yokozuna).

He is now the senior sekitori at Takasago heya, following the retirement of Asashio, and he feels a great sense of responsibility for the young recruits coming along, especially since the death of his friend and stable-master. Seeing discipline and hard work served him very well, he now dishes them out, with a stick where necessary. He says he is 'pretty strict' in the practice area, and of Nankairyu, who defected in the middle of the Aki basho in 1988, he says 'I worked his butt off.' Konishiki is nothing if not a traditionalist and firmly believes the old, harsh way is the best. He doesn't want to see sumo Westernized or watered down, and he doesn't care to see it internationalized either. One change he has made: he has set up his own weight-training room, believing firmly

in the value of power-lifting for sumo. Other heya in the last decade have begun to emphasize iron-pumping too as part of their programmes. Wrestlers are getting bigger as the species perfects itself physically for the task at hand.

To keep fit and agile Sally likes to swim, play golf and dance. He claims to be able to 'strut his stuff' for hours on end, and shares with many of his fellow-rikishi a love of music of various kinds. Konishiki's tastes are more catholic than most: he plays several musical instruments and has plenty of time to practise because unless there is a basho or a tour, his day starts around seven and finishes at lunchtime. He has weekly piano lessons (he was good at music at school) and even blows his own trumpet. Then he enjoys listening to other people as well: he makes a point of seeing American bands visiting Tokyo, and he was thinking of releasing a record himself, called 'Endless Night', until the Japan Sumo Association clamped down on the wrestlers' outside contracts. A company – Teichiku – even signed him to cut the disc because Konishiki has not only charisma and pulling-power but a very good singing voice.

Konishiki's success has inspired other foreigners to take the plunge in sumo. His own 19-year-old Californian cousin, Vince Divoux, has now joined him in Japan to try to follow Sally up the ladder. Vince, who weighs 27 stone already, is prepared to work and eat his way to promotion, though he hates the drudgery of stable life and, had it not been for the fact that Konishiki went all the way over to Los Angeles to collect him, might well have thrown in the towel. The sight of the great Dump Truck holding his own on the dohyo is very good for Vince's morale – and that of any gaijin.

Sally has one abiding ambition – to become a yokozuna. At all costs he doesn't want to be like other ozeki who have lost faith in themselves and remained on the second rung until they retired. Konishiki says he is ready to make the jump within the year, now that his chronic injury problem seems to be under control. His philosophy is stoical. 'I don't think about next year', he says. 'I take every day as it comes.' But to see him storm the last barrier would be a delightful experience for the many British sumo fans who have taken the big bachelor to their hearts. They hope The Dump Truck keeps on trucking.

THE BIG FAVOURITES

AKINOSHIMA

Rank: Maegashira
Stable: Fujishima
Weight: 133 kg (20 st 13 lb)
Height: 176 cm (5 ft 9¼ in)

They call Akinoshima 'The Killer Whale', after the small, ferocious carnivore of that species. He is also known to the Japanese as 'Mountain' or 'Mini-Tank'. He's only in his early twenties but he looks as if he's been in a few fights, an impression reinforced by the pocket battleship build, the lightly poised fists, the serene, deadly expression and the cauliflower ears. Waiting for his turn on the dohyo, Aki smacks himself round the face as though tenderizing beefsteak, and the rest of him obviously comes in for similar weltings against the *teppo* pole, the odd wall, and anybody likely to toughen him up. Were it not for all this riveting masculinity, Aki would bear a striking facial resemblance to the eponymous little deaf and dumb heroine of the film *Mandy* (who knows but that this may have been the very spur to his success). He is what American women call 'pretty cute'.

Akinoshima has apparently set himself the unusual target of 100 practice bouts a day – above and beyond the call of duty even of an ambitious sumotori. He isn't afraid of hard work or hard wallopings. In fact, if appearances are anything to go by, he isn't afraid of anything at all. He has his narrow eyes on the proverbial summit of Mount Fuji, and his whole demeanour is that of a short but very promising potential yokozuna. At least, that's what the sumo *cognoscenti* are saying, despite a few setbacks in 1989 when Aki met with some fierce counter-attacks.

They say that being born in a ghetto can make a champ out of a fighter, and if that is the case, being born in Hiroshima, as Aki was (on 16 March 1967), must give you a very formidable edge indeed. As a young boy growing up in that devastated prefecture, Yamanaka Katsumi, as Aki then was, must have formed the impression life was for those tough enough to survive their next breakfast without their arms falling off. Hiroshima, when he was born, was still an atomic fall-out zone with young people affected physically and mentally by the legacy of the war. Many observers, including Channel 4's Lyall Watson, have commented on Aki's enormous confidence and self-belief. Where he gets it from, nobody knows, but he exhibits what the Japanese call 'shin', the inner strength that can eclipse an opponent in the shikiri naoshi and make him doubt his own abilities. His poise and balance – with a spectacular self-righting mechanism inside his head – are dismaying even to his yokozuna superiors.

Aki came into sumo in March 1982 when he entered Fujishima heya. Interestingly his oyakata there, former Takanohana Toshiaki, was known as the 'eternal ozeki' during his own fighting career when he failed to make yokozuna after a most promising start. Before that the ozeki had been called the 'Prince of the Sumo World', rather in the same manner as Akinoshima is lauded now, so we may assume that there will be particular emphasis at the stable on Aki making the very summit and not just a high rank. Anything else

Small and deadly: Akinoshima daunts larger foe.

would be doubly disappointing to his oyakata.

As an apprentice Aki immediately set about rikishi twice his size, and turned his short stature to advantage by literally using his head – burrowing into the shoulder or chest of his adversary. From this position he learned to cling on tenaciously until he could secure an attacking belthold. Sometimes this was not easy, as The Killer Whale's arms are short and some of his opponents' bellies were very large, but gradually Aki adapted himself to these difficulties and yotsu-zumo – belt-grappling – became second nature to him. Sumo fans are accustomed to seeing him in close clinches now. The Killer Whale's head goes boring in as Aki focuses on his rival's weight distribution and the tensions in his arms, to see what the other wrestler plans to do. He is sharp and quick, wriggling his own mawashi out of reach, and strong enough to withstand powerful pushing attacks. Most important of all he is clever and, for a man of relatively little experience in the top division, has a large repertoire of grabs and counter-grabs to baffle and upset an opponent: all of which makes the young man very special to watch, and his bouts with the shrewdest adversaries – people like Chiyonofuji and Sakahoko – can teach even a television viewer something about their sacred skills.

The tough little customer's favoured techniques are hidari-yotsu (left hand inside on the belt) for yori-kiri – the frontal force-out. He is also adept at knee trips, leg grabs, the hand pull-down, the push-out, the scoop throw, the outer arm throw, and the pulling outer arm throw, though he'll try plenty of other things in a crisis, including the force out and down. Gaining in weight, strength and expertise, he entered Makunouchi in the Haru basho in Osaka in 1988. In July of that year, in the Nagoya basho, he established himself with a resounding 11–4, taking the Fighting Spirit prize and being promoted very quickly to the senior number 2 slot, just beneath the highrollers. Now came the September tournament, seen by Britain's Channel 4 audiences, and 'Aki in the Aki basho' proved very entertaining indeed.

Ranked senior number 2, of course, Akinoshima faced the sternest competition of his life. With one initial loss on day one, he stood face to face with The Sea Slug, Asahifuji – keen to get hold of the young whipper-snapper and perhaps squash him into subordination or fling him into the expensive seats. This was Aki's first ozeki opponent but he looked far from ruffled, going through the shikiri naoshi with a calm, phlegmatic expression. At the tachi-ai Aki flew forward and engaged The Slug in the middle with an inner arm belt grip, shadowing the ozeki's moves to avoid his rubbery clutches, and keeping his own belt well out of reach. The smaller man began boring his head into Asahifuji's shoulder and forcing the pace and then, breaking a brief stalemate, drove forward to bundle The Slug out by yori-kiri.

Next day, Aki faced an even bigger challenge in the form of mountainous Yokozuna Onokuni. Sumo fans are used to seeing startling mismatches of size and weight on the dohyo and here was one for them to savour. Not only was Akinoshima half The Panda's girth but nearly six inches shorter as well. Nothing daunted, out he charged at the tachi-ai and, using the reliable head-boring technique, clenched the giant's sash in his left hand, fishing with his right around The Panda's massive waist for his second grip and moro-zashi. The yokozuna threw his 31½-stone weight this way and that, pushing and dragging the upstart with increasing violence yet unable to shake him off. A very long (by sumo standards) and gruelling fight ensued in which Onokuni tried all he knew to drive the young man and wear him to a standstill. The longer it lasted, the greater the heavier wrestler's advantage. Akinoshima must succumb under the enormous payload and drop to the clay. Not at all. Suddenly cutting loose, Aki stormed his monstrous opponent round the ring backwards, and with his last ounce of strength forced him across the straw ridge by yori-kiri. It was only when he had made sure of victory that The Killer Whale allowed himself to fall forward on the dohyo, lying exhausted from his supreme effort. Here was a young Grand Champion in the making, and everyone in the Kokugikan cheered him to the rafters.

Not content with these two giant-slayings, Aki accounted for two more ozeki in this basho – Konishiki and Hokutenyu (the latter being dismissed from his presence by uwate dashi nage), only to lose several close-run battles and end up on the final day (senshuraku) needing his last bout to make his majority. The man waiting for him, Tochinowaka, also stood on the knife-edge of 7–7 and jealously guarded his rank and authority from Akinoshima's prying gaze during their shikiri naoshi. Junior champion Tochi slapped his belt, stuck out his lower lip in a menacing sneer and put salt on his tongue. The Killer Whale looked on unblinking, rocking his head slightly as he crouched down in the last shikiri to detect the smallest movement of his opponent just prior to the tachi-ai.

They locked horns. A furious struggle on the belt reached deadlock in the centre, each wrestler pinioned in a two-handed grip. What followed was easy to misinterpret. It looked as though Tochi suddenly pushed the little Killer Whale towards the ridge, but, on film, slow-motion replay reveals a different story. The forcing movement had come not from Tochinowaka pushing, but from Aki astonishingly wrenching and twisting the junior champion, manoeuvring him into position. When Tochi began pushing forward, Aki went for his *coup de grâce*: utchari, the spin throw on the rope. Both men went plunging off the dohyo and into the lap of Asashio, waiting for his bout. The gyoji gave the decision to Tochinowaka. As he did so, one of the five ringside judges shot up his hand to dispute the call. A judges' conference on the dohyo, or mono-ii, was followed by an announcement over the public address system. The bout was Akinoshima's. Technically, his foot had been the last to leave the clay inside the ring. The victory gave him his third consecutive majority, promotion to komusubi and a well-deserved Shukun-sho or Outstanding Performance prize for beating a yokozuna and three ozeki.

In the Kyushu basho that followed, Aki again overturned three ozeki and had a terrific try at upsetting Chiyonofuji with throws, but came up empty. He was unlucky to miss promotion to sekiwake by a whisker, and also the Fighting Spirit prize, allowing Kirishima to catch him off-guard on the final day and reduce his scoreline to 7–8. In 1989 his fortunes were again rather mixed. He started out in the January basho, ranked senior number 1, by spectacularly yanking Chiyonofuji's leg from under him and then polishing off the job with an outer arm throw. Yet he ended with make-koshi (7–8) there as well.

Another impressive victory over Ozeki Asahifuji in the March basho in Osaka, another win over Ozeki Konishiki, and another majority scoreline (8–7) brought him a Fighting Spirit award (Kanto-sho), this time shared with Masurao.

Unfortunately Aki was also losing bouts to young tiros like Terao and Kotogaume, and one of his victories was by default. Promoted to sekiwake for the Natsu basho in Tokyo, The Killer Whale fared rather worse – perhaps because of promotion jitters but perhaps, too, because opponents were beginning to work him out, finding their own answers to Aki's cranial chest attacks. Mitoizumi, always a hard challenge for the smaller man's burrowing skills, had given Akinoshima such a spiteful shove to finish their bout in the 1988 Aki basho that TV commentator Lyall Watson had observed it was 'the nearest thing to violence you'll ever see in sumo'. Here in the Natsu 89, The Salt Shaker simply lifted Aki up in the air and deposited him out of the ring, and Hokutenyu and Kirishima added insult to injury to leave the young Killer Whale beached in his first bouts as a sekiwake, 0–3 down. But as the going got tough, tough Aki got going. The next day he up-ended Konishiki, and the day after that he set about Asahifuji again, leaping out at the tachi-ai with his patented head-boring attack and gripping The Sea Slug's belt in front as the ozeki writhed and wriggled. Then, to Asahifuji's horror, the small sekiwake took the initiative and marched him towards the edge, shoving him over like a sack of coal. The earlier victories were no mistake: The Sea Slug definitely had a problem with The Whale. It was a good win for Aki in a losing cause, because on day eight he injured his right leg being thrown down by his frequent oppressor Hokutoumi and ended up with another make-koshi, a losing score of 6–9. Demoted back to senior number 1 for the Nagoya basho, he suffered a further setback, making only 7–8 there too.

Yet what a 7–8! He had not only knocked six bells off Yokozuna Hokutoumi but also, on day nine, come back from an apparently fatal Chiyonofuji leg trip to send his second and much bigger prize crashing by uwate nage. The Wolf would handle him with extreme care in future. The pair of them stood locked in motionless combat for over a minute in the middle of the ring in their next confrontation, in the Aki basho of 1989, before Chiyo could decide how to get rid of his small tormentor. And in November, at the Kyushu tournament, The Wolf actually jumped aside at the tachi-ai in a quite uncharacteristic avoidance manoeuvre, indicating that he now sees the young Whale as a bundle of trouble. But while Akinoshima appears to be having a 'whale' of a time against the big challenges, worrying Asahifuji, Hokutoumi and Onokuni half to death, he keeps letting himself down against the lower-rankers and coming up with losing scores. Hence his rather unworthy position on the banzuke. He did badly in the last 1989 basho, turning in a paltry 5-10.

Early days yet, of course. But Akinoshima is worth watching, not just because he throws the odd giant about, or because he is skilled on the belt beyond his years, but because he has the character, the heart, to push and punish himself beyond his physical limits. A rikishi who can do this wins victories not only over other men, but more important, over himself, and this is a great asset in sumo. To date he has a win–loss rate of 243–184 over 47 basho (up to November 1989), which record has garnered him four Gold Stars or Kinboshi as well as his Outstanding Performance prize and his two Fighting Spirit awards. Certainly no one can doubt his dedication, and he has explained to Channel 4 that he's seeking to achieve a style that will have his opponents out of the ring 'in one go'. Any female admirers hoping to whisper sweet nothings in either of this bachelor's cauliflower ears may have to wait a while. Aki is a man with a mission.

ASAHIFUJI

Rank: Ozeki
Stable: Oshima
Weight: 142 kg (22 st 5 lb)
Height: 188 cm (6 ft 2 in)

Asahifuji was a sometime fisherman; now he's a perpetual ozeki. He is nicknamed Fuji, but the Japanese also call him something terrible: 'Tsugaru Namako'. The Tsugaru part is fine: it's the old name for the place where he was born. It's the second part that's a bit below the mawashi because a 'namako' is a sea-slug or sea-cucumber. Clever as this reference is to Saya's

slippery skills and his family's connection with the fishing industry, being called 'The Tsugaru Slug' is not everyone's idea of a flattering handle. So when Saya was promoted to his present rank, he told journalists that from now on he'd like to be known as something a bit 'posher', and when they asked what it was he said, 'the Tsugaru *Prince*'. They all laughed, but poor Asahifuji got his wish: he's been a 'prince' on the heir apparent rank of ozeki ever since. 'Eternal ozeki' is a sumo label, rather like 'choke artist' in Western sports, which refers to exceptionally talented people who always seem to miss the top by a whisker. Such labels are deeply hurtful and offensive to the sportsmen concerned, but the fact remains that Asahifuji has been on the brink of promotion to yokozuna so many times that he may at last have lost heart. If he comes to Britain on the 1991 tour, we shall have to boost his morale.

Saya is a great favourite of British fans, who followed his successful fight for promotion to ozeki in 1987, and began phoning Channel 4 about this handsome, lazy-eyed 'Robert Mitchum type' who travelled to the stable on a push-bike in his kimono and wooden sandals. (He had a scooter as well.) They liked his style. Some rikishi look like bombs about to go off. Asahifuji looks as if he can just about be bothered to get up in the mornings, which British people find very swanky. Seeing him waiting for his turn on the dohyo rubbing his eyes – this is normally a tension-ridden time – Lyall Watson commented, 'Asahifuji seems to have difficulty staying awake.' It's true: The Slug looks sluggish.

In practice he is often doleful and lethargic – though he intends to turn in an electric performance once the real fighting begins. In the shikiri naoshi he goes through his staring and squatting without too much attention to detail, his lazy eyes focusing somewhere at the back of the stadium as he flicks his bit of salt with as much nastiness as he can muster. He hasn't the terrifying countenance or evil eye for this sort of thing, but he does his best, pulling faces manfully. Sometimes, when it's particularly important to look menacing (as, for example, before a fight with Chiyonofuji), he contrives a fierce grimace by pulling his mouth into an upside-down crescent. This has the effect of making him look as though he's about to burst into tears. This is Saya's version of the fire and ferocity you are supposed to generate during the

Lazy-eyed and unorthodox, Asahifuji appears not to give two hoots about winning. But he cared enough to add tsuppari to his armoury.

psyching ceremonials. Fortunately his opponents don't need any convincing of Asahifuji's dangerousness – they know he can beat them by technique alone, often by techniques neither they nor his oyakata have ever seen before. In fact, The Slug has forgotten more about sumo than most of his rivals will ever learn. He knows the subtle art of belt grips, the throws, the niceties of timing, and more recently the science of tsuppari with which to blast out his attackers as well. Besides, even if they get to grips with him, as perhaps Asahifuji hopes they will, his body is so supple and his manoeuvres so quick, that they think they've got hold of an octopus rather than a slug. On form he is big trouble anywhere in the ring, and

deadly on the rope, even when apparently beaten.

Away from the dohyo, Asahifuji is renowned for being quiet, soft-spoken and easy-going, unassuming even in the modest world of sumo wrestlers. He doesn't boast or show off, or talk about rivalry with anybody. Onokuni entered the Juryo Division at the same time as Saya and because he got into Makunouchi at the same time as well, press people tried to make something of it. How would Saya feel if Onokuni were promoted to ozeki before him? Asahifuji said he couldn't care less. When it was suggested that he got good grades at high school, Saya replied that the tests were very easy. He was the one of whom it was always said that 'he disappears into the woodwork' or 'he's overshadowed by so-and-so'. And the smart cars would flash past as he peddled round Ryogoku district on his bike like any run-of-the-mill commuter, instead of the outstandingly gifted sumotori that he was.

Saya was born Masaya Suginomori in Aomori Prefecture, in a fishing town called Kizukuri, on 6 July 1960. In the garden his father built a dohyo, and required his son to practise on it. He was by trade an electrician (Channel 4 commentary said he was a fisherman, which he may well have been in his spare time), but he loved sumo, and he was determined to reserve a future in it for his boy. He set Saya to learn the fundamentals and made him work through them again and again until he got them into his head. Saya's father was very strict. He had been a keen amateur and still devoted much of his time to official duties with the Prefecture Sumo Federation, where he was vice-chairman and a respected figure. Saya would like sumo or he would lump it – and fortunately he liked it well enough, and made good progress.

Anyone who has studied sport's thoroughbreds – children groomed for sports stardom by parents who missed it themselves – would have to have every sympathy for Saya. Such youngsters, however obedient to their parents' ambitions, tend to progress very fast up the junior ranks, only to hover inexplicably on the brink of greatness. Their tragedy is well-documented (e.g. in one of my books, *Sportsmen Under Stress*, Century-Hutchinson, 1986), and the rare ones who succeed (like Chris Evert in tennis) have at some point to decide that they want to win for themselves, rather than their parents. The rest, inwardly or outwardly, rebel, often blaming their disappointments on 'bad luck' or unfair treatment.

In his early years at junior high school, Saya would attend for registration and then go missing. Where was he? Relaxing, playing pinball in the *pachinko* parlour, or sound asleep in the grounds of the temple, or messing about on the shore, watching the fishermen mending their nets (he would help out occasionally). He was training at sumo both at home with his father and in the school club, and doing well there, finishing third in a national schoolboy competition, so he was a bit tired during school hours, and liable to doze off. He managed to wake himself up in time to get respectable academic grades, but when he left school it was to attend university at the sumo

hothouse, Kinki, whose club had nurtured such future stars as Asashio. There he would have to be on his toes.

At university Saya had an advantage over most of his fellow-students in the sumo club in that he had been drilled not only at school but at home as well, and already knew a good deal for a boy of his age. He quickly began to shine, winning the West Japan Student Newcomers tournament and being singled out as a rikishi of real potential. And it was at this point, just on the brink of stardom, that Saya decided to clear off home. What his father said when Saya darkened his doorway is not recorded, but the young man became a village fisherman, and many a slug he saw as his boat plied the cold dawn waters off the north coast of Honshu Island trawling for sea bream and yellowtail.

In fact this was not the first time Saya had run away: he'd done it on a couple of previous occasions, but never so dramatically. He was fed up with the never-ending chores, and being told what to do. He was fed up with early morning practice and bowing and scraping to all the seniors. He was only young and he wanted to be out enjoying himself like other Japanese teenagers. And whereas everything you did on the dohyo was carefully ordered and ritualized like the tea ceremony, on the sea you were free, and could see from one far horizon to another. Not that Saya wanted to spend the rest of his life fishing for bream. He just wanted a break from being dutiful all the time, so off he went.

How long he would have remained a fisherman is hard to say, but Asahifuji is a man who likes his creature comforts and a good snooze, and the cold and damp are uncongenial to him and make his injured joints flare up. In any case he knew that he was unusually good at sumo, and somewhere at the back of his mind he believed that if he really put himself out, there was no reason why he shouldn't become a yokozuna. Many others had faith in his abilities: his father had always had high hopes for him, and an office worker at his high school also thought Saya should be fighting rather than fishing. One day he became so exasperated by Saya's lack of motivation that he got in touch with a sumo boss who needed fighters for a stable he had just revived, and told him about this 'fisherman's' talents. The oyakata offered Saya a berth in his heya. Notwithstanding

Saya's reputation for running off, he was prepared to give him a fresh start, another shot at greatness. Most lads would have jumped at the chance, but this sleepy-eyed young man was so laid back as to be almost horizontal. He told a reporter some years later, 'Actually either way would have been all right. I didn't have any special reason for joining.'

Once he was at the heya, though, he made an effort. One of the reasons for this was that he had a pair of 'evil-looking eyes' watching his behaviour, which seemed to follow him about the stable with special interest. They belonged to stable master Oshima Oyakata – small of stature but magnetic of gaze. This man knew everything about sumo technique that was worth knowing. He knew how to overpower larger opponents and use their weight against them, because as an ozeki in his own day, he'd had to be dauntingly good. He wasn't as strong or as big as his rivals. Even to be admitted as an apprentice and meet the size requirements he'd had to get a friend to welt him over the head with a piece of wood so that the resulting lump would add to his height sufficiently. Whereas Saya had a desultory attitude towards this sport, his oyakata had been willing to endure any amount of pain and hard work to succeed in it. Whereas Saya was six foot two, this man had had to fight just to be *allowed* to fight with people twice his size.

He had seen in Saya uncommon abilities, and he was not about to allow this 'fisherman' off the hook. So his eyes were on Saya's every move, just in case he kicked over the traces. The oyakata's fighting name had been 'Asahikuni', and Saya was now given the name 'Asahifuji' – Sunrise over Fuji. Clearly, whatever vicarious hopes Saya's father may have cherished about his sumo future, this gentleman's were even higher.

Asahifuji made his sumo début in the Hatsu basho in 1981, and it took him precisely 12 tournaments to get to the top division, Makunouchi. He worked very hard indeed, and only ran away once, and then not permanently. The following year, 1984, he invested in a set of weights and pumped iron several times a week to strengthen his rubbery tentacles. He was lanky for a rikishi, but putting on the pounds as well, aiming for his optimum fighting weight of about 22½ stone. His waistline disappeared and he began to suffer from stomach pains. Perhaps he had

strained himself weightlifting. He began to go up and down the senior ranks rather alarmingly, and his stomachaches got worse. His oyakata, who once nearly died from pancreatitis, became concerned, and Asahifuji went for a medical examination. Sure enough, bulking up his weight had damaged his pancreas as well. From now on he would have to watch his diet carefully. Acute pancreatitis has the same symptoms as appendicitis, and without immediate surgery the patient is unlikely to survive.

It is against this background that Saya's progress has to be judged, for it was rather remarkable. His early win–loss record was 346–213, and the Kyushu basho in November 1984 saw him take his first prize, for Fighting Spirit. He had beaten two ozeki to finish 11–4. Promoted to komusubi for the next basho he shifted up a gear, dispensing with three ozeki and a yokozuna in the first week of the 1985 Hatsu basho, only to run out of steam, finishing with a losing score. In the next tournament in May he was back at the senior number 1 slot, but there he delivered 9–6 and won another award, this time the extremely coveted Gino-sho, for technique. At 24 he was coming of age.

Two years later, having stalled for a time at sekiwake, Saya was enlarging his repertoire by sparring with heavy hitters from Takasago heya and perfecting a technique that was to become a great favourite with him – tsuppari. The more Saya used it the better he got, and the better he got, the more he resorted to slapping rather than close-quarter fighting. His range of skills was now fairly awesome for a man of his age, and he was ready, in 1987, for the next step up the ladder. With 31 wins over three basho, he stood on the threshold of promotion in the Aki basho in September, seen on television by British audiences. They were not aware that his margin of error was three losses in the basho if he were to make the big breakthrough to ozeki, and when he was bellied out by Onokuni on day one, it was reduced to two.

Asahifuji beat his next eight opponents, using a combination of throws, blows and belt grips. On day ten he faced the frightening challenge of Chiyonofuji, and he had The Wolf in his intended grip, but didn't take advantage. Chiyo told the press afterwards, 'I won by a hair'. Another loss to Yokozuna Hokutoumi on day eleven sent a shudder through Oshima stable, because Asahifuji simply couldn't afford one more false move. Two more good wins brought a sigh of relief, but his next opponent was the absolutely enormous Konishiki who was giving everybody a good hiding and looked very formidable indeed. In fact, in the shikiri naoshi, the giant Dump Truck stared up at Asahifuji so forcefully that he got The Slug slightly annoyed, and when the moment of truth came he decided the only suitable ripost would be to step aside at the tachi-ai and let Konishiki go sailing past. Konishiki blundered by, the pair exchanged slaps, and then The Slug forced the ozeki over the rope. (Saya has used this ruse on The Dump Truck since, and with similar effect.) He followed this triumph with a win over Tochinowaka to finish 12–3, which was just what the sumo doctor ordered (Oshima Oyakata was known as 'Dr Sumo' for his technical wizardry). Asahifuji was not only granted his promotion: he won two prizes as well – for Fighting Spirit (Kanto-sho) and for Technical Skill (Gino-sho).

Sadly, this was to be Saya's last promotion. He has lingered on the second-highest rank of ozeki ever since, often threatening to make the big push to yokozuna, often being carefully considered by the Yokozuna Promotion Council after a string of good scores, only to be pipped at the post in the next basho. He looked to be about to make the breakthrough in 1988 when he beat everyone except Hokutoumi to take the yusho in the Hatsu basho in January. His winning score was 14–1, and his victory over Chiyonofuji, muscling the fearsome yokozuna out on the belt, was spectacular. But in the next three tournaments he couldn't match this form, losing three or four bouts a basho and losing to The Wolf in May, as tournament runner-up, in a way that will long be repeated on Japanese television for its stunning skill. Chiyonofuji ended their long battle by carrying the larger man towards the rope and then jumping at him like a frog to topple him over the edge.

In the 1988 Aki basho, seen on British television, Saya was still in with a chance, but the only man capable of beating The Wolf failed to do so and he finished in second place with 12–3. Second best was becoming second nature. In the Kyushu basho in November, he was runner-up yet again, The Wolf hoisting him out on day fourteen to clinch the yusho, leaving Saya with his fourth

12–3 of 1988. It wasn't good enough to make him a yokozuna, though it did earn him something: a Rikishi of the Year award for his 73 winning bouts (beating Chiyo's tally because The Wolf had sat out one basho).

Saya's announcement at the beginning of 1989, that he was going to make yokozuna this year or bust, may if anything have added slightly to the pressure he already felt about making the big push. In the New Year Hatsu basho he stormed to 14–1, got into a play-off with Yokozuna Hokutoumi and then succumbed to a bludgeoning attack. It was particularly upsetting because he had beaten Hokutoumi in their regular bout. He had even beaten Chiyonofuji, edging him to the rope and then tipping him over by an outer leg trip. The only yokozuna he *didn't* beat was The Panda – and he'd had him on the rope as well, and failed to polish him off. Never mind. After another great surge in the March basho in Osaka, Saya was within an ace of the yusho and the white rope belt yet again. By now it was becoming apparent that, with three reigning yokozuna in office, Asahifuji was expected to beat them all to prove he deserved their rank – though in the past Grand Champions have been created on far shorter qualifications. The Slug slugged it out determinedly with two of them, beating Onokuni on the belt and bundling out Hokutoumi by an unorthodox backward thigh hoist, after a terrible struggle, and needed only victory over The Wolf on senshuraku to clinch his promotion, standing on a score of 12–2. Poor Saya got his win all right, but only on paper. The Wolf, who won the yusho, defaulted with a dislocated shoulder.

Even worse was what happened to Saya in the May tournament, the Natsu. Given the East Ozeki ready, in 1987, for the next step up the ladder. With 31 wins over three basho, he stood on the threshold of promotion in the Aki basho in September, seen on television by British audiences. They were not aware that his margin of error was three losses in the basho if he were to make the big breakthrough to ozeki, and when he was bellied out by Onokuni on day one, it was reduced to two.

bouts to go. How could he fail? Unfortunately sport's thoroughbreds can usually find a way, and the next day Asahifuji allowed Onokuni to shear through his defences with his great right mitt and bustle him out like a sack of potatoes. He recovered himself sufficiently to beat Hokutenyu, but he had lost his lead and sunk into a play-off with Hokutoumi, also on 13–2. It was a bout that Saya will remember for the rest of his life. The Bulldog flew out of the tachi-ai and seized The Slug's belt with one powerful paw, going for an arm throw. Asahifuji was unable to stop his forward momentum, needing only a little shove from behind. It was all over, and with this final turn of the screw, something inside Saya seemed to break. No ozeki has ever tried harder, or come closer, only to fail.

East Ozeki for yet another basho – more times than any fighter in recent history – Asahifuji slipped in the Nagoya to an ignominious (for him) 8–7, losing to people in an almost desultory way, and recovering only slightly in the Aki basho in September. The Yokozuna Promotion Council made no secret of their displeasure and he is now in considerable trouble, not least because lately there is someone much younger who can out-think and out-wrestle him – Akinoshima. The pundits are tipping The Killer Whale for the top, so Saya is in danger of disappearing into the woodwork once again. In November, he made his majority by the skin of his teeth. It is a great pity, for this man has everything in the way of sumo skills, and the American magazine *Sumo World* lists a long and varied gamut of them: tsuki-dashi, yori-kiri, oshi-dashi, uwate-nage, sukui nage, katasu kashi, yori taoshi and shitate dashi nage – to name but a few. He likes his right hand inside and his left hand outside on the belt – the same as Chiyonofuji – and his win–loss record to date, 459–280, will give you some idea of his technical cunning. So too will his haul of two Kinboshi, two Kanto-sho, two Shukun-sho and no less than five Gino-sho or Technical Skill prizes. But he has won the Cup only once, and been runner-up six times – which is significant in itself. He is now complaining of his pancreatitis flaring up again. Small wonder, knowing he must now either give up on promotion or start again from scratch.

His oyakata, being a technical wizard, attributes Saya's problems to unorthodox technique, explaining that if only his star ozeki would listen to him and adopt a more regular style of beltwork and throws, he would climb every mountain. Oshima Oyakata's view is that since Saya wins by his own curious methods, he's never going to straighten himself out. But Saya's methods worked just fine until he got within range of 'the barrier'. He doesn't like what we call crunch matches, and says he's mentally unprepared for them (play-offs, for example). On those occasions he can't fight his natural way because he gets very tense and nervous. Sumo is a spiritual test and will find out a man's weakness if he has one, whatever techniques he may use. The only remedy is to strengthen the spirit, if necessary by intensive psychological training.

Asahifuji is married to stable boss Kasuga-yama's niece, Junko Enomoto. He likes sleeping, playing Mah-Jong, fishing, good food, and listening to music – mainly pop and disco. Like several of the top fighters, he has a lovely voice and sings Japanese *enka*, winning prizes for it in televised contests and looking suitably composed and sad. But then, on or off the dohyo, Saya is always underwhelmed. He has been more than once likened to Wakanohana II, who as a yokozuna was tall, talented and ticking over.

HOKUTENYU

Rank: Ozeki
Stable: Mihogaseki
Weight: 144 kg (22 st 9 lb)
Height: 183 cm (6 ft)

'Hokutenyu' means 'Heavenly Help from the North', and there are bevies of the most beautiful Japanese fans willing to testify to Hoku's heavenliness by standing up and screaming his shikona at the top of their lungs as he goes through his sacred ring rites. What unsettling effect this may have had on his career nobody knows, though he is by no means the first high-ranking sumo wrestler to have had a half-crazed female following, and a few have somehow managed to buckle down and make yokozuna in spite of such distractions. But it cannot have helped Hokutenyu's concentration to know that when he steps on the dohyo his opponent is not the only one eager to lay hands on him, or that, win or lose, the girls will go into frenzies anyway.

His Heavenliness. Despite his fan following, ideal build and strength, The Polar Bear has somehow frozen to the second rung of the ladder.

Their idol comes from the opposite end of Japan to sumo's other sexpot, Terao. But whereas the southerner looks lean, hot-blooded and almost Mediterranean, Hokutenyu appears cold, hard and built to withstand a Russian winter and a couple of yeti. He comes from Hokkaido, Japan's most northerly island. When he looked out to sea as a large small boy, on one horizon was the USSR, where the great Taiho's father came from. Hokutenyu is known as 'The Polar Bear', for obvious reasons. He is hefty and burly, with thighs like tree trunks and most of his 22 stone centred round his waist, hips and legs, as every good rikishi's should. In fact, if you asked to see the image of an ideal sumotori, the Japanese would probably show you Hokutenyu, because he certainly looks the part, at least.

Hokutenyu's power to mesmerize sumo's female followers comes partly from his rarefied smile and sneering good looks, and partly from his reputation for prodigious, iron-fisted strength, but mainly from his demeanour on the dohyo, where he is reckoned to be the second-best place to store your ice-lolly if you don't have a freezer. Cool, casual and unhurried, he goes through his salt-flicking with an air of calm disdain. In the shikiri crouch he is noted for prolonged narrow stares, his eyeballs boring upwards into his opponent's skull like two black bullets, communicating something unpleasant and cold-blooded. These evil glances have upset a few of his rivals and Chiyonofuji, who comes from the same part of Japan, is known to dislike him, following a long-standing feud. This reportedly began after a clash in 1979 at Kokonoe heya in which Hokutenyu's kid brother was hurt. The Polar Bear considered Chiyo was entirely responsible for that, but all the daggers on the dohyo over the years cannot have helped cement a warm friendship between them, either. Whatever The Wolf's invincibility against everybody else, Hokutenyu is always capable of plunging out and upsetting him, in more ways than one. In fact he has made beating Chiyo something of a party trick, and features it regularly on his agenda. He did it for the 14th time in the Nagoya basho 1989 when, on 8–6, The Polar Bear appeared to have nothing particular to gain by it, other than annoying Chiyonofuji and obstructing his passage to the yusho.

Hokutenyu was born Katsuhiko Chiba on 8 August 1960 – under the sign of the Lion according to Western astrology – and destined either for grandeur or bitterness. Having been scouted by the oyakata at the age of nine and given 3,000 yen to secure his commitment, he joined an ancient and highly successful stable, Mihogaseki, seminary of some of sumo's great names, like Kitanoumi, to whom he became *tsukebito*, or personal servant. There he was seen as the boy with everything: an ideal build and style and, even as a teenager, formidably powerful. His first appearance on the dohyo was in the Haru basho in March 1976, and it immediately became apparent that Hokutenyu was no ordinary prospect. Yotsu-zumo, so hard for some rikishi to get to grips with, proved no trouble to him at all. As a fighter he was inclined towards the belt of any adversary, clenching the sash in a grip that was to become known as the strongest in sumo, and driving with all his might. Such an attack, coming from such a weight distribution with its low centre of gravity and wrenching power, was hard to resist, and opponents found themselves shucked aside like children wrestling with their father. Hoku's passage to ozeki was as swift as it was unencumbered, with an early win–loss rate of 451–285.

Having broken into the top division in the Kyushu basho at the end of 1980, Hoku reached his present rank in just two-and-a-half years. At 22 he took his first yusho and looked every inch the ideal sumotori. People began comparing him to the great Futabayama, whom he was said to resemble, and it was naturally assumed that The Polar Bear could scarcely fail to become the next yokozuna unless someone stopped him with an elephant gun. With such power, how could he not prevail? His technical range was already remarkable. Exploding out of the tachi-ai he could use his force for tsuki (thrusting) or oshi (shoving) according to his whim. Yori-kiri, the force-out, was tailor-made for him, as was yori taoshi, the force out and down. Then there was tsuri (lifting) and a variety of hip throws using his mighty arms. Shitate-nage, shitate dashi nage, uwate-nage, underarm, overarm, pushing, twisting or pulling – any sort of leverage would do. Opponents, including Chiyonofuji, could be sent stumbling, or be flung out into the front seats. There was technically very little that Hokutenyu could not do. And those who believe that sumo is won chiefly by physical strength – and there are a lot of them – were reassured by this spectacle that their philosophy was correct in every detail. Unfortunately sumo's invisible barriers can bring even the strongest sekitori to a full stop, and the biggest barrier of them all is at ozeki, the one just before you reach the top.

Just when everything looked perfect for Hokutenyu, problems began to set in. Like all rikishi he had bulked up his weight at the chanko pot. Japanese food contains a lot of carbohydrates, a lot of sugar and starch, and the body will stand just so much of this treatment before it reads a wrestler the Riot Act. Asahifuji developed pancreatitis, and this is not uncommon among rikishi, but the other great fear for their health is that chronic, terrible malfunctioning of the pancreas: diabetes. Hoku developed the disease, and the accompanying disability. Weakness, lassitude, depression – all the things you definitely do not need on the dohyo when you have a few seconds to exert your full power or you are doomed – Hoku began to suffer, and his form was affected accordingly. Worse than the disease itself, which is bad enough because it must be controlled by rigorous attention to one's diet or by insulin injections or both, is that the weakened state makes a wrestler vulnerable to circulation problems and injury, and The Polar Bear began to get hurt in spite of his strength, or perhaps because of it. And worse than all this was that his opponents began to sense something was wrong with Hokutenyu. He had cold feet, perhaps even clay feet. They could bring him down, and if they did it with enough force, he might not be able to get up again. So Hoku's victims on his way to sumo's second highest rank began to think to themselves, 'I'm going to give this ideal sumotori a good hiding'.

It was in 1983, just as the public were wondering when the yokozuna ceremonials would begin, that Hokutenyu, having won the Emperor's Cup, suddenly seemed to lose his appetite for winning. At first, critics were sympathetic: of course his strength had been depleted by diabetes; of course he would be promoted very shortly, just as soon as he strung three good results together. But Hoku's string didn't materialize. He began to look dispirited on the dohyo, and preoccupied. His mind was on other things: he likes music, and messing about with cars, and also cameras, and

takes himself a bit seriously as a photographer. And then of course there were the injuries to worry about, and the sudden stardom, and all these womenfolk to fight off with a shovel – and it was a lot for a chap to contend with, all in all. So Hoku didn't get promoted in 1983 as expected, or in 1984 either. But in 1985 he was what the Japanese call *genki* – he was ready, and firing on all cylinders.

There was now a race for promotion, the other front-runners being Onokuni, Asashio and Kitao. The diminutive Chiyonofuji was being mooted as about to topple over under the combined weight of these young tiros, and The Polar Bear was strongly fancied – and not just by his female following – to take his place. In July, in the Nagoya basho, Hokutenyu turned in a yusho-winning, blistering performance, dropping only two of his bouts and looking mentally and physically overpowering. He was now at the top of his talent and another good showing in the Aki basho in September would almost certainly clinch his long-awaited promotion. His progress through that tournament, too, looked unstoppable. Sure enough, on day eleven he stood 9–1 and with the yusho in his sights, having bounced a lot of his opponents about like corks in a display of power sumo. But it was just then, as his ichimon stable-mates had practically got their white gloves on to make his ceremonial rope belt, and as Hoku saw his 11th opponent's enormous belly advancing towards him, that he suddenly decided, for some reason, to postpone the festivities. The belly belonged to his great rival for promotion, Onokuni, and no sooner had it bumped Hokutenyu over the rope by yori-kiri than Hoku found himself tied with The Panda for second place, both of them now on 9–2. Outwrestled by Chiyonofuji and up-ended by The Plum, Hokutenyu never looked forward. He lost his last five bouts in succession to finish with a mortally disappointing 9–6.

A mere hiccup, The Polar Bear's admirers said: perhaps he was injured again, or suffering from diabetic lassitude. Their man would surely set the record straight in the Kyushu basho in November. And indeed he got to the last five bouts there and only fumbled three of them. But he knew that this was not good enough to make him a yokozuna and, what was more distressing, questions were now beginning to be asked about what in the West we would call his 'temperament' — his spiritual fitness for the task at hand. Why did Hokutenyu seem to 'choke' his crucial bouts? Why did he suddenly start making misjudgements when he was on the point of promotion? Was he over-confident, or overanxious? Why did his fighting spirit give up the ghost? Was he worried about losing, or about winning? In short, what the devil was the matter with him? Whatever it was, it was now becoming fairly academic. The Giant Panda had drawn alongside The Polar Bear in the race for promotion and in the end, in the autumn of 1987, after Hoku had recovered from yet another strange slump and looked ready to prepare for greatness once again, Onokuni overhauled him. And so it came about that the unglamorous Michelin Man, the technically flawed and less versatile Onokuni, and not the classic stylist, the wonderfully powerful and gifted 'ideal sumotori' Hokutenyu, put on the white rope belt. And if Hokutenyu's heart had not broken before, it broke in 1987.

Such is The Polar Bear's sheer store of skills, however, that he can never give up. As long as he remains an ozeki, his talent will continue to beat him against the barrier, trying to push him through. He often looks superb in practice, or when it doesn't matter. It's only in the grip of possible promotion that he really backs off, but as he has been on the brink of promotion many times since 1983, this has meant a lot of backing off, and caused a lot of sumo speculation. When he got married to a young lady by the name of Eimi, the envy of thousands of his fans, some said this might straighten poor Hoku out; others that it would definitely finish him off altogether as marriage is 'known' to weaken a fighter. Fortunately it did neither, but he now has a little daughter to think about, prettier than any of his fans.

Hoku is now 29, and his reputation for having the strongest grip in sumo cannot sustain him forever. In 1988, when he was still recovering from a back injury that forced him to pull out of the action in the March basho and miss the Natsu altogether, British fans saw him flex his muscles in the Aki tournament to dispose of Enazakura, Tochinowaka, Takamisugi, Kirishima, Hananoumi and Kotogaume in rapid succession, by yori-kiri (3), oshi-dashi, okuri-dashi and uwate-nage, all to the accompaniment of screams from Hoku's fans

in their best dresses. But then The Polar Bear seemed to weary of winning, allowing Sakahoko to force him out, Akinoshima and Asashio to send him crashing, The Slug to slough him off and Onokuni to bury him beneath his mounds and force him over the straw ridge. His best battle, against his old enemy Chiyonofuji, looked evenly balanced until Hoku turned aside momentarily to get rid of Chiyo's sagari tangled on his wrist — a blunder ruthlessly exploited by The Wolf. Hokutenyu finished on a bare majority, 8–7, bad news for an ozeki.

In 1989 though, having faded from 9–1 to 10–5 in the 1988 Kyushu and been largely written off as an 'old man' of 28 whose strength was deserting him, Hoku shone once again, for he likes to steer clear of both extremes – too much winning *or* too much losing. He beat Chiyonofuji in the January basho to finish 10–5 and then got down to business. For the first ten days of the spring tournament in Osaka he unleashed himself like an icy blast and froze all his opponents in their tracks. Standing unbeaten on day eleven he had defied those who said he was finished as much as those who said he was about to become a yokozuna in 1983 and 1985. In some strange way this seemed to unsettle him: he lost three of his remaining bouts. His eleventh-day nightmare Onokuni plunged his massive arms for Hoku's belt and then threw him on his knees, and The Wolf scented weakness the next day and sent him sprawling. Finally on senshuraku, Konishiki got hold of his sash and heaved him carefully out of the circle. But The Polar Bear still finished with a highly creditable 12–3, and the Yokozuna Promotion Council turned their weary eyes towards him yet again. Sekitori past 30 have been known to make yokozuna at last. Perhaps...

In May, in the Natsu basho, Hoku's grand foe Chiyonofuji was out of contention with a shoulder injury and The Polar Bear was actually joint leader on day eleven with a score of 10–1. But he lost on day twelve, and then tangled with Kirishima, a man who likes to flick giants over his shoulder when he's in the mood, and the number 1 maegashira pulled off one of his famous utchari upsets on the rope and sent the hunky Hoku crashing out of the reckoning for the yusho. He ended up with 10–5. He was still in with a faint chance: a convincing score in the Nagoya basho might have gone down well with the Promotion

Council and tipped the balance in his favour. Hokutenyu managed to avoid such a catastrophe by collapsing in his first three bouts, getting off to a dreadful start and turning in a comparatively miserable 9–6. His light came out only once from under the bushel – in his bout with Chiyonofuji. The Wolf was naturally in the lead and on his way to yet another yusho, and Hokutenyu suddenly felt like giving a show of his strength. Chiyo was snow-ploughed out by yori-kiri, which put him to the trouble of a play-off for the Cup with his own stable-mate and fellow-Yokozuna Hokutoumi – a fact no doubt gratifying to The Polar Bear, now turning 29. But he had shown his age against Terao and Kotogaume, and at times looked brooding rather than menacing. Nothing daunted by this setback, in the September (Aki) basho he was once again doing what he does best – proving everybody wrong. At one point he was in the lead; at another he was in second place on 7–1 and breathing down The Wolf's neck. But though he may have given Chiyonofuji something to think about as his only real challenger in that tournament, and though he'd demolished Terao with satisfying ease, he faded on the home stretch to finish 10–5, and in November he could only manage 5–10 on account of an elbow injury.

What Hokutenyu still has in his locker, nobody can rightly say. He is still perfectly capable of beating anyone other than himself, but that opponent has proved his undoing on so many occasions, he may well have conceded defeat by now. No one can second-guess his abilities: he has won just as many yusho as his old rival Onokuni (who has rested on his yokozuna laurels quite a lot). They both have two to their credit (The Polar Bear's second coming in July 1985), and Hokutenyu has been runner-up or a close contender on several other occasions as well. He has an array of awards – two Shukun-sho, one Gino-sho, three Kinboshi and – as if to defy those critics of his Fighting Spirit – four Kanto-sho. His win–loss record now stands at 607–384.

But he would need three good consecutive scores and perhaps another turn with the Emperor's Cup before the Yokozuna Promotion Council would elevate him to sumo's highest rank after such long dithering. And that last great barrier still looms like an electric fence before him. Having burned his fingers on it several times, Hokutenyu may hesitate to get within sizzling range again.

KOTOGAUME

Rank: Sekiwake
Stable: Sadogatake
Weight: 183 kg (28 st 11 lb)
Height: 180 cm (5 ft 11 in)

Kotogaume looks deceptively harmless. A chubby dumpling of a lad, waddling and dimpled like a human Cabbage Patch doll, he arouses maternal instincts throughout Japan. Yet Kotogaume has trounced both Hokutoumi and Chiyonofuji with his crashing power and is taken seriously by every man on the dohyo. They are not fooled by the coy expression as of one caught with his hand in the biscuit barrel. They know what he is capable of. If all else fails, he might eat them. Kotogaume is renowned at Sadogatake stable as 'Ebisko' or 'The Gobbler', from his habit of tucking in at all hours. Legend has it that he sits down to a midday meal of chanko-nabe with several bowls of rice and side dishes and then goes out in search of proper nourishment. He has put on over a stone in weight since last seen on British television, and as he is only five foot eleven, it shows.

Wrestlers from the Sadogatake heya all traditionally prefix their fighting names with 'Koto', a Chinese character for a musical instrument something like a lyre. 'Ume', however, means 'Plum' and comes from the Japanese 'Umegatani' – the name of two famous yokozuna, one of whom actually came from Plum's own prefecture of Toyama. Kitayama Satoshi, which is Plum's real name, was one of the '1963 crop' of boys born in the year Showa 33, like Konishiki, Hokutoumi and Terao, who are collectively known as 'Sanpachi-gumi'. Little Plum came into the world on 5 October 1963 and showed no interest in sumo whatsoever. Like the equally rotund Onokuni he wanted to be a judo-ka and was spotted by people from Sadogatake stable performing as a judo black belt, first dan. No doubt they thought that, with all his size and power, he could go on to perfect his grappling skills and become an all-round sumotori, adept on the belt as well. This was not to be.

The heya took him in as an apprentice after he

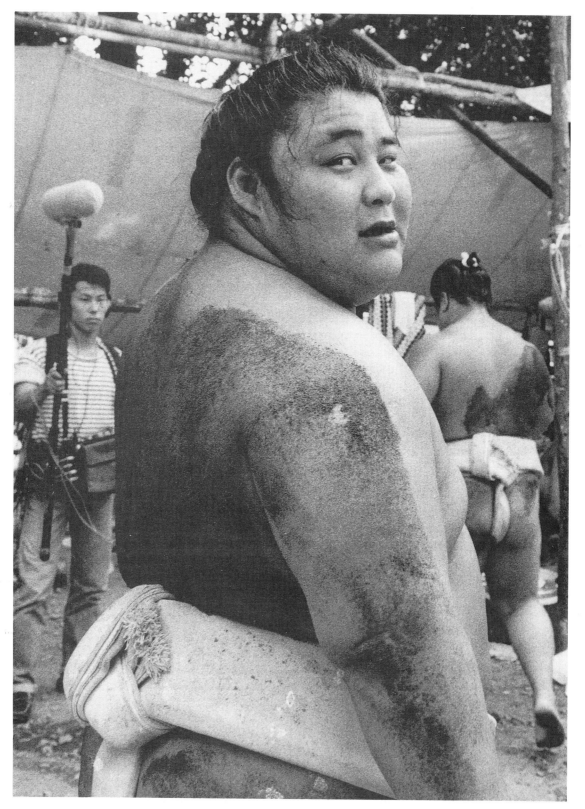

The Plum goes in search of a square meal.

finished junior high school, in March 1979, whereupon Plum promptly lost confidence and hurt his knees doing strenuous keiko and being pushed to the clay by other young men equally burly. Plum was made *tsukebito* (personal servant) to the then rising Ozeki Kotokaze, whose own knees were worse than Kotogaume's but who inspired the young Plum with his fierce courage, fighting his own pain as well as his opponents. Kotokaze showed Plum how a sumo wrestler should behave — with self-restraint and courtesy at all times. The younger man has tried to follow this example.

It took Kotogaume five years of rumbling round in obscurity to reach the threshold of Makunouchi or the First Division, but once he got this far, he put his head down and charged. He made his komusubi début in 1985 at the November basho in Fukuoka, where one of Kotokaze's crippled knees finally gave under him and he was forced to retire. The ozeki said that he was very sorry to leave sumo, but that seeing Plum's success had been some consolation to him and taken a great responsibility off his shoulders. Now Sadogatake heya would have a new champion.

Since then, though Plum's weight has gone up and up, his form has gone up and down, bouncing him back and forth between the ranks of maegashira (top division senior) and sekiwake as though Plum can't quite make up his mind what he wants to be. There have been some interesting tussles with Izutsu stable's Sakahoko (Kotogaume spars with the Izutsu men quite a bit) which have had sumo fans scratching their heads trying to remember who ranks as what. In 1989, for example, at the Haru basho, Plum, ranked komusubi, got hold of Sakahoko, ranked sekiwake, and twisted him on to the clay. Sakahoko failed to make his majority and was demoted to komusubi, while Plum, though he made only the bare majority of 8–7, was promoted to sekiwake by virtue of his achievement in coming from 0–6 down at the start of the tournament. Two months later the pair met again in the Natsu basho. This time Komusubi Sakahoko threw himself at the bonny sekiwake and Plum went bouncing down towards relegation again, clinging to his 8–7 majority by a whisker. One of his best recent results came in the 1989 Nagoya basho, when he clapped his pudgy hands and charged at ten of his opponents like a bull. A score of 10–5 is very

commendable for a man who confesses he's no good at fighting on the belt, and it earned him a Fighting Spirit prize for beating two ozeki and showing unusual gumption against Mitoizumi, Akinoshima, Terao and Sakahoko.

Plum is nothing if not unpredictable. He is very good indeed at pushing and shoving techniques — practically all his victories have come from thrusting and bouncing at his opponents, using his weight and power and often moving in low for his attack. But then you never know whether Plum will send somebody flying or fall flat on his face, because he tends to lean forward to the point of overbalancing. Oshi-dashi is what Plum likes best, though he also enjoys a good thrust-out, twist-down or rear push-out (okuri-dashi). If all else fails he has a nice pulling outer arm throw in his locker. Because he is shorter than most of his opposition he tends to be looking up at them anyway as he comes out of the jump-off or tachi-ai, and this has hampered him over the years. Some of his adversaries have been able to seize him by the back of the neck and use this as a fulcrum to press or throw him down, as Chiyonofuji demonstrated for British television audiences in the Aki basho of 1988, finishing poor Plum off by uwate dashi nage (the pulling outer arm throw).

Not that The Wolf has always been so effective in dealing with the chubby pusher. In the Nagoya basho earlier that year, Plum looked to the referee to have Chiyo beaten, only for the decision to be over-ruled by the judges. Almost the same thing happened in the November basho in 1989. But in the Natsu basho, 1988, Plum left them in no doubt whatever, upsetting Chiyonofuji rather badly and putting The Wolf in the mood for his long unbroken winning streak of the coming months. Kotogaume seems to specialize in beating his superiors in rank — Yokozuna Hokutoumi was up-ended in the Hatsu basho in 1988 and Plum is always good for the odd ozeki or two, thudding into them with underdog determination. The trouble comes when Plum meets someone of lower rank, whom he might be expected to shove out with ease. It is then that Plum goes into his shell and starts acting defensively. Kotogaume says that he concentrates very hard for his bouts with the big fish, but that the smaller fry don't seem to get him going. Konishiki says that to be a great sumo wrestler 'you have to be hungry'. Plum is hungry as the next man, but he leaves the little bits on the side of his plate while he looks for something more satisfying.

In the Kyushu basho at the end of 1988, he managed only five wins – but one of these was against Yokozuna Onokuni. He had promised great things earlier in the Hatsu tournament, finishing third there with 12–3 as a number 7 maegashira and earning a Kanto-sho. He had followed this up with an Outstanding Performance prize in May. But he's a hard man to rank. As a sekiwake he often fights like a senior, and as a senior, he often looks like a sekiwake. As maegashira number 3 in January 1989 he disposed of two ozeki and a yokozuna (Onokuni by oshi-taoshi) in waddling to his majority, 8–7.

Like Konishiki, another '1963 Boy', Plum is obsessed with the pushing style and disinclined to mess about on the belt. He says he really doesn't like yotsu-zumo and hasn't any confidence at it though he can do it in an emergency. He wants to get better and better at tsuki and oshi techniques, so that opponents don't get the chance to grapple with him in the first place. He is improving his balance now and not toppling forward so much, though he still tends to bundle downwards at the tachi-ai. If he can perfect the low centre of gravity that all sumo wrestlers try to cultivate, he can use his head like the nose of a missile to crash into an opponent and frighten the life out of him. Whether or not Plum can force through the invisible barriers to ozeki and yokozuna like this, of course, is another matter. At 26 he can have a few good charges at them yet, certainly. His win–loss rate over 66 basho stands at 387–321.

He has never won a tournament but has taken one Outstanding Performance prize, one Technical Skills prize, two Gold Stars and four Fighting Spirit awards – a signal of his undoubted potential. He did very well in the Aki basho in September 1989, following up his strong 10–5 showing in Nagoya with another 10–5 performance, and up-ending a listless Onokuni and a bewildered Konishiki. These two consecutive double-figure efforts could have helped spring The Plum to ozeki at the end of the year had he gone out with a bang in the last tournament, in Kyushu. But Kotogaume managed only a respectable majority there, and now looks as though he needs a fresh attack. Critics remain unconvinced of his soundness as a belt-wrestler and say he needs to work

harder and really push himself. But he may prove everybody wrong by tunnelling to victory in his inimitable style, always provided his knees stand the strain.

Plum is still enjoying his bachelorhood, though many are keen to look after him. He says his hobbies are 'saké and music', and he likes *karaoke* – singing to pre-recorded backing tracks. He prefers Japanese pop to traditional enka, though he can sing both, has done so many times on television, and has the voice of an overweight angel.

MITOIZUMI

Rank: Sekiwake
Stable: Takasago
Weight: 173 kg (27 st 2 lb)
Height: 194 cm (6 ft 4½ in)

If you were a television producer trying to promote sumo in a foreign country, what you would really like is a personality who was flamboyant, bold as brass and tall as a tree trunk, who looked a bit like John Wayne, did his ring rituals with more panache than the next fellow, and chucked handfuls of salt up into the ring canopy, to screams of delight from the audience. What you would need, in fact, is Mitoizumi. Twenty-seven stone of trouble and towering above his rivals at just over six foot four, Mito is the ultimate televisable character, and bored viewers cheer up the moment they clap eyes on him. To the Japanese, Mito is 'The Salt Shaker', the man to melt their snow and season their potato crisps. But Channel 4's Lyall Watson has nicknamed him 'The Jolly Green Giant', because in his vivid green mawashi he could well be John Barleycorn, or the burly boy on the sweetcorn cans. His appearance is redolent of legends and fables, of Gulliver or Goliath or somebody very formidable who lives up a beanstalk, and his behaviour is as big as his person. Little do viewers realize, as they watch him striding merrily away from his first victory over a yokozuna, laughing and swinging his

THE BIG FAVOURITES

elbows, that Mito has been through years of pain and heartache to get where he is today. Indeed at one point he became so very unlucky and unhappy that his stable boss changed his fighting name to try to give him a fresh start in life.

Mito was born Masato Koizumi on the outskirts of Mito in Ibaraki Prefecture on 2 September 1962. His present shikona is of course derived from his home town. One day at the beginning of 1978 he and his younger brother were at a loose end and decided to go along to their local department store to see sumo star Takamiyama, the huge Hawaiian, making a personal appearance. Masato and his brother hung about hoping to get a signed handprint or *tegata* of the hero. The 16-

year-old Masato was 20½ stone (130 kg) at the time, and the pair of them made a hefty impression on the store executives and Takamiyama himself, who took mental note to find out who they were. He sent his personal servant to inquire, and next day the Koizumi boys and their mother were being introduced to the great man, who asked Masato how he'd like to join Takasago stable and throw his weight about a bit. It seems they were very keen to have him, because the oyakata himself came calling on the family soon afterwards to discuss the possibility.

It was a great honour, and most boys would immediately have jumped at the chance, but for young Masato it wasn't an easy decision. He had

Life has been a bit of a struggle for Mitoizumi.

lost his dad when he was only five, and he had a lot of responsibility on his shoulders. He had to think about becoming the breadwinner to support his family and look after his mother properly. Takasago Oyakata listened to all this sympathetically, and explained that if the young man were successful at sumo, he would not only do his family proud, but earn an awful lot of money as well. In any case, while he was an apprentice, he would get free board and lodging at the stable, and as he was clearly a growing lad this would relieve a great strain on the household budget right away. So Masato thought it all out and decided he'd like to try.

He was a natural athlete, and a natural fighter. The year before he had finished runner-up in the national junior high school wrestling championships and been offered a senior school sports scholarship which, because of his circumstances, he'd had to turn down. But he loved sport, and at school he'd been so good at judo that he reached a senior grade while he was too young officially to qualify for it. At that time he hadn't a clue what to do with his grappling skills, but the fateful visit to the department store decided his future.

Masato joined Takasago heya – home of the big, burly forcers-out – on 11 February 1978. He was given the fighting name of 'Koizumi' at first, which was his own family name and just about the only congenial thing about his new life. He had entered the strict, sacred world of sumo unprepared for what confronted him there: massive, monstrous fellows like Asashio and later Konishiki sleeping round one on the floor; millions of loathsome chores, like chopping chanko veg., and slaving and scraping; senior wrestlers yelling and hitting one on the backside with sticks; homesickness and worry about his brother and his mum, and about how they would manage without him. Poor 'Koizumi' hated it. He lost over three stone in weight worrying and working himself half to death in the practice ring. Training was tough and relentless, hurting one's joints and stomach, and causing a feeling of nausea. Mito was clearly not well. He developed liver trouble, which causes great pain in the midriff and makes the sufferer susceptible to food poisoning. He went in and out of hospital, and as time went on he developed other health problems. He missed two whole tournaments with appendicitis and, in 1980, during a basho in the junior ranks, he smashed one of his knees, already bearing a considerable burden. Unlike his high-flying stable-mates he wasn't making the grade. Missing tournaments and being ill had pushed him down to the lowly rank of Jonidan 31 for the May basho. Things could hardly get much worse.

The Japanese are very conscious of spiritual forces in the universe and in sumo they grapple with them all the time. When a wrestler gets a spell of really bad luck, it is thought prudent to placate the unseen powers which ultimately determine winners and losers, by changing his fighting name or shikona. The term 'shikona' was originally written with characters meaning 'strong name' – a larger-than-life title to fit a man for a larger-than-life vocation. Clearly 'Koizumi' was not quite the ticket, his oyakata decided. So from that day forward Koizumi was no more. He disappeared forever, to be replaced by the rikishi we know as Mitoizumi. And although he certainly didn't live happily ever after, in the long term he became a household name, and a Jolly Green Giant as well.

Mitoizumi started to climb out of the sumo cellar, rising at last above the lowest ranks who chopped the chanko veg. (a job he never could bear), and getting so excited that he 'choked' a couple of opportunities for further promotion. He was still languishing in the Makushita or Third Division along with about 120 others, mostly younger than himself, and then in 1982 in the Kyushu basho in November, disaster struck yet again. Mito withdrew from the tournament with a knee injury so serious that the only cure was hospitalization. Bedridden for four months, Mito missed two basho and watched his ranking slither back down to the depths of Sandanme 34 – which is not the end of the world, but you can see it from there.

Mito watched sumo on television. His contemporaries and juniors were doing well. Konishiki was on a meteoric ascent to stardom, though he slept on the next mattress on the stable floor. They'd all gone past and left Mito way behind. Perhaps he would be chopping chanko veg. for the rest of his life, and never earn enough to support himself, let alone his mother. His younger brother had decided to enter sumo and had been given the name Umenosato. Perhaps he could succeed where Mito had failed. Mito felt useless. As he says, 'If you lose, you're nobody.'

He'd struggled halfway up the sumo mountain and slid all the way back down again. Now he'd hit rock bottom, and it would take all his strength and character to get up and about, let alone up the banzuke ranking list. His fellow hospital patients cheered him up by saying that of course he wasn't just a big lug; of course he'd succeed, and make sekitori, and they'd all support him when he did. And Mitoizumi grinned his great grin, full of little tiny teeth, and set about pushing his giant body back up the slope.

In 1983 somebody at Takasago stable suggested Mito do some weight-training to tone up his muscles. Konishiki was a long-term believer in pumping iron as well. So Mito began to lift weights at a gym in Okachimachi in Tokyo, spending two hours a day in mortal agony. It was worth it. Both he and Konishiki got stronger and more resilient, and Konishiki began to eye his friend as a potential threat, which was very flattering to Mito, considering his lowly status. Perhaps he was getting somewhere after all.

At last, in March 1984 in the Haru basho, Mito made the breakthrough to the Second Division, going from Makushita to Juryo with a perfect score, and phoning his mum excitedly to announce 'I'm a sekitori!' Now he really began to believe in himself. He was earning a salary from sumo, for the first time. Striding through the Second Division in just two tournaments, he prepared for the biggest step of all – the entry into Makunouchi, the premier league. Of course, as it was Mito, he had to go and injure his leg in the Nagoya basho and recoup all summer to get back into shape, but his weight-training had toughened him up, and besides, he was ready.

The great day came in September 1984. After six years of struggle, Mito fought his first bouts as a senior wrestler in the Aki basho, coming from 3–8 down, forcing his injuries to the back of his mind and finishing with 7–8 – a creditable performance under the circumstances. Despite his losing score, he was not demoted. His oyakata now drove Mito and Konishiki like a pair of oxen, putting them both through intensive training. Sally was openly telling the press that he regarded Mitoizumi as a 'rival', which brought the flush to Mito's cheeks and caused him to work even harder. In November, fighting to retain his senior ranking, he made his majority and started 1985 by being promoted for the Hatsu basho.

Then, just as the gods seemed to be smiling on The Salt Shaker at last, he went and had a motor accident. It was his own fault. He was driving round Kawasaki, where they make the motorbikes, and not looking where he was going, and he hit a parked car, smashing his head on the windscreen and hurting his bad knee. He was a fortnight in hospital with stitches in his forehead, and when he got out he missed eight bouts of the May tournament and could only manage two wins in the remainder. It was the start of another slide down the sumo mountain, slithering and crashing down to the bottom of the Second Division again.

Not for the first time, the John Wayne of sumo showed True Grit. Not only did he fight his way back up to Makunouchi and seniority once more, but he made 1986 his greatest year, landing several high-ranking giants, two Fighting Spirit prizes, and promotion to his lifetime highest rank of sekiwake – sumo's third rung. Only his knee let him down. Heavily bandaged, Mito dropped back into the Second Division, and there he remained through 1987 when British fans first tuned in to Channel 4's coverage. He would not keep them waiting long. Still feisty and exuberant, still hurling his salt, Mito was clambering back up the mountain, determined to make his mother a rich lady. He'd given her all his prize money when he became a sekitori in the Haru basho in 1984, and he meant to give her a lot more.

In January 1988 the unstoppable Mito hit the high spots once again, re-entering Makunouchi and winning another Fighting Spirit prize. And he made it two Kanto-sho in a row in March. He was now seriously setting his heart on yokozuna. For the Aki basho, in September (seen by British fans), he was ranked komusubi, and showed his class with a magnificent 10–5 effort that earned him an Outstanding Performance award. He had beaten Hananoumi, Ozeki Hokutenyu, Terao, rising star Akinoshima, Ryogoku, Kotogaume, Tochinowaka, Daijuyama, Sakahoko and – most important of all – Yokozuna Onokuni in three seconds flat, his first-ever victory over a Grand Champion.

Unfortunately he also lost a couple of bouts which upset him badly: Hananokuni hurled him into the posh seats, causing Mito to punch the floor in very un-Japanese fashion, and Jingaku threw him heavily, hurting his vulnerable knee. His ankle also went for a burton the following basho trying to negotiate the pantechnicon Panda, and he had to withdraw on 0–2–13 the second day.

In 1989, having missed the Hatsu tournament nursing his joints, the March basho saw him ranked senior number 8, but he made a creditable showing of 9–6 and won promotion to senior number 2 for the following tournament, making his majority there too. In the Nagoya as a komusubi, he was in trouble again, making makekoshi – a losing score. He did badly against Terao after a false start, but otherwise his 7–8 did him scant justice: he had upset not only Ozeki Asahifuji, but two yokozuna as well. He beat Onokuni by a slap-down dodge and on day eight he even demolished The Wolf himself. Small credit did he get. Critics still wrote of him, 'Mitoizumi has a tremendous tachi-ai but little else.' In September, following a 9–6 showing, he was promoted back up to komusubi, this time absolutely determined to make it pay, and in November he really went to work. In the Kyushu basho he unleashed himself at Hokutoumi and Hokutenyu, bowling them over on his way to a thumping 11–4 finish and picking up the Fighting Spirit award. He was promoted to sekiwake for the January 1990 basho, though of course critics are still saying 'Mitoizumi is not really ozeki material'.

Technically Mito has set himself to master both belt sumo and the fierce shoving and slapping attacks favoured by his stable. He admits that he has much room for development and would like to improve his tsuppari particularly. He has a literally smashing tachi-ai, but though it is rough, it is not always ready. As Mito explained for British Channel 4 viewers, 'If you think too much, your tachi-ai becomes awkward and your wrestling suffers. You hesitate – that's called a matta. There's nothing for it but to wrestle flat out with a clear mind. I just try to move forward, to get a right-handed overarm grip.' He tries to keep his hips low, as he has a high centre of gravity and tends to get pushed back or down. His favourite techniques, apart from arm throws (shitate-nage and uwate-nage) include the slap-down (hataki komi), the thrust-out, force-out or crush-out (yori taoshi). He wants to develop his beltwork (left hand inside on the belt and right outside), using his driving power, and also the technique which seems tailor-made for him – tsuri, or lifting; particularly tsuri-dashi, hoisting an opponent over

the edge by a two-handed grip on his sash. Mito is the tallest man in the top division and if he decides to hoist a rival he can usually manage anybody not actually nailed to the floor, whatever grip they may have at the time. Sakahoko and Akinoshima, subtle and strong though they are, have had all their powers neutralized by a fork-lift from Mito, their legs kicking helplessly.

In the pre-fight rituals, Mitoizumi exerts enormous pressure by his flamboyance and exaggerated cockiness. He whacks loudly at his belt and crouches nonchalantly with one hand on his knee, observing his rival with a quizzical, cock-eyed expression as though hugely entertained at the opponent's expense. The message comes over loud and clear that the upstart looks even more puny than usual, and that Mito can't wait to do away with him and make it look like an accident. And then he rounds off this leg-pulling onslaught with his famous third visit to the salt basket, digging deep and flinging a giant handful in the air as a token of his derring-do. And because the Japanese audience responds to all this with unconcealed glee it is very hard for his opposite number, whatever he may inwardly believe about Mito's abilities, not to feel compromised, and even insulted to the core. It certainly tests his concentration and self-esteem, as the shikiri naoshi is designed to do. Western sportsmen call this 'psyching', and many a hardened pro here might have second thoughts about his skills if he looked up and saw a great, mocking monster like this bearing down on him. Of course, there is method in Mito's madness: if an opponent were so foolish as to be angered by his display, he would not be able to clear his mind for the coming attack. He might start thinking and, as baseball legend Yogi Berra used to say, 'Ya can't 'tink an' hit at the same time.' Certainly not in this sport – it's often over in seconds flat!

Mito's record is not as good as his talent, because of serious illness and injury. To date it stands at 377 wins against 263 losses with 77 'rests' over 72 basho. But he has no less than five Kanto-sho or Fighting Spirit prizes, as well as one Shukun-sho or Outstanding Performance award. He has come close to winning the yusho on two occasions and he says his destination is yokozuna, nothing less.

For some reason this adorable character is still single, snoring on the floor of the sekitori quarters at Takasago heya. He likes films, music and detective stories and is very handy with a sketch-pad and a paint brush, having won a prize at school for art. He's also a very fine son to Mrs Koizumi, is full of fun, and has a heart as big as his person.

SAKAHOKO

Rank: Maegashira
Stable: Izutsu
Weight: 129 kg (20 st 4 lb)
Height: 181 cm (5 ft 11¼ in)

Once upon a time there were two brothers, Yoshiaki and Yoshifumi, and a ladder, which they both wanted to climb. 'I'll go first', said the elder brother, Yoshiaki, and up he went, getting as high as the third rung from the top. He hovered there for such a long time that Yoshifumi grew impatient. 'What's happening?' he called, but Yoshiaki did not answer. So Yoshifumi started up the bottom of the ladder himself. The ladder began to bounce. The more Yoshifumi climbed, the more it bounced, until his elder brother fell off and landed in a heap on the ground. 'Now look what you've done!' said Yoshiaki, exasperated. 'Well, you'd just better make the most of it!' So Yoshifumi climbed as fast as he could, but when he reached the third rung from the top, he stopped. 'What's happening?' shouted Yoshiaki from the ground. 'What's the problem?' 'It's OK', replied the younger brother. 'It's just the same as when you were up here.'

A true sumo story, which Sakahoko would understand very well because Yoshiaki is none other than Sakahoko himself, and Yoshifumi is the real name of his younger brother Terao. Sakahoko got as high as sekiwake, the third highest rung of the sumo ladder or banzuke, and just when he looked to be stuck on it indefinitely, Terao's own surge up the ranks seems suddenly to have jolted him off his perch. Poor Sakahoko has tumbled back down to maegashira number 12 now, around the bottom of the seniors, hurting

his shoulder in the fall, and it remains to be seen, at 29, whether this foxy fighter can clamber back up again. British fans hope he can: they have acquired a special respect for undersized Sakahoko's outsize skills ever since they saw him throw the formidable Wolf into the front seats in September 1987.

Sakahoko, or 'Wily' as I prefer to call him, is the second of three sumo sons of Izutsu Oyakata, who as a fighter also reached the rank of sekiwake and whose shikona was Tsurugamine. He is now one of the most successful stable bosses of the modern era, fielding five fighters in the top division – a recent record. In fact Sakahoko's elder brother made it to Makunouchi too, but was sent plummeting back down to Juryo status by a shoulder dislocation. Wily himself was born Yoshiaki Fukuzono, on the southern island of Kyushu in the Prefecture of Kagoshima on 18 June 1961, making him Terao's senior by 20 months.

When their mother died, both boys left school to follow their father's sumo calling, although Yoshiaki seemed a rather unlikely candidate. He was little and prone to lark about, and he had a struggle making the under-18 minimum weight qualification of 70 kg (about 154 lb or 11 stone). He resolved this problem by the addition of a huge pot belly, which lowered his centre of gravity – an important consideration in sumo, and an aid to balance and authority in close-quarter fighting. Unfortunately it also gave him the appearance of a tiny tot in nappies, which illusion his baby face and mischievous grin did nothing to dispel.

In this case, though, appearances are even more deceiving than usual. For Sakahoko is not only highly intelligent, but a rugged individualist as well – and in Japanese society this is about as common as mugging. His musical tastes, for example, are inclined not towards pop, like his kid brother Terao and many of the younger rikishi, nor towards enka, like many traditional Japanese, but towards, of all things, jazz. He likes reading, and not just adult comic books either. And he prefers to select a film on video rather than watch boring tripe on television. He likes to go his own way and do his own thing, which would normally cause great tension and trouble in a sumo heya. Sakahoko is perhaps fortunate in having an oyakata who understands his little foibles better than most, and that the oyakata happens in this

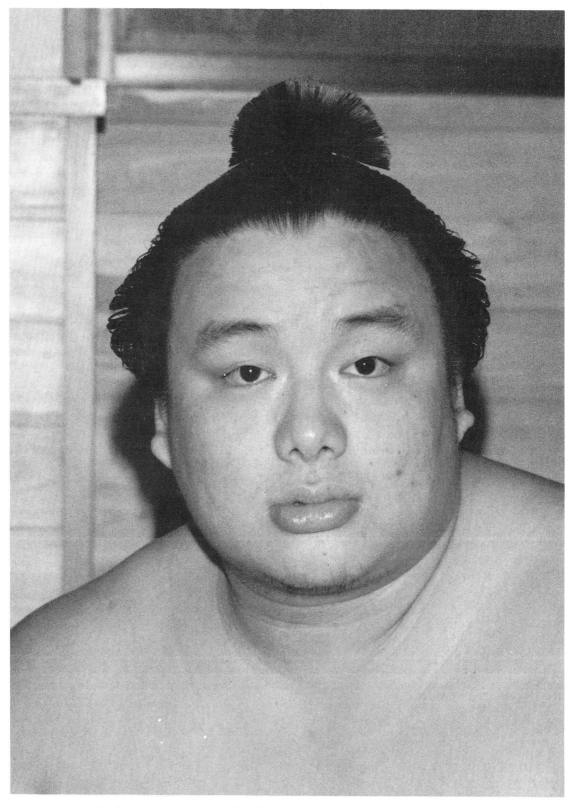

Far from happy since his brother's promotion. Baby-faced Sakahoko.

case to be his own father. For in any stable, as Wily explained to Channel 4 viewers during the 1988 television series, conformity is *de rigueur*:

Today, even for Japanese, it's hard to understand sumo. Forgive me for saying this, but while there are no doubt hierarchical structures in the West, they're unlikely to be anything like as strict as the world of sumo. When it comes to respect for one's seniors, Westerners can communicate quite freely. But in Japan we must address the seniors in a special respect language. In the West, juniors don't alter their language with seniors, even if their ages are quite different. In Japan, however, you must use special respect language when you talk to seniors. And the world of sumo is particularly strict about this. Even when you are only one year younger than the other person, you must obey.

Sakahoko thought that this rigid draconian system would be very hard for foreigners to stomach. He managed it himself by letting off steam with Terao and his mates in their leisure hours, and by maintaining a boyish sense of humour and fun. Sumo fans have grown accustomed to seeing 'behind the scenes' shots of Wily grinning and giggling, apeing it up for the television cameras, giving interviews with his hair awry and a towel slung round his neck, having pretend punch-ups for a video, or creeping about behind people's backs on top of the Arc de Triomphe like a little fellow scared of heights. Such Peter Pan behaviour is in complete contrast to his professional dedication. Once on the dohyo, Wily is transformed into a self-collected, detached and shrewd foe, eyeing his opponent narrowly and making a mental note of any shortcomings. Not for nothing is he called 'The Returning Spear'; not for nothing does Channel 4 commentator Lyall Watson admire him tremendously and refer to him as 'the wily Sakahoko'.

His first appearance in a tournament was in the Hatsu basho in January 1978. It soon became apparent that what this unlikely-looking rikishi lacked in size, he intended to make up for in brains, balance, speed and skill transmitted to him through his father. Unlike Terao, Sakahoko is a southpaw, with an inside left or hidari-yotsu attack. He is extremely quick and exceedingly

cunning, very often picking up his opponent's move as he thinks of it himself. Not for Wily his brother's addiction to slapping and slogging to excite the crowds. Sakahoko is Izutsu-trained in tsuppari as well, and uses it when appropriate, but his belt skills at their best are so formidable that British fans have seen him juggle out a giant like Konishiki and a master like Chiyonofuji by moro-zashi – two hands inside on the sash. (His father was also a moro-zashi specialist.) Three times Wily has got the better of The Wolf, and Konishiki must now dread their confrontations because Sakahoko has the power to seize him by the waist and frog-hop him out of the ring with unusual panache.

Despite nature withholding physical advantages, Sakahoko was always under pressure to make the grade. Once his elder brother was out of the reckoning, the responsibility fell on his small shoulders to follow in his father's footsteps and to set an example to the Izutsu youngsters. It took him five years and 30 basho to weasel his way into the top division – which he did in the last tournament of 1982 (the Kyushu in Fukuoka, not far from his home). His early win–loss record was 285–299–1, which shows what a struggle Wily had to overcome brawn with brains. The one 'rest' is also significant: it shows he was always fit and in contention and, unlike some rikishi, unwilling to miss a bout simply because he didn't feel like fighting. Sakahoko always felt like fighting. He was Izutsu's morale booster and spiritual lighthouse.

With the years he has learned to vary his attack across a broad spectrum, often using his moro-zashi (double-handed belt grip). He employs sukui nage (the beltless arm throw) and shitate-nage (the inner arm throw) as well as hataki-komi (the slap-down) to considerable effect. Exploiting his low centre of gravity and superb timing, he could shove out opponents larger than himself by oshi-dashi, and using his speed and slapping attack he could beat them by thrust-outs as well. The force-out, yori-kiri, is a favoured technique, as well as yori taoshi (force out and down), with Sakahoko performing it all the more violently against lumbering opponents he particularly likes to beat. He also favours the outer leg trip, and the twist-down. His mastery of technique has won him no less than three Gino-sho, and his delight in up-ending top-rankers has brought him an exceptional number of Outstanding Performances prizes or Shukun-sho as well: five to date.

One of Sakahoko's most formidable qualities on the dohyo is his refusal to allow anyone to intimidate him. He is not impressed by greatness, whether it be Chiyonofuji's or anyone else's. He thinks of himself as their equal, and in the shikiri naoshi (the pre-fight face-off) his defiance and poise are upsetting to any high-ranking adversary. Between the two basho filmed by Channel 4 in 1987 and 1988, Wily overturned yokozuna no less than four times and took the Shukun-sho in three tournaments. He was now at his peak, having reached his optimum fighting trim of just over 20 stone, and the sight of him, in the Aki basho 1987, flying out at Chiyonofuji, exchanging blows and engaging the great man on the belt, will long be remembered by British fans who watched it on television, not only for the unusual speed and complexity of the battle, but for the way in which Sakahoko engineered his moro-zashi sideways on, firmly encasing one lethal wing, and shovelled the Grand Champion, his free arm still snatching furiously for Sakahoko's head, into the front seating. A year later, in the Aki basho 1988, the now invincible Chiyo still had great difficulty putting Wily away, resorting when all else had failed to the soto-gake or outer leg trip. (In fact, if you watch a recording carefully, you can see that Sakahoko had gone for this move unsuccessfully moments before.)

So why, with this impressive army of abilities, did Sakahoko take three years to make sekiwake and then trundle along from tournament to tournament quietly making his majorities without threatening to do anything more spectacular? Why did he remain so long on the third rung that he began to be called a 'perennial sekiwake' and then slide back down among the seniors when Terao began to cut loose? The answer is that, whatever sumo's weight-watchers might think, a lot of what happens in this strange sport is determined not on the dohyo, but between the ears. For a start, Sakahoko may look small in comparison to some of his more gargantuan opponents but he is not far short of six foot. He may look light, but he is in fact heavier than Chiyonofuji (eight pounds heavier, to be precise). True, he is not nearly so strong, but he can shift Konishiki's 35½-stone bulk if the mood takes him. Sakahoko's problem is not moving mounds, but moving himself. His greatest disadvantage is

psychological, not physical.

Wily goes all out against the big names when he has nothing to lose and everything to gain as a 'giant-killer'. On these occasions he can often perform the unexpected, and pick off a Grand Champion here and there. His high-ranking rivals extend him, and unleash his full reserves. But he often allows himself to be beaten by lower-rankers who know less than he does, and who allow him more time to pick and choose his techniques. Against them he may well be too clever for his own good. Also, like many highly intelligent performers who think too much, Sakahoko suffers from nerves, and once he starts worrying, he stops fighting freely. As he told Channel 4 when he was a sekiwake:

Sumo is quite a mental sport. So when you are fighting in the upper ranks you get tense and you are not often able to fight the way you want to. I've been a sekiwake for quite a while now, and being too aware of this I feel I haven't been fighting the way I really can, so it's hard to judge my progress.

Crucial to his success has been the speed and accuracy of his tachi-ai. A winning jump-off is important to any wrestler, but to one who relies on guile rather than might or ferocity it is even more imperative to get the launch right. When Sakahoko is committed to the task, he is as fast and formidable as anyone, but if he doesn't feel confident he doesn't let fly. On these occasions, Wily says, your opponent looks larger than he really is, and you get that depressing feeling that no matter what you do, you're going to lose. So you tend to dodge the initial clash: you mentally pull back instead of firing yourself down the barrel of the gun like you should. Sakahoko knows that the only way to overcome this feeling is to say to yourself, 'Win or lose, I'm going to charge, and that's it. Who knows, but I might produce something creditable.' And then you go off like a firecracker and hope for the best.

The added pressure of having his younger brother in the top division with him gave Sakahoko something else to think about. A picture of the pair of them shaking hands on the occasion of Terao's Makunouchi début in 1985 shows Terao smiling proudly in his mawashi and Wily sitting in his kimono looking less than delighted, but putting a brave face on it. Of course he was pleased for his brother, but what would this mean for him? If Terao overtook his rank, what would this do to their relative status at the stable? Even age bows to seniority on the higher banzuke. It was a phenomenon very few sumo brothers had ever had to think about, because only Tanikaze and Tatsugesake, 200 years before, had ever been knocking about in the top division at the same time. Nobody knows how they felt about it.

The rank of sekiwake is in itself an interesting perch. Not too far up and not too far down, it is effectively the middle status of the First Division – two slots beneath the dignity of yokozuna and two above the number one maegashira or senior. On this perch you could look successful whilst still remaining one of the lads. It's a fine balance. Wily admits to being very shy with outsiders. He's single, and prefers the company of his fellow-wrestlers to anyone else. He doesn't feel at ease with non-sumo people. Perhaps, had he made it to ozeki, the gap might somehow have separated him from his stable-mates, who were also his friends. Perhaps there was therefore a positive incentive to remain in the middle of the pack, with just enough status to ensure his authority. An ozeki might have more restrictions placed on his behaviour; high jinks might be less easily tolerated. So sekiwake was a very nice rank to maintain – and since it was the same as Izutsu Oyakata's, who could grumble? With Terao's own promotion to sekiwake, however, everything has changed. Stable-mates do not ordinarily fight each other in a regular basho (unless, as happened recently, there is a play-off), so when they spar, in keiko, nothing much is at stake. Terao and Sakahoko wrestle each other like this all the time, but Terao is now a rival and a threat who has equalled the family achievements and may now go even higher: time is on his side. In any case their reversal of roles, with Sakahoko now the lowly senior of the pair, will have altered their status at the heya.

1989 was not a good year for Sakahoko. He began well enough, winning the Technical Skill prize in January and ensuring his status for the ninth straight basho. But then in March, when Terao got his hands on the rank of sekiwake, Wily lost his precious third rung for the first time in recent memory. At first he faltered only slightly, missing his routine majority by just one bout with

7–8. He had been lifted out by The Polar Bear, overpowered by The Bulldog, hooked in an arm throw by The Slug, and twisted on to the clay by The Plum fighting for his own skin on 7–7. But he had had some good wins too, including a nice one over mighty Mitoizumi by a shove-out from behind. The humiliation of slipping to komusubi for the Natsu basho seemed to sting Wily into action, and this time he managed to claw his way back to sekiwake by achieving kachi-koshi, 8–7. But the panic was far from over, and in the next basho, the Nagoya in July, Sakahoko hurt his shoulder, slithered to 1–6 in the first week and then sank out of sight, 2–13. This was the basho in which his younger brother, having been demoted back to senior ranking, stormed the barrier again with 10–5 and ensured his own return to sekiwake for the upcoming Aki tournament. Sakahoko, ranked at senior number 7, did badly there, too, turning in another losing score. But he did a lot better in November, and at the start of the Kyushu tournament his win–loss record over 72 basho was 443–420–14, with five Kinboshi or Gold Stars to his credit.

We shall have to wait and see, when the sumo ladder stops bouncing, whether there's room for both Yoshiaki and Yoshifumi at the top.

TERAO

Rank: Sekiwake
Stable: Izutsu
Weight: 115 kg (18 st 2 lb)
Height: 185 cm (6 ft 1 in)

After Chiyonofuji, the most popular fighter on the dohyo is Terao. Men find him thrilling to watch because of his spirit and fire, his storming courage and his tsuppari attacks capable of blasting out opponents twice his size. Women find him thrilling to watch for other reasons. Lean, dangerous and good-looking, Terao sets young hearts a-flutter all across Japan, the sumo equivalent of a pop star. In the UK, Channel 4 have received many enquiries about him since British fans tuned in in 1987, particularly since, during one televised series, female viewers saw him larking about at a stable singsong with a carnation between his teeth. This is not the sort of behaviour one associates with Japan's oldest sport, and if he comes to Britain with the tour of 1991, as it is hoped he will, sumo's glamour boy will cause a stir.

Terao's face has become familiar to British television viewers from a certain airline advertisement in which he plays the part of the cosseted passenger being doted on by a nubile hostess, a financial sideline of his that has somehow escaped the Sumo Association's clampdown on their wrestlers' outside contracts. Any advertiser would be glad of Terao, of course. He has that rare commodity known as star quality that turns a sportsman into an idol, even if he *is* only clumping up a plane gangway in his wooden sandals. Whether his stardom actually helps in his drive to the top is another question, since he has already earned the adulation normally accorded to a yokozuna, and win or lose, the same hysteria greets his appearances on the dohyo, the squeals rising to a crescendo. As the poet Milton would say, 'Wisdom at one entrance quite shut out.'

At just over 18 stone, Terao is one of the lightest men in the top division. This fact has encouraged many so-called experts to suggest that Terao's inconsistent form would be sorted out, and his progress up the ladder would be swifter, if he put on a few pounds. When one hears this, one is tempted to remind Terao's critics that Japan's great master of aikido, Morihei Ueshiba, weighed barely 9 stone, but could not be budged from his stance by force, though his counter-attacks sent huge fellows flying through the air. His exploits have been much filmed and photographed. He could also glue himself to the ground by the power of his mind so that no adversary, however large, could lift him up. Whether by tradition or training, most rikishi know about these things, and that such forces are at work behind what they do on the dohyo. Weight is only half their battle. Besides, just 22 pounds separate Terao from one of the lightest yokozuna in history, and one of the greatest – Chiyonofuji. He too suffered 'expert' opinion about his weight in the early days and showed by his physical strength and eloquence what nonsense commentators can come out with. Newcomer Kyokudozan, 15½ stone and

with one Kanto-sho already to his credit, is showing them too. Perhaps Terao can do the same, though in his case other factors are at work. Sumo is not about lard, but about skill and timing, balance and harmony, technique and power – both inward and outward. And unfortunately Terao's power, though he tries with all his heart, is not yet equal to his popularity. He is seeking to remedy this, of course, by constant work, and lifts weights every day to turn his 18 stone into solid muscle. Because muscle is heavier than fat, he estimates that he can gain three kilograms a tournament if he keeps at it!

Another interesting sidelight on Terao's weight is that the Second Division has had a lightweight star of its own, by the name of Ishinriki. He stands just over 5 ft 8 in and tips the scales at 81 kilograms (about 12½ stone). His obsession with sumo and his spiritual strength have made him a tough Juryo contender for a number of years and he was recently, at 28, even in the running for the division title and promotion to maegashira. Compared with Ishinriki, Terao looks very bonny indeed.

Terao, known as 'Abi' to his mates, took his mother's name as his shikona. There was a reason for this. He was born Yoshifumi Fukuzono in Kagoshima Prefecture on the southernmost island of Japan, on 2 February 1963. While he was still a boy at high school his young mother died leaving the family bereft, and Terao and his elder brother left school and entered sumo because of the inspiration of their father. He had been a formidable sumotori called Tsurugamine, and reached the rank of sekiwake, the third rung, before retiring to become eventually master of Izutsu stable – one of the most successful of the modern era. It is to this Izutsu heya that Terao now belongs, working and weight-training under the tutelage of his bald-pated, fierce-looking dad. Izutsu Oyakata is a superb teacher, fielding an outstanding five men in the top division (Terao, Sakahoko, Kirishima, Jingaku and Sasshunada).

Terao was not the only boy in the family; there were two others knocking about, one of them a wily, pot-bellied lad with apple cheeks who liked nothing better than a rough and tumble and who entered sumo with Terao. He later became famous as Sakahoko. The natural brotherly rivalry between them sparked their competitive instincts as they fought then, and as they spar at the stable

Terao coils.

now. There is also a great deal of affection and kindness between them: Channel 4 viewers have seen Terao in the showers, in a pair of blue boxer shorts, carefully rinsing his brother's long hair – a job normally assigned to one's tsukebito.

The pair have much in common. Both are relatively lightweight and have adapted their styles accordingly; both have a strong presence in the face-off and unquenchable courage in dealing with larger opponents; both tend to suffer from styes, squeezing their eyes shut occasionally under the bright television lights (in private life Terao sports blue-tinted spectacles); both have a fondness for fun and leg-pulling in their leisure hours; both are extremely dedicated, and both

have reached the rank of sekiwake, like their father before them. But in other respects they are very different. Whereas Sakahoko has cultivated a quiet undemonstrative shrewdness and a repertoire of belt skills, Terao has tunnelled his energies into what he does best: tsuppari – the fast and relentless two-handed slapping onslaught which has made him famous and earned him the nickname of 'The Typhoon'. He is quite capable of fighting on the belt and British television audiences have seen him do it, but the more spectacular style appeals to the fans and appeals to Terao as the best way of dealing with behemoths. Attention to detail at yotsu-zumo (belt-grappling) might well improve Terao's win–

93

loss rate but might also cramp his style. Besides, for all the traditional respect towards belt-sumo and weighty waltzes round the ring, all-out lightning strikes are a feature of Japanese warfare and, anyway, The Typhoon's attacks make very good television!

At the moment before the tachi-ai, Terao is coiled tight, like a rattlesnake ready to strike. He commits a lot of matta, or false starts, because his muscles and mind are under such tension that the slightest flicker out of his opponent will trigger him off. But at its best Terao's tachi-ai is a thing of beauty, like the explosive spring of a wild animal towards its prey. Even if you slow him down on video, he is still what might be described as quick. Forward he goes to pummel the face, neck and chest of his adversary with both open hands and wrists (fists are not permitted), his cheeks puffed out as he blows at his foe with all his being. If the storm drives the rival backwards, Terao may win by a frontal push-out or thrust-out, push-down or thrust-down. If the rival's own counter-attack sends him forward into the teeth of the gale, Terao is quick to take advantage, spotting the moment of greatest commitment and dodging out of the way. This enables his opponent to go blundering over the rope by himself, or with a little assistance, such as a push from behind. If the sidestep is fast enough he may even stumble onto the clay, requiring only a slap-down or hand pull-down to send him crashing. The Izutsu man's attacks are blistering; they are also blinding, and an opponent has first to be able to see where he is going before he can marshal his own defences. With blows raining down on one's face at three per second (which is Lyall Watson's estimate), this is not easy. Each rival has to devise a method of dealing with Terao's surge – and many have, which is why he often loses. Chiyonofuji may do it by locking up the young fighter's arms and clenching his belt; Asahifuji may seize an arm or a wrist and draw Terao into his tentacles – and if they can grab The Typhoon they can contain him and make him look fairly ordinary. He has the heart but not the sheer strength for long-winded belt battles, and he avoids them if he can.

Despite Terao's youthful appearance, he never-theless has a decade's experience in sumo. His first basho was in July 1979 (the Nagoya), but it took him until March 1985 (the Haru) to climb into Makunouchi, with an early win–loss rate of 173–202. He spent a year smashing his way through the division beneath, the Juryo, culmi-nating in a spectacular 12–3 yusho-winning performance there in the 1985 Hatsu basho at the start of the year. This earned him promotion to the top division and he made his Makunouchi début in the Haru (March) tournament 1985 as the bot-tom senior, or number 14 maegashira. It was a big day for the family because ten ranks above him, at senior number 4, was his elder brother Sakahoko. They were only the second pair of brothers to appear in Makunouchi together like this – and their predecessors were the legendary Tanikaze and Tatsugesake, two centuries before them. There may shortly be another equally dynamic pair of brothers up there in the First Division – called Takahanada and Wakahanada – getting their names in the record books. They are the sons of *their* stable master, Fujishima Oyakata (the former Ozeki Takanohana) and they look very promising indeed. Takahanada in particular, tanned, muscular and mischievous-looking, was the youngest Third Division title-winner in sumo history and, at seventeen years and two months, the youngest-ever sekitori, is already (though perhaps a bit prematurely) being touted as a future Chiyonofuji.

Terao's début as a First Division fighter proved disappointing, but he did electrify the crowds with his fightback from 1–6 down to finish 6–9, a taste of things to come. He was demoted back to Juryo for the Natsu basho but he was soon spoiling for a fight with Makunouchi people again, upsetting an ozeki (Wakashimazu) and a future yokozuna (Hoshi) with his stunning attacks as a senior number 2 in the Aki tournament, albeit in a losing cause. After that he continued on his unpredict-able way, going up and down the senior ranks but always rising to the big occasion, always fighting his heart out, and always holding his audiences, and particularly his female fans, spellbound. At the time of his appearance in the 1988 Aki basho, where British viewers watched him go down fighting, his highest rank had been senior number 1, and his best showing had been a bare majority, 8–7. His overall success rate stood at 46 per cent, and here he was afforded the maega-shira number 4 slot. But it was in this basho, though British television viewers had grown fond of him before, that they saw Terao's fighting spirit at its most magnificent, and bombarded Channel

4 with letters and phone calls saying what a wonderful fellow he was. Indeed, few who were privileged to watch Terao's bout with Konishiki on the opening day will quickly forget it.

Terao went through the shikiri naoshi on that day in his usual brisk style, slapping his shins, slapping his hams, throwing his salt and squatting lightly in the shikiri crouch to size up his opponent. Sizing up Konishiki, of course, requires a very long tape measure indeed: the daunting ozeki was literally twice Terao's weight, a mountain man ready to come down on him like an avalanche. Terao bounced on his heels, got up, then went into the final crouch with his right foot slightly forward. He grounded his left fist, touched down with his right – and flew out at Konishiki, his arms working like propellers, thrashing and slapping at the giant with all his might. Konishiki, who likes a slap-up fight as well as the next man, returned blow after blow, his massive arms driving Terao's neck backwards and almost out of its socket. As The Typhoon's heels edged towards the ridge, though, he spun out of the way, hoping to allow the giant to blunder forward. The Dump Truck faltered but regained his poise, turning to bludgeon Terao once again as the Izutsu man went on beating and smacking back, his hair flying out of its o-icho-mage and his face a sheen of sweat. Once more they neared the straw ridge and as the crowd's screams rose to a high-pitched shriek, Terao dodged aside – but again Konishiki arrested his forward momentum and renewed his battering assault near the centre of the ring. And there the two fighters lambasted each other with arms and hands and wrists, tsuppari versus tsuppari, the lighter man's frame shuddering occasionally from his 4½-hundred-weight attacker's bombardment. Still Terao would not give in, standing his ground and hitting the ozeki round the head. At last Konishiki, having realized that Terao would not succumb to his guns however heavy, turned to the belt. The Typhoon wriggled and wrestled, keeping it out of reach and cuffing the ozeki's face and chest with every ounce of his strength. Konishiki struggled to get at him; Terao wrenched and writhed. In the end, since this was the only way to get hold of the slippery young snake, Konishiki closed in, virtually offering Terao a two-handed *inside* belt grip – moro-zashi. Since the Izutsu man's arms would not go round Konishiki's tree-trunk arms on top

of his massive girth anyway, this was just as well. But now the mountain man settled into his own double-handed clamp on Terao's belt, his arms outside Terao's, imprisoning him firmly. The fighters now stood leaning against each other, Terao gasping over Konishiki's shoulder, his hair tousled from his frenzied efforts. And even at this obvious disadvantage Terao's mind was on how he could turn The Dump Truck sideways on and use some fulcrum for a throw. Twice he pulled and twisted, but to no avail. The odds were now simply too great for him. He was buried alive. Konishiki sensed his prey was completely played out and, half lifting and half shoving, he deposited Terao at last over the rope, setting him down gently as if demonstrating his respect. It was the end of a marathon struggle, and Terao had lost, but he had also won.

The Typhoon recovered his strength sufficiently to demolish Ozeki Asashio and also Daitetsu, principally on the belt, and five others, principally by tsuppari, but he finished with make-koshi, a losing score of 7–8 for the basho. He was demoted to number 6 senior in November. Since then though, and without adding much poundage to his athletic physique, Terao has moved up far and fast – to sekiwake. He has done it by technique, intelligence, a few tricks and blazing courage, though once again his fans have had to put up with heart-stopping inconsistencies of form.

A splendid showing at the start of 1989 saw him promoted to sekiwake for the March (Haru) basho. He had excelled himself by beating not only Konishiki in the January tournament, but The Wolf himself. As number 1 maegashira he had used his brains to turn the yokozuna's lethal heave-ho manoeuvre – one paw on the belt and one cuffing the victim's neck forward – into a stunning upset by soto-gake, an outside leg trip. In sending Chiyonofuji crashing on his backside, Terao won the Shukun-sho for Outstanding Performance as well as promotion all the way to the third-highest rank. He had made more than his 8–7 majority. He had made people sit up and take notice of this 'lightweight' sumotori. In the March basho, though, he got a little above himself and dropped to 5–10. In May he was back among the seniors at maegashira number 3, this time turning in a brilliant display on day two against Ozeki Hokutenyu, who came out of the tachi-ai expecting Terao's customized tsuppari attack. He didn't get it; Terao suddenly fixed his attention on The Polar Bear's left thigh, and decided to grab it ferociously. Hokutenyu, whose thighs are among the biggest and most unassailable in the business, was so surprised that The Typhoon was able to close in and send him very smartly packing. As brother Sakahoko was busily demolishing Konishiki in his own bout that day, it was a double for Izutsu Oyakata's offspring. But next day Terao was back to his usual storming style, falling foul of Asahifuji who twisted him round and showed him the way out, and then Onokuni, whom he had initially almost driven over the rope. Terao exploded at all sorts of others, some of whom succumbed, to finish 7–8, but he retained his rank for the Nagoya basho and this time he got his timing just right, blowing away Onokuni, Hokutenyu, Konishiki, Mitoizumi and Akinoshima – all 134 stone of them – to finish with a superb 10–5. And for this he was awarded the Gino-sho and once again promoted to sekiwake for the Aki basho 1989, on the rank seemingly reserved for this Izutsu fighting family. He kept his standing with aplomb there, twisting

Hokutoumi and Mitoizumi to oblivion and sending young Akinoshima on a flight into the seating arrangements, and he managed to hold his status, though with more difficulty, in November 1989 as well.

Terao's record at the time of writing stands at 64 basho, 367 wins and 334 losses. He has under his mawashi three Kinboshi or yokozuna defeats, as well as Outstanding Performance, Technical Skill and Fighting Spirit prizes (one of each). Where he will go from here is anyone's guess, but his female followers hope that he will improve his yotsu-zumo in some way that does not involve putting on unnecessary weight and ending up like a pudding.

He is single, likes professional wrestling and adult comic books, and loves a laugh, pulling the legs of his personal attendants in agonizing pro wrestling holds, and pulling the legs of British television audiences by telling them he really wanted to be a *sushi* chef. He is occasionally to be seen around the Ryogoko district with personal stereo headphones round his ears listening to loud Japanese pop groups. However loud, they can't blast any better than Terao.

THE HEAVY SET

Other First Division Contenders

DAIJUYAMA

Stable: Futagoyama
Weight: 161 kg (25 st 5 lb)
Height: 183 cm (6 ft)

Veteran Daijuyama has been written off as over the hill several times, but takes it all on the chin. His shikona means 'Splendid Happy Mountain', and though he's losing his hair, he's lost none of his cheek. He has upset a lot of very important people in the top division (including Onokuni in the Aki basho 1989), cruising the ranks between sekiwake and the more lowly senior grades, where it's harder to get to grips with the top-rankers. One of his best showings was at the age of 28, when, as lowliest maegashira, he answered those anticipating his early retirement by scoring 10–5 and looking stronger than when he was 21. He isn't particularly fast, and this is probably his undoing. He has relied on toughness and technique, though he's very inconsistent. He can toss Konishiki about, as he did in the Hatsu basho 1989, and yet lose to Terao who weighs half as much. We shall probably never know Daijuyama's true potential. As a humble number 8 maegashira in July 1989, 30 years old and with his o-icho-mage eked out from a few strands of hair, he bulldozed his way to 11–4 and the Fighting Spirit

prize. You never can tell what he'll do next. Of course, if his hair comes out altogether he'll be forced to retire anyway, as baldies are banned from the banzuke.

Daijuyama, or 'Mountain Man' as Channel 4 call him, was born Sakatsume Tadaaki in Niigata Prefecture on 8 April 1959. He entered sumo in the spring tournament of 1975 and bounced about quite a bit before breaking into Makunouchi in September 1980. He comes from Futagoyama heya, a prestigious stable which has produced yokozuna like Takanosato and Wakanohana II. Dai's technical range includes yori-kiri, tsuki-dashi (the thrust-out), tsuri-dashi (the hoist out), yori taoshi (the force out and into the front seats), hataki-komi (the sidestep and slap-down) and tsuki-otoshi (the twist-down). He also likes the outer arm throw, the pulling inner arm throw, the scoop throw (sukui nage), and kote-nage (the swing-down using a forearm). His yotsu-zumo is the main source of his success.

He was runner-up once, has won three Kanto-sho or Fighting Spirit prizes, an Outstanding Performance prize, and a startling number of Kinboshi or Gold Stars for upsetting yokozuna (seven). Dai is a Jack the Giant Killer, if anyone has a right to that title. His highest rung on the sumo ladder has been sekiwake, the third from the top, and his record so far is 522 wins to 531 losses over 89 basho. He's married, with three little girls, and says his favourite leisure activities are playing golf and eating.

Daijuyama, losing his hair but not his yotsu-zumo.

ENAZAKURA

Stable: Oshiogawa
Weight: 134 kg (21 st 1 lb)
Height: 180 cm (5 ft 11 in)

The Cherry, as he's called (his nickname is 'Nobushi' or 'Freelance Samurai'), is a relative newcomer to the top division, despite his years. He's just an old-fashioned boy really, and enjoys a nice quiet evening cooking or listening to traditional Japanese music (he sings enka himself), rather than a lot of rowdy Westernized larking about. He was born in 1960, on 29 July, in Gifu, not far from the Nayoga basho taking place around that time. He made his own sumo début in March 1977, and after a decade of clumping about the clay at Oshiogawa heya, he popped his head up in Makunouchi in November 1987.

He has never gone any higher than senior number 3, though there's still time if he can tear himself away from his wok. His record at the moment stands at 362 wins to 339 losses over 77 tournaments, and apart from all that experience he has one award, a Kanto-sho for Fighting Spirit. His technique is sound rather than special, with a preference, all things being equal, for pushing (oshi) and thrusting (tsuki), though he is fairly competent on the belt. Tsuki otoshi, the twist-down, is one of his favourites, along with the slap-down, push-down and push-out. He also goes for the hand pull-down (hiki-otoshi), arm-lock force-down (katasu kashi) and force-out. But apart from the odd scoop throw and outer arm throw, he's not a great nage man.

He can hold his own around the bottom of the maegashira but will need to toss some giants about shortly if he means business. His real name is Toru Hayakawa.

FUJINOSHIN

Stable: Kokonoe
Weight: 147 kg (23 st 2 lb)
Height: 181 cm (5 ft 11¼ in)

Fujinoshin is either very lucky or very unlucky, depending which way you look at it, in having two terrifying yokozuna to spar with at Kokonoe stable – Chiyonofuji and Hokutoumi. This means that he

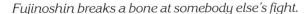

Fujinoshin breaks a bone at somebody else's fight.

is either on his toes or on his back. He was on his back for rather different reasons after the most recent Aki basho. Sitting waiting for his turn on the dohyo on day twelve, he suddenly felt a crash. Misugisato had come hurtling out of the ring and landed on Fuji's ankle, following which the 'True Mount Fuji', as he is called, had to be removed in a wheelchair.

He was born in Chiba Prefecture, with Tokyo and the Kokugikan Stadium on his doorstep, on 6 November 1960. His first tournament was the Aki basho at that venue in 1976, but it took Fuji a whole decade of pummelling and wrenching to make it into the top division. He finally managed it in the Aki basho 1986 (though by then there was a new Kokugikan for him to shine in). As to why it took him so long, we need look no further than his technical armoury. As a southpaw on the belt, he tries a wide gamut of kimarite but his repertoire is greater than his competence. Fuji has a go at yori-kiri, oshi-dashi, hataki-komi (the slap-down), yori taoshi (the force out and down), uwate-nage (the outer arm throw), shitate-nage (the inner arm throw), uwate dashi nage (the pulling outer arm throw) and tsuki-otoshi (the twist-down), as well as katasu kashi (the arm-lock force-down). Sometimes they come off and sometimes not. As Jack Nicklaus once said, it's better to know three clubs well than a lot badly. Fuji is improving all the time though, and may yet hit a high spot or two, despite having a fairly thin time in 1988 and 1989 and a broken ankle. His win–loss rate is 389–354 over 83 basho, and his highest rank so far has been senior number 1.

Fuji is still single and off the dohyo he likes karaoke. His real name is Yagi Tetsuya though Channel 4 have nicknamed him 'The Truth'.

HANANOKUNI

Stable: Hanaregoma
Weight: 146 kg (22 st 13 lb)
Height: 185 cm (6 ft 1 in)

Late-flowering Hananokuni, whose beautiful shikona actually means Land of Flowers, shocked

Hananokuni (the morning after).

everybody at the Aki basho in 1988 when, as a 28-year-old senior number 9, he whirled his way to 11–4 and spent much of the tournament in second place up among the ozeki. He carried back to his stable a share of the Fighting Spirit prize to give Hanaregoma heya something to cheer about, their massive Panda having had a lean time. In honour of his efforts Channel 4 have nicknamed him 'Flower Power'. The reason for Hananokuni's Indian summer is simple: he's in love, and has just got engaged to a young lady by the name of Miss Keiko. Since that *tour de force* he hasn't done anything quite so spectacular but has just about held his own among the high maegashira, beating Hokutoumi and Konishiki in the Aki basho in 1989 and steadying himself for a further climb.

Hanano's glowing performance in that September 1988 tournament was all the more surprising because he had only just made it into the top division – at 28, and after many years of struggle. His highest rank ever has been senior number 2, his record to date being 89 basho, with 424 wins to 375 losses. He has one Fighting Spirit prize to his credit, and that's about it. But there's no telling what he may accomplish as a married fellow.

He was born on 15 October 1959 in Osaka Prefecture, and his real name is Akihiro Noguchi. He got into sumo in March 1975 but then spent his entire time quietly nudging about in the lower ranks. Yet technically he's clever and experienced, lacking only the strength to shove his way to the front. He features the frontal force-out, push-out and crush-out (yori taoshi), and he likes the outer arm throw and the pulling inner arm throw from migi-yotsu (right hand inside on the belt). His other favourite techniques include the slap-down, twist-down and a speciality – the double-handed leg-grab, toppling his opponent over backwards.

Hanano looks like the late Donald Wolfitt. He likes music and baseball and, although the experts say he's left it too late for his big push to the top, never underestimate a man who's enjoying himself. He may make sanyaku yet (a collective term for the three ranks below Grand Champion), and shock the lot of them.

HANANOUMI

Stable: Hanaregoma
Weight: 141 kg (22 st 3 lb)
Height: 181 cm (5 ft 11¼ in)

Sidelined since May 1989, Hananoumi is familiar to Channel 4 viewers as the pretty fellow with the shikona meaning 'Lake or Sea of Flowers'. Little do they know he likes tinkering about with filthy car engines. Motors are his thing, ever since he was personal attendant to Yokozuna Wajima. He had an American automobile and they spent five years with their heads frequently under the bonnet.

Hana is a fine technician at sumo, and very strong, dragging even Chiyonofuji about the dohyo, but he never wanted to become a sumotori in the first place and has had a long-standing attitude problem about the sport. Born among the paddy fields of Ikawamachi, Akita Prefecture on 16 December 1960, he was committed to the now defunct Hanakago heya by his rice-farming father, whereas what he really wanted

to do was to play baseball, chiefly on the grounds that it had more female fans than sumo wrestling. His five years as tsukebito to the then-Yokozuna Wajima (Asahifuji's hero) were a time of struggle and remorse. He kept changing his fighting name in the hope that the right shikona would bring him luck and strength, and he still thinks he isn't really the right size for his profession. He developed a low-plunging sort of style, ducking into the behemoths and sometimes falling forwards at the tachi-ai, but he became extremely well-versed in sumo technique, and had his own specialities. One of these was *hazu-oshi*, which means shoving the opponent under his armpits. Hana did this with both hands, which is called *moro-hazu*. He also favours the throat thrust (nodowa). Along with all the regular force-outs, push-outs and thrust-outs and the hand pull-down, good belt technique and an assortment of throws make Hana a difficult customer, whether on the sash or off it. Since getting into the top division in March 1985, he has won four Kinboshi or Gold Stars, and two Technical Skill prizes.

His highest rank has been komusubi, which is probably slightly beneath his dignity, but he suffers from disasters when he gets there, as happened in the March basho 1989 when he lost for nine days running, defaulted on the tenth and then withdrew injured. In May, demoted to senior number 10, he defaulted on day five and hasn't been seen since. His record over 80 basho stands at 404–370.

Behind the most recent and most beautiful shikona, by the way, there lurks plain Ken. Yes, Ken Sawaishi. One can almost hear Yokozuna Wajima shouting, 'Ken! Fix that carburettor!'

ITAI

Stable: Onaruto
Weight: 137 kg (21 st 8 lb)
Height: 177 cm (5 ft 9½ in)

Itai likes boxing. Of course you can't punch people in his game, but in 1988 he began training

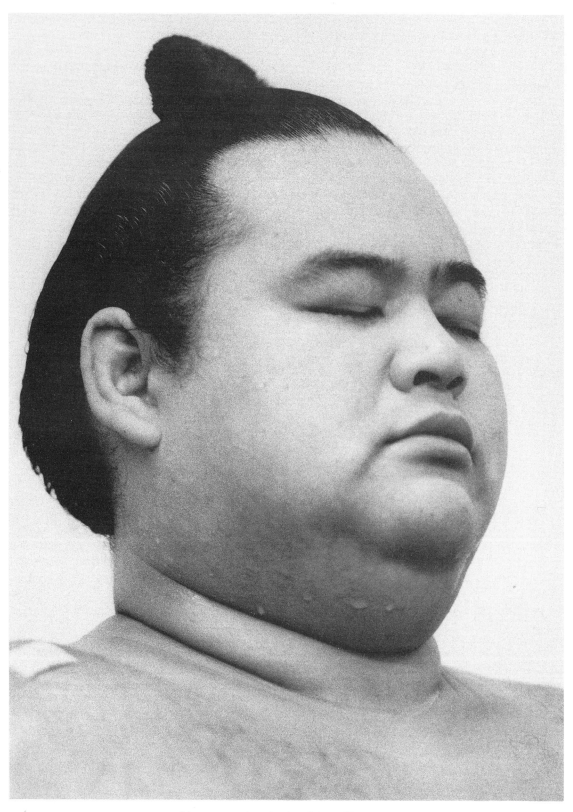

Hananoumi resigning himself to sumo.

with a boxing coach because at 34 he has bad knees and he wants to give himself more 'oomph'. He has quite a lot already, which is why they call him 'The Steam Roller'.

Born Keisuke Itai in Oita Prefecture on the first day of spring, 1956, he won many times in national youth championships as an amateur, but worked in the ceramics industry until he was 22. At five foot nine you aren't immediately thought of as a sumo wrestler, now that the Japanese are growing much taller, and it wasn't until September 1978 and the Aki basho that sumo fans saw hide or hair of him. He'd given up his job and decided bravely to try and tough it out among the gargantuans, going through the apprentice machinery at Onaruto stable and proving that he was a lot better than half the fighters twice his size. He zoomed up the lower ranks, smashing his way into the top division in record time in September

1980, chiefly on the strength of his pushing and shoving talents. But there he seemed to meet too many immovable obstacles, and couldn't budge the better ones. He did get as far as komusubi in May 1989, on the merits of a very fine 11–4 showing in March, but in the Natsu basho he got a good hiding, 3–12, and was seen off to the seniors again.

He's a bonny fighter, though he can sometimes go all to pieces, as happened in the Kyushu tournament at the end of 1988. His overall record is very respectable. Over 68 basho he has a tally of 431 wins against 412 losses, and he has picked up three Kinboshi for upsetting yokozuna, as well as an Outstanding Performance award and a Gino-sho for technique. He still favours the tsuki and oshi sort of stuff, and likes the frontal push-out, push-down, push-out from behind, thrust-out and thrust-over, the force-out, slap-down and

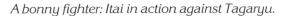

A bonny fighter: Itai in action against Tagaryu.

twist-down. It would be very nice to see Itai go out with a bang, because it was such a hell of a job for him to get into sumo in the first place.

He's married with one daughter, and he relaxes by going fishing.

JINGAKU

Stable: Izutsu
Weight: 147 kg (23 st 2 lb)
Height: 189 cm (6 ft 2¼ in)

'Jin-chan' or Jin-boy to his friends, Jingaku looks like a Kabuki actor and suffers very badly from stage fright, losing a lot of weight during each basho because of stomach upsets. He should see a sports psychologist like Gosaku Naruse at Kyushu University, or use self-hypnosis tapes like Seve Ballesteros. His record over 76 basho of 439–435 would look an awful lot better were it not for this handicap. At over six foot two and 23 stone, he is big and formidable, and though his detractors are saying he's 30 and past it, he has experience on his side if he could stop beating himself. He might pull off a few upsets in his downward years.

Born Nakayama Takashi on Christmas Eve 1959, Jin-boy comes from the same place as his stable-mates Terao and Sakahoko – Kagoshima Prefecture on the southern island of Kyushu, noted for its Samurai warriors. Unlike those two, of course, he lacks the advantage of having his father as stable boss (Izutsu Oyakata). But like them and the other Izutsu men, he has in his armoury a ferocious tsuppari attack. The frontal push-out springs readily to his mind, as do the force-out, scoop throw, and lifting or tsuri techniques. He occasionally has a very good crush-out, using his migi-yotsu grip (right hand inside on the belt), counters a slap-attack by hataki komi and, like stable-mate Kirishima, has a nasty trick up his sleeve when he's on the rope – utchari, the backward pivot throw. He isn't as forceful as he might be because of digestive illness, and he has had a bad right foot recently too, but he once

fought one tournament at the rank of komusubi and is trying to get back up the ladder now from his customary senior positions. He was ranked senior number 1 for the Kyushu basho of 1989.

Married with two daughters and a son, Jin-boy is a keen golfer and *kendo-ka*. He was very good at kendo at school and he believes the mental attack training helps him on the dohyo. Evidently not enough. He needs relaxation exercises.

KASUGAFUJI

Stable: Kasugayama
Weight: 139 kg (21 st 12 lb)
Height: 177 cm (5 ft 9½ in)

Shoki Iwanaga, to give Kasugafuji his real name, is just trying to establish himself among the maegashira men after a long struggle in the lowly ranks, followed by a heady rush through Juryo, the Second Division, in a little over a year. He was born in Kawasaki Prefecture on 20 February 1966 and joined Kasugayama stable in the spring of 1981. There he became the star apprentice. He made his sumo début in the Haru basho that year, and it took him eight years to overcome the disadvantage of being shoulder-height to most of his attackers and shove his way into the top division.

There's not much wrong with him now, despite his lack of inches, though his strength at the moment lies in tsuki and oshi fighting rather than yotsu-zumo. As pushing and shoving is the first thing youngsters learn at the stable, it often takes a while to develop confidence in their belt skills and he still has time to get to grips with the grappling. He's a very fierce and spirited push-and-shove artist and like Terao, spectacular to watch whether he wins or not. But he's increasingly competent on the belt and his repertoire features a gamut of things from push-outs and push-downs through slap-downs, thrust-outs, lift-outs, inner arm throws, force-outs and crush-outs, to the twist-down and head throw. His record at the moment stands at 235 wins to

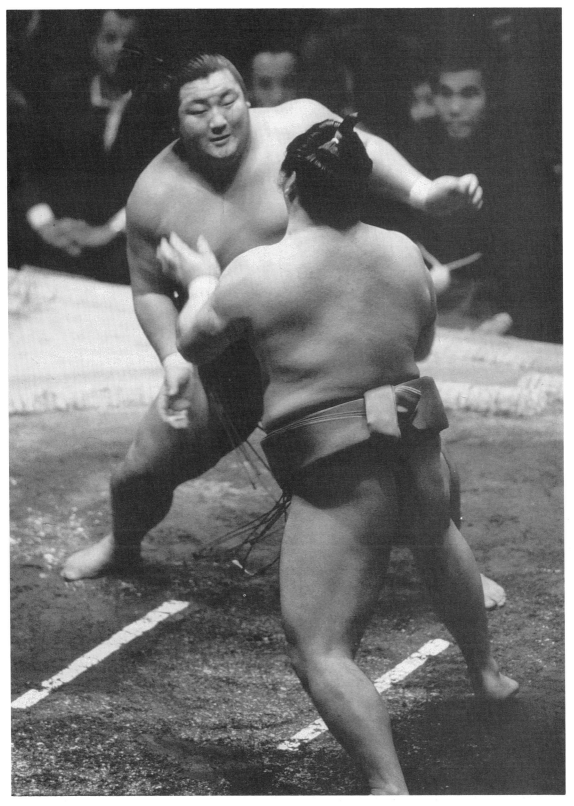

Not short of spirit: Kasugafuji likes pushing and shoving.

210 losses over 53 basho, and his highest rank to date has been senior number 4, though he's young and has yet to find his rightful place.

Kasu is single and says he likes listening to music. He looks shock-proof and hefty, rather like a snub-nosed version of Asahifuji.

KINOARASHI

Stable: Oshiogawa
Weight: 161 kg (25 st 5 lb)
Height: 183 cm (6 ft)

At over 25 stone and with above-average grappling abilities, Kinoarashi looked a highly promising prospect when he forced his way into Makunouchi for the first time in March 1982, and after a spate of success that year he was being touted as an ozeki candidate. But the bigger they come, the heavier they hobble, and a serious injury to Kinoarashi's left knee sent him plummeting down the banzuke into the cellars of the Third Division. Since then he's been struggling, putting in an appearance in the First Division when he can.

Born Ishiyama Kazutoshi in that sumo seminary Hokkaido on 9 July 1961, he became an Oshiogawa apprentice and entered pro sumo in the Haru (spring) basho in 1977, soon showing his yotsu-zumo class. He uses an inside right-handed attack on the belt (migi-yotsu) and favours lifting (tsuri) and forcing (yori), in particular yori-kiri and yori taoshi. His nage throws include the outer arm throw (uwate-nage), the pulling outer arm throw (uwate dashi nage) and sukui nage (the scoop throw). His shoving skills include oshi-dashi (the push-out) and tsuki-otoshi (the side thrust-over).

He has one Gold Star or Kinboshi to his credit over 77 basho, with a win–loss rate of 415–332, which is creditable enough, but he sports a huge elasticated bandage on his left knee, and that really tells you the whole story. He's in his late twenties now, not married, and presumably sick as any two parrots about his highest rank of

senior number 2 when it should have been better than that. Far from finished, but far from fit.

KIRISHIMA

Stable: Izutsu
Weight: 128 kg (20 st 2 lb)
Height: 187 cm (6 ft 1½ in)

Kirishima is the handsomest man in the First Division and not just a pretty face either. He's a keen weightlifter and his speciality on the dohyo is utchari, the spectacular backward pivot throw on the rope. A frequent victim has been the 30-stone Onokuni, who outweighs Kiri by a matter of 150 lb and who has been flung out in this way on several occasions. British television viewers saw it during the 1988 Aki basho. The Giant Panda drove forward and looked about to force the lighter man over the edge, but despite thunderous blows to his face and chest and backbreaking shoving, Kiri refused to be yori-ed. Rising on his toes on the straw ridge and bracing his knees, he suddenly lifted the behemoth and heaved, spinning Onokuni to destruction. Kiri has repeated the indignity since then, in the May 1989 basho and again in the Nagoya two months later. He also has another trick: flinging down the 35½-stone Dump Truck. Yet to look at Kirishima you'd think he was a ballet-dancer rather than a sumo wrestler. He weighs just 20 stone of solid muscle.

Kiri's techniques have won him three extremely prestigious Gino-sho, the first a result of his performance in the 1988 Kyushu basho when as a lowly maegashira number 6 he finished with a fine 10–5. His finest showing was as runner-up in the November basho in 1986, where he astonished everybody with 12–3. He's now in his thirties, and according to sumo experts has long since shot his bolt. They say he's too light to reach the top (though he outweighs Chiyonofuji by six pounds), and that he suffers from stage fright, being unable to perform up to standard when he's promoted (his highest rank has been sekiwake). His nickname, 'The Fog', derives from his shikona, 'Misty Island', and the suggestion is that Kirishima

Not just a pretty face. Kirishima has honed his strength with weight-training and now threatens to do some damage in his thirties.

evaporates under the bright lights.

On the face of it, Kiri *does* seem to be a victim of the Peter Principle, getting thrashed as a komusubi, 1–14, back in January 1989, yet doing well hustling down among the lower ranks. But the truth is probably that he lacks confidence among sumo's stars. Coming from Izutsu stable where the top fighters happen to be the Oyakata's own sons, it can't have been easy for Kiri to grab the limelight as the apple of anybody's eye. That he has real giant-crushing talent may be seen from his run of success at the end of 1989 and from the trouble he gives the top men, and his technical repertoire is considerably larger than

some senior fighters: it includes such kimarite as the arm-grab throw (hikkake), lift-out, the scoop throw, the pulling outer arm throw, pulling under-arm throw, the backward pivot throw, the slap-down, force-out and crush-out (yori taoshi).

His third Technical Skill prize came as a result of Kiri's very fine showing as a komusubi in November 1989, when he delivered 10–5 and merited another try for the rank of sekiwake in the New Year. Perhaps this time he can show them what he's made of.

Kiri was born Kazumi Yoshinaga in Kagoshima Prefecture on 3 April 1959, and he entered sumo in March 1975. It took him a long time to nudge

Kitakachidoki muscles out the opposition.

up into the top division and he finally made it in the Nagoya basho 1984 – presumably after lifting more weights than usual. At the end of 1989 he had won 469 bouts and lost 451 over 90 basho. He has garnered one Outstanding Performance prize, one Fighting Spirit prize and two Gold Stars, as well as his three awards for Technical Skill. He's married with one little daughter, and lists his hobbies as painting, pumping iron, karaoke and golf. Experts may not think of Kiri as a wrestler to watch, but women should ignore this.

KITAKACHIDOKI

Stable: Isenoumi
Weight: 134 kg (21 st 1 lb)
Height: 183 cm (6 ft)

This son of a lorry driver from Obihiro City, Hokkaido, is prone to running away from the stable, but if he can overcome the desire to go AWOL, he might well make the grade like his fellow beya-bunker, Asahifuji. He's extremely tough, with big, iron-pumping shoulders and a strong-willed nature. His real name sounds a lot better to Western ears than his shikona: Kuga Hayato. The Kuga was born on New Year's Day in 1966, and was recruited by Isenoumi heya, where he's a big fish in what is now a small pond. He made his sumo début in May 1981 and only got into the top division for the first time at the beginning of 1989, dropping back down to Juryo a few times and picking himself up off the clay to try the maegashira game again.

Kuga undoubtedly suffers from the disadvantage of not having many testing opponents at the stable to practise with, and has to rely on wrestlers from his ichimon (family of stables) to bash his offence and defence into shape. He hasn't finished honing his techniques yet. They include an assortment of hip throws, notably uwate-nage, sukui nage and uwate dashi nage, as well as force-outs, push-outs, side thrust-overs and leg trips. He's an inside right-hander on the belt and vulnerable there, but he's a keen weight-lifter, very muscular and fast through the air (he was a school goalkeeper).

At the time of writing, Kuga's highest rank was maegashira number 10, and his record over 52 basho is 267 wins to 215 losses. But expect him to find a way up the banzuke. He stands out in a crowd, and looks like a man who can handle himself.

KOBOYAMA

Stable: Kumagatani
Weight: 142 kg (22 st 5 lb)
Height: 179 cm (5 ft 10½ in)

A heavy 'old man' of 32, Koboyama is reckoned to be slowing down both mentally and physically. But he's been a bit of a technical specialist in his day and has two Gino-sho under his mawashi, once reaching the rank of sekiwake. He's the only fighter in the top division who lists 'tottari' (a throw twisting the victim's pinioned arm) among his favourite techniques, along with hiki-otoshi, oshi-dashi, sukui nage, yori kiri, yori taoshi, tsuki-dashi, tsuki-otoshi, hikkake (the arm grab pull-down) and tsuki-otoshi (the side twist-down). He is a moro-zashi exponent, using two hands inside on the belt to particular advantage, which is something few top division men specialize in (Sakahoko being a notable exception).

He's a wilful, contrary sort of fellow. He was Prefectural Junior School Sumo Champion for two years before anybody could persuade him to join a stable. Eventually he agreed to become an apprentice at Kumagatani, and made his first appearance in a basho in March 1973, getting into the top division in November 1981. Since then he has amassed the absolutely enormous tally of 1086 bouts and 101 basho at a win–loss rate of 540–546. He was in grave danger of demotion to Juryo in January 1989, clinging to the lowest rung of the ladder, but by May he was back up at senior number 3, showing his defiance again. If he finally goes down for the count this coming year, it will be the end of a tough and

Koboyama, a technical specialist in his day.

clever old tiger.

He was born Misuyoshi Hasuda on 15 August 1957 in Miyagi, but he's known as Yomogida, and his fighting name means 'Far-seeing Mountain'. He's married, with a son and a daughter, and lists his hobbies as saké, song, music and karaoke.

right hand inside (migi-yotsu). Perhaps he's just ambidextrous. His win–loss rate over 59 tournaments is running at 292–243, and if he exploits what nature has given him, he should go far.

On the dohyo you can pick out Kotofuji by his long sideburns and the fact that he wears his mawashi pulled up over his waist like old-fashioned underpants. He's single, and lists his hobbies as music and playing golf.

KOTOFUJI

Stable: Sadogatake
Weight: 145 kg (22 st 10 lb)
Height: 191 cm (6 ft 3 in)

At six foot three and almost 23 stone, Kotofuji has nature on his side for this business. He's still only 25 and has already given a taste of his talents by a thumping 11–4 Makunouchi début performance in the 1988 Aki basho. There, seen by British fans on Channel 4's coverage forcing out Akinoshima, he finished third and came away with a share of the Fighting Spirit prize with Hananokuni. Not bad for a senior number 12, and it earned him promotion up a few rungs of the maegashira ladder. His highest rank so far has been senior number 2 (in November 1989), but he's too inconsistent yet to show us where he really belongs.

He was born in Chiba Prefecture on 28 October 1964 and his real name is Kobayashi Takaya. He joined Sadogatake stable where he spars with young Plum: they share in their shikona the stable prefix 'Koto', meaning harp or lute. Kotofuji began his sumo career in the Haru basho of 1980, before getting into the top division for the first time in September 1988. He was a bit shell-shocked by the experience but has managed to stabilize since then with a couple of 9–6 performances. He's consolidating his technique: his favourite methods are yori (forcing) and tsuri (lifting), and he's already strong enough to surprise a few foes. His kimarite include the force-out, the force-out and down (yori taoshi) and thrust-out (tsuki-dashi), as well as the slap-down, hand pull-down (hiki-otoshi) and outer arm throw. Some analysts say he has a hidari-yotsu attack (left hand inside on the belt) and some say he fights with his

KOTOINAZUMA

Stable: Sadogatake
Weight: 128 kg (20 st 2 lb)
Height: 180 cm (5 ft 11 in)

At just over 20 stone, Kotoinazuma is just six pounds heavier than Chiyonofuji, but he lacks The Wolf's exceptional power and skill to overcome the big predators of the top division. At this level, it's all he can do at the moment to break even, though he has in his favour a lot of vigour and fire appropriate to the lightning in his fighting name, and is improving his tactics to suit his size.

Nicknamed 'Pyo' by his friends, he was born Shozo Tamura on 26 April 1962 in Gunma Prefecture and joined Sadogatake stable, where one's shikona usually has a Japanese harp ('Koto') in it; The Plum, Kotogaume, also hails from there. Pyo's first basho was in March 1978, and he became the proverbial good little 'un getting beaten by good big 'uns, breaking into the top division at last in the Kyushu tournament at the end of 1987. His technical taste varies from yori, or forcing techniques on the belt, through hip throws (nage) to a lot of pushing and shoving (oshi and tsuki), and his repertoire features the force-out, push-out (oshi-dashi), thrust-out (tsuki-dashi) and push-down (oshi-taoshi), as well as the outer arm throw, the pulling outer arm throw (uwate dashi nage), slap-down, scoop throw, hand pull-down and soto-gake, the outer leg trip. He's very game.

His highest rank so far has been maegashira number 3, but he doesn't give up easily and

Kotofuji. England cricket selectors please take note.

will do his best to push further up the queue. His record over 65 tournaments works out at 360 wins to 339 losses. Experts say he needs a lot more weight to make it to the top, which is what they always say if you fail to make sanyaku and you're under 30 stone. What he does need is a touch more hair – he's receding at the front of his o-icho-mage.

Koto is single, and likes music and getting out on the golf course.

KOTONISHIKI

Stable: Sadogatake
Weight: 132 kg (20 st 11 lb)
Height: 176 cm (5 ft 9¼ in)

Kotonishiki is one of the 'Koto' (or Japanese harp) boys of Sadogatake stable, of which there are a good number in the top division at the moment. This particular Koto is into computers, and he's so fond of the games that he may well disappear like Tron into a visual display unit at any time. He's single, young and, provided he either grows a bit taller or overcomes his height disadvantage by technique, should do very well indeed. So far his highest rank has been maegashira number 9, but that was as recently as September 1989.

He's a pushing and thrusting specialist, with oshi-dashi, oshi-taoshi and tsuki-dashi as his first line of attack. But he can now also turn his hand to force-outs, crush-outs, scoop throws and hataki-komi to counter an opponent's onslaught. He doesn't have any special awards yet, but he will.

His real name is Hideyuki Matsuzawa, and he was born in Gunma Prefecture on 8 June 1968. He appeared in a pro basho for the first time in the spring of 1984, and became the youngest entry to the top division in May 1989, at 20. Since then he's been getting his majorities and coming up the banzuke. His current record over 35 tournaments stands at 171 wins to 124 losses. 'The Lute' is one to watch. He lists his leisure activities as music – and computer games.

KUSHIMAUMI

Stable: Dewanoumi
Weight: 171 kg (26 st 13 lb)
Height: 187 cm (6 ft 1½ in)

Like his Dewanoumi stable-mate Ryogoku, and Tochinowaka of Kasugano, Kushimaumi is one of the ex-college fraternity and a former amateur champion at university, winning 29 titles. Like Ryogoku he is also huge – at 171 kilos (nigh on 27 stone). Dewanoumi Oyakata seems to have a penchant for training up hulking great book-worms at his heya.

Kushi was born in Wakayama Prefecture near Osaka on 6 August 1965, and fought his first pro sumo bouts in the New Year basho in 1988, shortly before he graduated from Nihon University (the top place for amateur sumo). Since then he has risen sharply through the lower ranks to hit the top division in the Nagoya basho in July 1989, where he knocked himself out slightly as a senior number 13, winning 8 of his first 11 bouts and then stumbling through the rest to finish with a bare majority. Good enough for promotion, though, to maegashira number 11 for the Aki tournament in September, seen by British television viewers, and there Kushi paced himself much better, coming in with 9–6 and polishing off some old pros in the process. He looks like a certain sanyaku contender provided he doesn't rest on his enormous hams.

Technically he is strong and powerful, sticking a right paw through his opponent's defences for an inside grip on the belt and going for force-outs or crush-outs. Like Yokozuna Hokutoumi he has a heavy-handed tsuppari attack, clonking and shoving people out or down by tsuki-dashi, oshi-dashi or oshi-taoshi. He also has a fierce twist-down and forearm throw (kote-nage).

His aggregate, admittedly over just 12 basho, is 71 wins to 38 losses, which is a fairly crushing start, and which includes a record run of consecutive majorities for a college star. He's single, and his shikona comes from his real name – Kushimaumi Keita. Nicknames: 'The Jellyfish' and 'College Boy'.

Worth his salt. Kotonishiki entered the top division at 20.

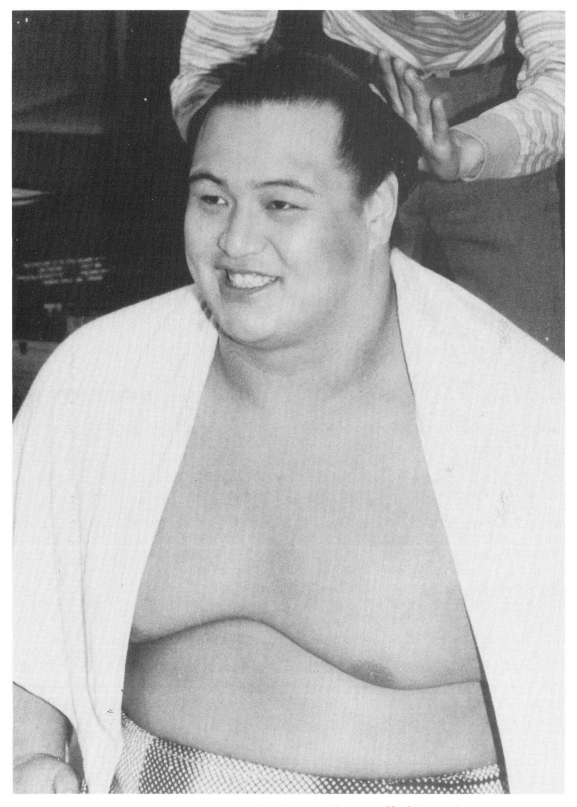

A big future is expected for former college star Kushimaumi.

KYOKUDOZAN

Stable: Oshima
Weight: 100 kg (15 st 10 lb)
Height: 181 cm (5 ft 11¼ in)

Chiyonofuji's tip for the top, judging by the help and attention The Wolf has given him, is this young man from Kagoshima Prefecture (where Terao and Sakahoko hail from). Kyoku shares with Chiyo the advantage of a clean pair of heels in the 100-metre dash (they can both do it in 11 seconds) and the distinction of being unacceptably light for sumo – in Kyoku's case a mere 15½ stone (compare Terao's 18). But this young fellow is only 25 and will undoubtedly bulk up his muscles as Chiyo has done. He already has everybody goggle-eyed over his fierce leap into the top division, where he looks very brave and very classy.

Born Kazuyasu Hata on 14 October 1964 on the Kagoshima island of Tokunoshima, Kyoku was a month premature, anaemic, and weighed in at 4½ lb. He and his brother Hisakazu toughened themselves up at school by kendo, that marvellous martial art with all the yelling and the bamboo sticks, surpassing all the other boys in the classes and learning virulent do-or-die speed and attack. Kyoku's tachi-ai at sumo owes a lot to his kendo training. He was an all-round athlete (again like Chiyonofuji), excelling at volleyball and long-distance running and building up his speed and stamina. His muscles benefited from a couple of labouring jobs while he was a teenager, humping bails of sugar cane and working on a building site.

He joined Oshima heya in the spring of 1980 because his mum wanted him to. Divorced and with four children to bring up, her household could do with a well-paid sumotori to bring home the bacon. Turning down various volleyball scholarships and weighing just 10½ stone, skinny Kazuyasu began sweating up a storm on the practice dohyo with such stable-mates as The Slug, and making painful progress. He could hardly stomach the contents of the chanko pot, but very gradually acquired a taste for both the slop and the sumo, and twirled his way through

the lower ranks. He got through the Second Division at a lick in just three tournaments and landed with a bang in Makunouchi in January 1989, where he romped through to a 9–6 finish and took the Fighting Spirit prize. Since then he has hardly drawn breath, getting as high as senior number 5, though of course he hasn't settled yet and may well get a few good hidings from the big men and go back to Juryo for a while to cool his heels.

Kyoku's technical range and skill, together with his tenacity, have singled him out for practice sessions with The Wolf (which the younger man likens to charging into stone). Kyoku favours yori-kiri, followed by the twist-down, push-out, force out and down, the hand pull-down and a variety of nage throws (inner arm, pulling inner arm, outer arm and the scoop). He is already a mean belt fighter. His record over 58 basho is an impressive 249 wins to 210 losses, and the crowds already react to him as they do to their other handsome hero from the south, Terao. Both are equally exciting to watch, and Channel 4 call the newcomer 'The Sundance Kid', though his Japanese nickname is 'Nankai no habu' or 'South Sea (poisonous) snake'.

Kyoku is single, and lists his special interests as films, music and animals.

Interestingly, Kyoku has a stable-mate of almost identical shikona, Kyokugozan (real name Taizan Kimura) who shows great promise. They look very different, and whilst Kyokudozan prefers yotsu-zumo, this other Kyoku is a 24-stone oshi and tsuki artist. He's already been downstairs in the senior ranks and may accompany young Kyoku Mark I up the banzuke, to the eternal confusion of British fans.

MASURAO

Stable: Oshiogawa
Weight: 127 kg (20 st)
Height: 188 cm (6 ft 2 in)

No disrespect to the real Wolf, Chiyonofuji, but Masurao is nicknamed 'The White Wolf' himself. He was born in Fukuoka on 27 June 1961, and as a boy was a fairly remarkable high school judo

Huge of heart. Feather-light Kyokudozan.

Misugisato, fast becoming The Bulldog's nightmare.

champion. He might well have carried on as a judo-ka, but Oshiogawa Oyakata stirred him up with a chance remark, 'How about trying your strength in a man's world?' This was just the sort of thing to get him going, and he joined Oshiogawa stable in 1978. As an apprentice Hiroyasu Teshima, as Masurao then was, showed unusual spirit and fire. Though he was very light, he broke into the top division in the September basho of 1985, and launched himself at the high-rankers, getting as far as sekiwake before sinking back down again.

The reason for his downfall was that he kept being injured. The worst harm by far was to his knee, which has been troublesome now for several years and which has sent him crashing down into the Second Division despite his obvious skill and guts. It's bad enough having a wonky knee if you're huge and strong, but Masurao relied on his agility and spirit to over-come the heavy people. He's getting back up among them again and should not be written off while his topknot is still attached to his head. Only recently he beat Hokutoumi, and his record against that yokozuna is two wins in just six bouts.

Technically Masurao is sharp and versatile, with a migi-yotsu attack and a flair for the inner arm throw, shitate-nage, as well as yori-kiri, oshi-dashi, oshi-taoshi (the push-down), sukui nage (the scoop throw), tsuki-otoshi (the side twist-down) and tsuri (lifting) techniques. He's still a judo black belt and likes professional wrestling, so his belt sumo is very handy. His awards so far are: two for Fighting Spirit, two for Outstanding Performance, one for Technical Skill and two Gold Stars. Over 65 basho his win–loss rate is 362–296.

His fighting name means 'Brave Hero' or 'Warrior'. He's an unusual chap, rather like Sakahoko in that he likes jazz, and is single. The crowds are very fond of him.

MISUGISATO

Stable: Futagoyama
Weight: 141 kg (22 st 3 lb)
Height: 185 cm (6 ft 1 in)

Misugisato is just beginning to rumble out of the top seniors and into the lower reaches of sanyaku (the three ranks below yokozuna). He got to komusubi in January 1989 but found the strain a bit much, managing only 3–12. Obviously, the higher you go, the more big guns you face, but Misugi has picked off the odd top-ranker recently, including Hokutoumi in May and September 1989, and an admittedly half-asleep Asahifuji in July and September as well. His record to date is 333–284 over 66 basho, and he already has a Gold Star under his belt for a yokozuna upset, if nothing else.

He was born in Shiga Prefecture on 1 August 1962, his real name being Koji Okamoto. He fought his first basho in September 1979 and came good nine years later, breaking into the top division for the first time in the Natsu tournament in 1988. If his progress was a little slow, it was probably due to a lack of power. His favoured techniques are the force-out and thrust-out, inner and outer arm throws and the scoop throw (sukui nage). He is also good at hataki-komi (the slap-down against thrusting attacks) and the force out and down (yori taoshi).

Misugi is single and says he likes music and cartoons. His fighting name means 'The Village of Three Cedars', though Channel 4 calls him simply 'The Cedar Tree'.

OZUTSU

Stable: Taiho
Weight: 142 kg (22 st 5 lb)
Height: 183 cm (6 ft)

Extremely experienced and with a very sound defence, Ozutsu has all-round technical ability, befitting someone from the great Taiho's stable. This sad-eyed man is an old pro now and his weak knees are heavily bandaged, but he's still very dedicated to his sport, coming as he does from a sumo family. His astonishing tally of ten Kinboshi or Gold Stars shows what havoc he has wreaked on his good days, with many upsets to his credit. At the height of his powers he got as far

Ozutsu's knees take the strain. A tally of ten Gold Stars to his credit for overturning yokozuna, Top Gun is an old-timer now.

as sekiwake, and he has a collection of awards: two Shukun-sho or Oustanding Performance prizes, as well as a Kanto-sho for Fighting Spirit and a Gino-sho for Technical Skill.

He was born Takeshi Matsumoto on 18 April 1956 in Mie Prefecture, and he entered the ring in the May basho of 1971, breaking eventually into Makunouchi in March 1979. Once there he became known as 'The Big Cannon', though Channel 4 calls him 'Top Gun'. He has been around the top division for a decade now, earning a win–loss record of 651–671 over 112 basho. His technical armoury, apart from the obligatory yori-kiri and oshi-dashi finishes, includes strong beltwork, inner and outer arm throws, the pulling outer arm throw, the arm-lock throw, scoop throw and twist-down. Rather more distinctive is his neck throw – kubi nage.

Ozutsu is an artistic son of a gun, with such hobbies as painting, photography and singing. He also enjoys mucking about at baseball. He's married but without any children. On the dohyo he's easily identified by his very prominent rosebud mouth and jutting jaw, as well as his array of bandages and wristbands.

RYOGOKU

Stable: Dewanoumi
Weight: 172 kg (27 st 1 lb)
Height: 185 cm (6 ft 1 in)

One of the biggest lads ever seen on the dohyo is Dewanoumi Oyakata's protégé Kobayashi Hideaki, better known as Ryogoku. He's 27 stone, and he isn't named after the sumo district as Channel 4's commentary has suggested (they call him 'Local Hero') but after a predecessor at Dewanoumi stable who became a prominent Director of the Sumo Association, ex-Ozeki Ryogoku Kajinosuke.

Like the young 'Killer Whale' Akinoshima, Ryogoku was born under a dark star: in his case Nagasaki, on 30 July 1962 as a tiny, premature baby. He was an intelligent boy as well as an athlete, and became one of the select band of rikishi to step onto the dohyo from university as a college champion. Tochinowaka did the same, and journalists are always keen to point out their so-called rivalry. Whether Ryo has the tunnel vision to get to the top in sumo remains to be seen: he's been a long time coming, though nobody can deny he has the physical qualifications for the job and he gave The Wolf a good hiding in November 1989 to win the Outstanding Performance prize and promotion to komusubi. He made his first appearance in a basho in March 1985, and it took him exactly two years to fling the lower-rankers out of his way and climb into Makunouchi, the top division. There he found the going tougher, getting twice bumped to the rank of komusubi but tending to slip back down again among the seniors where he can exert his dominance more easily.

He can pull off the odd upset: apart from beating Chiyonofuji last November, he skunked Hokutenyu in January 1989, and Channel 4 viewers who saw the 1988 Aki basho were able to watch him overturn an admittedly below par Konishiki. They also observed that Ryogoku tends to get beaten rather a lot by yori-kiri for a man his size – and yori-kiri happens to be his favourite attacking technique. He also favours the lift-out, push-out, push-down, forearm throw (kote-nage), inner and outer arm throws and the outer leg trip. The crush-out (yori taoshi) is a formality if he's in the mood, which he often isn't. Experts say his main shortcomings are a sluggish jump-off and a lack of balance. But if anyone can teach him these things and spur him up the banzuke, Dewanoumi Oyakata can. His win–loss record over 29 basho stands at 190–171.

Ryo (nickname Koba) is single, and likes music and reading (and no, not *Moby Dick*).

SASSHUNADA

Stable: Izutsu
Weight: 149 kg (23 st 6 lb)
Height: 183 cm (6 ft)

One of the extraordinary five-man Izutsu con-

27 stone of trouble – Ryogoku nevertheless has trouble with a Dump Truck onslaught.

tingent in the top division, Sasshunada is known to his more famous stable-mates as 'Matzu'. His fighting name means 'Sea of Sasshu', but his real name is Katsuyuki Yoshizaki. He was born in the same part of Japan as those fighting brothers Terao and Sakahoko, also of Izutsu: Kagoshima Prefecture at the southern end of the most southerly island, on 7 June 1957. He's now in his thirties and losing his hair after a long career and 84 basho, with 433 wins against 400 losses.

He joined Izutsu Oyakata's cohorts at the beginning of 1976 and appeared in the New Year basho, but it took a decade of hard work to break into the top division in the Aki basho 1986. He has only ever got as far as senior number 1 and has never won any special awards, but he's steady and tough, with a stunning pushing attack. As he backs it up with over 23 stone, he has usually been able to hold his own among the maegashira men with better than break-even scores, but he's not a giant-killer and lacks the fire in his belly that has driven his more senior stable-mates. He sank into Juryo at the tailend of 1989, and looked set for a haircut.

His preferred techniques are the push-out and slap-down, though a lot of his wins have come by way of yori-kiri, sukui nage and tsuki otoshi as well. He also features the hand pull-down in his repertoire.

Sasshunada is married with one son, but spends a good deal of his time in *pachinko* parlours, flicking little silver balls into slots – a popular Japanese pastime.

TAGARYU

Stable: Kagamiyama
Weight: 139 kg (21 st 12 lb)
Height: 178 cm (5 ft 10 in)

Tagaryu was once a star, on the rank of sekiwake and with an array of awards: one Kanto-sho, one prestigious Gino-sho, one Kinboshi and even a title to his name, getting his portrait on the Wall of Fame and being pictured shaking hands with Chiyonofuji. But since those days he's been up and down the sumo ladder like a man mending his roof, and as recently as the November 1989 basho he was down in the Juryo division nursing an injury.

He was born Noboru Kurotani on 15 February 1958 in Ibaraki Prefecture – which makes him 32 now and due for the dreaded haircut fairly soon. He was recruited by Kagamiyama stable and entered pro sumo in the Haru basho of 1974, making Makunouchi at last in May 1982. He has had a less-than-flattering tally of 500 wins to 541 losses over a 95-basho career, reflecting his crashes from grace as well as his longevity. His technical arsenal includes his favourite yori-kiri and uwate-nage manoeuvres, along with oshi-dashi, hataki-komi, hiki-otoshi, and yori taoshi, though his power is diminishing these days and it takes a lot out of him to have to climb back to maegashira from the Second Division, as has happened recently. An old warhorse, though, who won't give up easily.

He's married to an actress, and looks a bit like Edward G. Robinson himself. They've got a son and a daughter, and Tagaryu says his hobbies are drinking saké, reading and baseball.

TAKAMISUGI

Stable: Futagoyama
Weight: 147 kg (23 st 2 lb)
Height: 179 cm (5 ft 10½ in)

Very popular with the female fans is baby-faced Takamisugi, whose singing voice was good enough to make a few records before the Sumo Association's clampdown on such activities. They call him 'Doraemon' (Temple Gong), though his real name is Kaneo Takashi.

This roly-poly character from Kanagawa Prefecture (where he was born on 1 March 1961) checks in at 5 ft 10½ in and 23 stone – big for a little fellow. One of his hobbies is eating out; another one is eating in, to judge by the look of him. He also shares the common Japanese habit

'Okay you dirty rats.' Tagaryu's mugshot.

of getting up and singing in public to pre-recorded backing tracks – it's all the rage and called karaoke.

Takamisugi joined sumo's well-stocked Futagoyama heya in the spring of 1976 and made his début in the March basho. He got into Makunouchi in July 1981, most of his successes coming from fiery pushing attacks. His highest rank has been maegashira number 1, and he did well in 1988, but since then he has found the opposition tougher, and particularly the top-rankers when they get their meathooks on his belt. He isn't much good at yotsu-zumo and, like The Plum and a number of other younger tiros, can't seem to be bothered with it. His favourite techniques are oshi-dashi, nodowa (the throat thrust), oshi taoshi, tsuki-dashi, tsuki-otoshi and sukui nage, the scoop throw. He also enjoys a good slap-down and the hand pull-down, and can manage the odd yori-kiri or yori taoshi to finish things off. He tends to have a terrible time when thrown to the lions of sanyaku, as happened in January 1989, when he got promoted above his head to maegashira number 3 and came home with his tail between his legs. If his match-ups are less exacting, he can turn in the occasional 10–5 and look rather good. He even has a Gold Star to his name. His win–loss rate over 83 basho is 477–452.

Married recently, he's still singing for his supper and unlikely to trouble the Yokozuna Promotion Council in the immediate future.

heya in March 1979 to be hurled about by resident stars Choyonofuji and Hokutoumi. Taka got into the top division in the Natsu basho in May 1986 and became known as 'The Mountain Lion' – presumably from his habit of attacking from a great height.

Despite the disadvantage of being built on stilts he managed to reach the rank of maegashira number 1 and even to be runner-up in a couple of tournaments, but in the end his temperament, rather than his high hips, let him down. He has two Kinboshi or Gold Stars to his credit, and has had some stirring spells – as, for example, in the Kyushu basho in November 1988 – but he doesn't seem to have the power, mental or physical, to finish off the job and gain promotion to the key rungs on the ladder. No doubt Kokonoe Oyakata is working on it.

Taka favours a southpaw attack on the belt (hidari-yotsu, with the left hand inside on the opponent's mawashi). His range includes yori-kiri and yori taoshi (despite his lack of cylinders), as well as the outer arm throw (uwate-nage), the hand pull-down, the slap-down, the push-out and push-down. He tends to go back into his shell after a rush of blood: having won good majorities in November 1988 and January 1989 he turned in an appalling 3–12 in March as a number 3 senior – and one of those wins was a walkover. His win–loss tally is 320–317 over 65 basho.

Taka is married, and his real name is Tadao Yasuda.

TAKANOFUJI

Stable: Kokonoe
Weight: 137 kg (21 st 8 lb)
Height: 192 cm (6 ft 3½ in)

Tall Takanofuji from Tokyo is the daddy-long-legs of the top division, with a centre of gravity much too high for this low-slung game. He also tends to choke every time he approaches the sanyaku ranks, which is an even greater disability. He was born on 9 October 1963 and entered Kokonoe

TAKANOHAMA

Stable: Fujishima
Weight: 184 kg (28 st 13 lb)
Height: 188 cm (6 ft 2 in)

Seeing Takanohama seated, one is struck by the wonder of his being able to walk, let alone fight. He's only 24, but he seems to lack the grace and poise of his mountainous rivals in the top division and at 29 stone he would do well to observe the enforced diets of The Dump Truck and The Giant

Takanofuji, having pounced from a great height.

Panda and take off a couple of stone before he does himself some damage. He isn't fleet of foot, and if you're slow at this game, you're an accident looking for somewhere to happen.

He was born on 22 September 1965 in Fukuoka, an auspicious start, as they stage the Kyushu basho there. His real name is Shinji Hamada, and he joined Fujishima heya, where he daily has the inspiration of seeing young Akinoshima bashing his head against the teppo pole to toughen it up. Taka's first basho was in March 1981, and although he got to the top division at his 'home' tournament in November 1988, he hasn't looked very sure of himself and went back into Juryo in July 1989 to refresh his confidence. Experts say he looks rather ungainly but that he should make the sanyaku ranks if he gets his act together. He likes the push-out, nage throws and a technique favoured by his fellow-colossus Konishiki, the elbow clamp force-out. He's also into slap-downs and belly-outs, *kime taoshi, kime dashi*, and the force-out, yori-kiri — though his belt technique is apparently suspect. He goes for the southpaw attack — left hand inside on the sash.

His top rank to date is maegashira number 8, and over 53 basho he has a 249–212 record. Not bad — and he'll do a lot better as well, provided he avoids eating himself to a standstill.

TOCHINOWAKA

Stable: Kasugano
Weight: 148 kg (23 st 4 lb)
Height: 190 cm (6 ft 2¾ in)

Tipped as a strong candidate for ozeki status, Tochi came into sumo from Meiji University as a graduate and runner-up in the All-Japan College Championships. He was the 34th rikishi to make the grade from college; another is Ryogoku, with whom he maintains a friendly rivalry. Arriving on the scene in March 1985, Tochi tore through the Second Division as if about to set the place on fire, tying the record for speed through Juryo and spending just two tournaments there (September and November 1986) before climbing into Makunouchi, the top division, in the January basho of 1987. But after a good run of giant-grounding that year, when British fans thought he was definitely going places, Tochi hurt his knee and in 1988 he was much more erratic, getting middling scores that pushed him up and down between sekiwake and the seniors. His Aki basho bouts in September that year included something historic: the first full four-minute shikiri naoshi ever shown on UK television, Tochi versus Ozeki Konishiki. Tochinowaka won both the wrestling and the staring session, sticking out his lower lip and looking very fierce indeed. But he was also featured in two other bouts in which he was particularly unlucky to be worsted. One was against Mitoizumi, which Tochi lost after his belt kept coming undone, and the other was his senshuraku match against Akinoshima, when the gyoji gave the decision to Tochi and then the judges reversed it. Being on the knife-edge of 7–7 at the time, this meant that Tochi was demoted. The following basho, the Kyushu 1988, he was also injured, sitting it out with a badly sprained wrist. He's getting back on target now, but ranked komusubi for the Aki basho 1989 he did himself scant justice with 5–10.

Tochi's real name is Kiyotake Kaseda. He was born on 23 May 1962 in Wakayama Prefecture, which hadn't produced a top-division wrestler for nearly 40 years. He belongs to Kasugano stable, where many of the leading lights have prefixed their fighting names with 'Tochi', or 'horse chest-nut'. Tochinowaka has missed out on a lot of ring experience while completing his education, but his techniques include yori-kiri (the front force-out), oshi-dashi (push-out), yori taoshi (the force out and down), oshi-taoshi (push-down), uwate dashi nage (pulling outer arm throw), inner and outer arm throws and tsuri-dashi (the lift-out). Far more important, he is stubborn, determined and tall enough to assert himself in a stand-off. He looks like the stuff of which top wrestlers are made.

On his day, Tochinowaka can upset anybody, and nowadays he even worries The Wolf. In July 1989 the college kid set about Asahifuji, levelling the ozeki with a crushing yori taoshi which seriously damaged his chances of becoming a

Tochinowaka (right) in civvies – on the dohyo he is much less friendly.

Wakasegawa likes his hands on your mawashi.

yokozuna. To date Tochi has to his credit one Outstanding Performance prize, one Gold Star and two awards for Fighting Spirit. His record over 29 basho is a creditable 190–143.

He's single, and says he likes karaoke for an off-duty break. In Britain he's known as 'The Mighty Oak', for reasons not easy to understand. His shikona suggests he's more of a young conker!

TOCHITSUKASA

Stable: Kasugano
Weight: 155 kg (24 st 5 lb)
Height: 180 cm (5 ft 11 in)

An old-timer and, at 32, veteran of just 53 basho, Tochitsukasa may nevertheless have a few tricks left up his sleeve. Born Tetsuo Goto on 25 April 1958 in Aichi Prefecture, he got into sumo as a collegiate champion in March 1981 and became a formidable prospect. He collected a cupboardful of awards – a Kanto-sho for his Fighting Spirit, a Gino-sho for his technical abilities, and two Kinboshi or Gold Stars for giant-slaying – and rose as high as sekiwake, on the third rung of the banzuke.

He's still big, power-packed and versatile, with a technical range that includes oshi, tsuki, yori and nage skills: oshi-taoshi, the push out and down, oshi-dashi, the push-out, the hand pull-down, twist-down, slap-down, force-out and crush-out, as well as shitate-nage and uwate-nage, the inner and outer arm throws.

Injuries have caused his demotion back to the Second Division, where he recuperates by flinging Juryo people about and winning their division title, as he did in January 1989 and again in July. Over his 53 basho his win–loss tally stands at 361 to 329. Known to Channel 4 viewers as 'The Tree Chief', he's tipped as a possible late-blooming star by commentator Lyall Watson.

WAKASEGAWA

Stable: Isegahama
Weight: 152 kg (23 st 13 lb)
Height: 189 cm (6 ft 2¼ in)

The November 1988 basho saw Wakasegawa, as a senior number 3, heaving about the dohyo with Konishiki, Onokuni and big Jingaku, and beating the lot of them. Onokuni, he of the mountainous girth and 30 stone, has been bundled away on three out of four occasions. Waka can do all this all right, but it seems to wear him out, and he sometimes finishes with a losing score after spectacular exertions. Experts say he has one of the best belt attacks of any of the senior men and he's determined to get somewhere with it as well, preferably the sanyaku ranks. If he doesn't strain himself giant-killing, why not? He's a big chap himself at around 24 stone and over 6 ft 2 in, but he needs to get going fairly shortly if he is to capitalize on his grappling skills to the full. At the moment he has only one Gold Star to show for them.

His real name is Wataru Sato, and he was born in 1962, on 28 July in Yamagata Prefecture. He joined Isegahama stable and fought his first basho in March 1978. When he got into Makunouchi at the start of 1983 he looked very stern and very strong, but after that first flush of success he developed diabetes and seemed to lose his grip, sinking back among the lower-rankers. He did well in 1988, and as a number 7 maegashira in the Hatsu basho last January he managed 10–5, got promoted to senior number 1, and promptly had a fiasco in March, missing seven bouts and losing seven more. He has steadied himself slightly since then, though: his record over 71 basho is 437–379. His techniques include his favourite, yori-kiri, plus tsuki-otoshi, tsuki-dashi, hiki-otoshi, and various nage throws (shitate, uwate, kote and sukui) at which he is very good.

He relaxes by tinkering with his car and listening to music, and he's a married man but without children.

PART 3

THE
BACKGROUND

THE SPORT OF GODS

Sumo battles between mountainous men are as old as the hills. Baked clay statuettes and wooden sumotori dolls excavated in Japan have been dated to over 1,000 years ago, and the sport itself is undoubtedly of much more ancient origin even than that. Rice farmers may well have grappled in belly bands as early as 200 BC, not so much to test their strength as to find out who had the favour of the gods for the next harvest. This was known as *shinji-zumo*, and using sumo for divination has always been common. Like a lightning conductor, it could 'earth' spiritual forces which might otherwise prove disastrous and difficult to understand, and there are many sumo-like ceremonies which depend on invisible powers to determine the outcome, or which celebrate the connection between the physical and spiritual worlds.

'One-man sumo' can still be seen at Oyamazumi shrine, Omishima, with a priest wrestling an unseen god and always losing as an act of appeasement, and the Ceremony of the Crows, held at the Kamo shrine in Kyoto, involves village boys in wrestling matches as part of a ritual for safeguarding the crops. There is even, in Nagasaki, so-called 'Crying sumo', in which local people hold staring matches between their babies. The tot who breaks into tears first actually wins: like the priest vanquished by an invisible opponent, he shows great wisdom by playing the fool. The association of sumo with the unseen, and with Shinto (the Way of the Gods), has been long and deep, and wrestlers have displayed their skills in temple compounds and at shrines since time immemorial, even raising funds for their building and repair.

Sumo fans have ranged from the humblest farmer to the greatest emperor, and since the people of Japan have always believed their emperors to be gods, their patronage made sumo more than just a 'sport of kings'. The first such grand patron on record was Emperor Suinin who in 23 BC watched a legendary bout between an enormously tall fellow called Nomi-no Sukune, and a powerful champion, who could straighten out hooks, by the 'handle' of Taema-no Kehaya. The pair set to kicking one another, there being no particular rules in those days, and Sukune got in a couple of stomps that broke his opponent's ribs and loins and killed the chap stone dead. Shrines still commemorate this battle. Under Emperor Shomu in the eighth century, a sumo basho was held annually at court on the seventh day of the seventh month, and although the date changed over the years, it really caught on at court. The wrestlers (mostly farmers from the outlying villages) fought in two teams, 'left' and 'right', and were seated accordingly in relation to the Emperor. Not being recognizable star names, they wore hollyhock flowers and calabash blossoms in their hair to show whose side they were on.

Sometimes the stories need to be taken with a good Mitoizumi-sized handful of salt, such as the bouts involving eight-foot tall Japanese, or opponents vanquished with the help of a passing water buffalo, and so on. But there are some intriguing myths and legends about how particular sumo customs came about. For example, how do you suppose Grand Champions came to wear the white hawser belt of their office? Well, in AD 850 there was apparently a tremendous

133

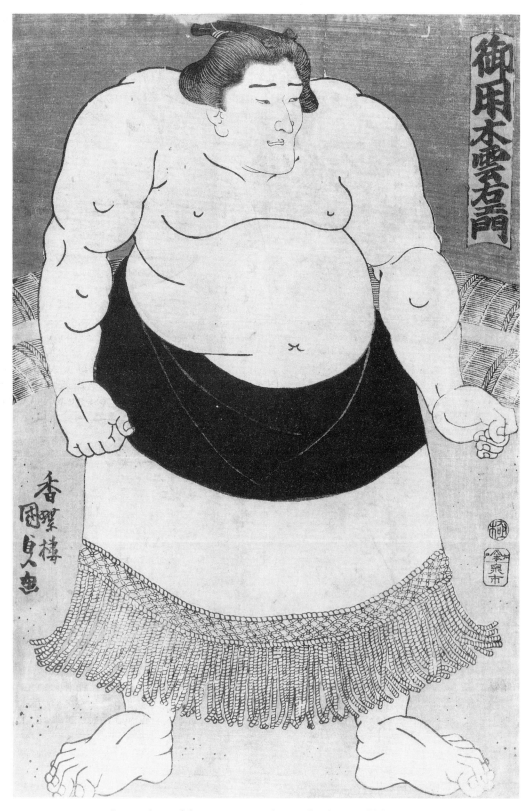

A woodcut of the sumo wrestler and reformer, Takasago.

champion called Hajikami, from the province of Omi, who so outclassed all his challengers that one day, while he was performing at the Sumiyoshi shrine, the referee took down the sacred white rope or *shimenawa* and tied it round his middle. If anyone could so much as get their hands on this, said the referee, he would consider him the winner. There are, of course, other possible sources. Anything *kami* or held sacred may be adorned with the white rope, and sumotori have always been considered very special indeed. Traditionally, when a new castle was about to be built, they took part in the ground-breaking ceremony, performing their high shiko stamps to tread down evil spirits and being protected from spiritual harm by a shimenawa belt. And this ground-breaking also involved spreading ropes crosswise over the land, some of which were called *yokozuna*.

When Japan was ruled by Shoguns or warlords, sumo was at first despised as an emperor's pastime, but it was later rehabilitated and the wrestlers performed at the warriors' behest, just as they had done for the emperors. Many feudal chiefs held sumotori as vassals and retainers. They were used as bodyguards, as 'champions' (representing their leaders in symbolic matches), as morale boosters, and for the training of troops in unarmed combat, earning Samurai status and the name they still use today – *rikishi*, or 'strong Samurai'. The techniques they used were far less refined than those of today, and included moves indistinguishable from those of jujitsu. The two disciplines gradually separated and became distinct martial arts. The type of 'attack' sumo used in battle was known as *buke-zumo* or warrior sumo. It had a very serious purpose, and could save a man's life if he lost his sword.

The sport retained its powerful hold over the public imagination through its strong connection with Shinto worship. It grew in ceremony and meaning, too, as Zen Buddhist thought permeated Japanese culture. What Zen gave to other martial arts by way of *bushido*, we may suppose it gave to sumo: contempt for death, harmony with the unseen, purity, politeness, meditation, self-mastery. Stories abound during this period of the sport's development of small men overturning superior opponents, exerting *ki* (central energy) and *shin* (heart, or 'character'). Even women appear among the legendary strong ones, showing power above and beyond their physical strength. Around the time of the construction of Hideyoshi's Fushimi castle in Kyoto (c.1594), the champion Tateishi was challenged by a nun, wearing Nagasaki-style pantaloons, who mysteriously threw him to the ground. She went on to earn something of a giant-killing reputation at the big tournaments, and was greatly feared for her unaccountable powers.

At Shinto shrines, sumo matches were held as fund-raising events, but they also became popular as a way of earning a living for out-of-work Samurai fighters. These rikishi formed themselves into professional troupes and travelled from town to town, challenging local champions and wrestling in a 'ring' of seething spectators. Big stakes were involved, and people lost their shirts and also their tempers. Terrible fights would occasionally break out, with the odd fatality, until eventually the authorities cracked down and declared street-corner sumo illegal (several times). Masterless Samurai wrestlers were at a loose end, having lost their status as castle basho celebrities. Under Oda Nobunaga (1534–1582), for example, it had been possible to win enough bushels of rice to feed a small army, and such wrestling prizes were greatly missed.

It was during this period, when sumo had been reduced to street-corner fighting, that a masterless rikishi decided to try to do something to save his noble sport from a seedy future. His name was Ikazuchi Gondaiyu, and in 1684 he petitioned the shrine magistrate of Edo (the old Tokyo) to permit a benefit tournament in the precincts of Fukagawa Hachiman shrine. The magistrate refused. Gondaiyu, being an intelligent man, sat down and thought out ways to make sumo more acceptable to the authorities. There had never been anything laid down about rules and techniques and until very recently there wasn't even a ring of any kind, so that fights would naturally spill out into the crowds. Gondaiyu proposed to stop this by surrounding the wrestling match itself with rice bales to fence off a ring. Gradually, fixed rules, techniques, and a dohyo made of hard clay with rice bales imbedded in its platform, gave sumo new respectability. Such organization also turned sumo into a thriving spectator sport, not just for emperors and warlords, but for the public, who could now pay to come and watch it without being set upon themselves.

With sumo's new-found legality, not only were champion wrestlers adopted by feudal lords, but also they were suddenly lionized by rich merchants as well. In Osaka and Kyoto a formal system of ranking and tournaments was agreed, and by the late 1780s sumo was organized on something like a national basis, with its heart shifting to Edo. Gone was the free-for-all violence of the earlier wrestling events. Now champions began to emerge who were not only strong and fearless, but extremely skilled as well. One of these was Tanikaze, who in 1790 performed the very first *yokozuna dohyo-iri* or Grand Champion's ring-entering ceremony (the great man now having a ring to enter). By any standards, this was a formidable champion. The son of a poor farmer, Tanikaze Kajinosuke lost only 14 bouts over 44 of the big tournaments and earned the status of yokozuna long before the official list began to be compiled (in 1909). He was colourful in his private life, but overwhelmingly popular with the public, who said of him, 'No Tanikaze before Tanikaze, and no Tanikaze after Tanikaze'. Invincible against most opponents, he died of 'flu at the age of 46.

His like was never seen again, but the eighteenth century did have several great champions, including the legendary Raiden Tame-emon, who had hands like shovels and who was banned from certain types of attack, among them slapping, because of his 'unfair' physical strength. He is said to have been rather ruthless in his private affairs and to have been involved in the murder of one of his rivals. He held the rank of ozeki for 15 years and might otherwise have been promoted to Grand Champion (with its exacting moral requirements).

Even towards the end of the Shogunate, sumo wrestlers continued to be held in very high regard, with the rich and powerful basking in the reflected glory of the champions. There was even women's wrestling or *onna-zumo* in the eighteenth century, though this was very rude and uproarious and nothing to do with nuns or spiritual forces. Changes were in the air. In 1854 came the first of them. The American Black Ships of Commodore Perry arrived to violate Japan's isolation, and though he was treated to the sight of huge sumo wrestlers humping bales of rice, to frighten his sailors, the Commodore did not go away. This was the beginning of the end of the Shoguns who

had sponsored sumo for so many years. After civil war came the Restoration of Japan's emperors in 1868, and the dawn of the Meiji era. The warlords having been ousted, their champions were thrown out on their cauliflower ears. Suddenly Western values were all the rage, and ancient Japanese sports and rituals, with bare bottoms all over the place, were simply not the thing. Once again sumo was in serious trouble, as it had been when the warlords originally came to power and saw it as the fetish of emperors. And once again, sumo hugged the shrines and street corners in order to survive.

Just as the masterless Samurai wrestler Gondaiyu had saved sumo before by adapting it for officialdom, so another saviour came along in the form of Takamiyama, later called Takasago Uragoro. As a sumo wrestler and reformer, he asked for far-reaching changes to be made which would ensure that sumo was free from administrative corruption, and fair to the wrestlers themselves. He was immediately expelled, so he set up his own rival association in Nagoya and ran sumo there so efficiently that he was able to stage an exhibition in Tokyo. The officials eventually saw the sense of his changes, and Takasago became a respected authority. In 1889, partly through his work, the forerunner of today's Japan Sumo Association was formed to steer the sport into a new age.

Decent again, sumo reverted to what it had once been: the Sport of Gods, and a token of Japanese pride in their ancestry, despite the recent flirtation with Western ideas. Emperor Meiji, himself a keen amateur, decided to give it the seal of approval by staging a huge basho to show off the splendid old sport. He was lucky enough to share an era with two great champions, in Hitachiyama and Umegatani II, who became ambassadors as well as yokozuna, and whose battles were some of the most exciting ever seen. Despite being physically small (at 5ft 8in and 5ft 6in) they were very great stars, and in 1907 Hitachi took sumo abroad, to the United States, where he was warmly received by Theodore Roosevelt. 'Teddy' may have been somewhat nonplussed, in those times of tightening belts, to see Hitachi's belt very loose indeed, and his kesho-mawashi sumptuously studded with real diamonds. In 1910, despite sumo's fluctuating popularity back home, there was even a four-month tour of England.

Sumo gradually re-established itself in Japan and, baseball notwithstanding, became recognized once more as the national sport. The first National Sport Hall or Kokugikan was built in Tokyo in 1909, and a statute was issued to ratify the rank of yokozuna and keep a roll of honour of all such Grand Champions. When squabbling threatened to break out in earnest between two rival sumo associations, no less a figure than the Prince Regent, later Emperor Hirohito, stepped in to act as a unifying force, donating the money for a great silver cup to be made and presented to all future tournament winners. Like his ancestors, the Emperor was prepared to act as sumo's conspicuous patron and friend, and unlike them he was even willing to travel out from the imperial palace to watch it at the stadium with everybody else. He was to be rewarded in seeing three of the greatest Grand Champions who have ever lived.

Futabayama, the first of these, dominated sumo in the late 1930s and early 1940s as few men have ever dominated any sport. Born in 1912 in Oita Prefecture, the son of a boatman, he became a national hero, amassing at one stage 69 successive victories and only losing then because he was very ill. He won 12 yusho, terrifying his opponents even before they got into the ring, and his rensho record of 69 still stands today.

Next came another extraordinary yokozuna: Taiho. Born Naya Koki in 1940, he was the son of a Japanese mother and a Russian emigré father, and he became the (then) youngest wrestler ever to win the Emperor's Cup. He went on to build a reputation for unfathomable power, and to collect an amazing number of tournament wins – 32 – which at the time of writing has never been equalled. He also had a rensho record to be proud of: 45 successive victories and, as later photographic evidence was to show, he beat his 46th opponent as well, though the official ruling robbed him of the chance to extend his run even further.

Emperor Hirohito must have been well pleased to have seen these two staggering fellows at the height of their powers, but we can only imagine what he thought of his good fortune in seeing a third, Chiyonofuji, in his prime. The Emperor died before The Wolf began re-writing the record books, but he knew enough about this ancient sport to have seen in him sumo's first truly international hero.

STABLE LIFE

Most of the 39 sumo stables – confusingly called both *heya* and *beya* – are clustered in the half square mile to the south of Ryogoku Station in Tokyo, not far from the great Kokugikan Stadium. Some have been there for over 200 years. The stables each have an elder or *oyakata* in charge, who rules his domain with a split bamboo cane called the *shinai* and in much the same feudal spirit as the lords of old Japan. Each elder is a former wrestler and one of the traditional quota of 105 dignitaries (though at the moment there happen to be 107) who make up the Japan Sumo Association (Nihon Sumo Kyokai).

The boys coming into the heya are mostly from the humble outlying fishing or farming villages. Any tough city kids are soon disabused of their fancy notions. The rookies are generally 15 or 16 and fresh from high school. College and university boys (like Tochinowaka) enter the system at a different level.

The newcomers immediately find themselves in a regime so harsh, even by Japanese standards, that many wait only for darkness to fall on their first evening to do a moonlight flit. As Konishiki says, 'You cannot find their bags. You cannot find their person. They're gone.' Sixty per cent do not last a year. The ones who do are boys with very strong characters who have fixed their minds on becoming sumo wrestlers at all costs, who are willing to obey at all times, respect their superiors, and work harder than they ever dreamed possible. They bow a lot, and when they are given mortifying chores in the stable or a repeated good hiding on the dohyo they must think themselves lucky, and reply, in answer to instructions or cuffs round the ear, 'Hai!' (yes) and

'Gotsu'an' desu!' (thank you very much). They have no money to speak of, and no word from home except through the medium of the oyakata's wife, the *okami-san*, who acts as their matron. She mothers them when things become unbearable – which is most of the time – and gives them any messages about funerals or weddings in the family (if it clashes with a basho they are not allowed to go).

The first thing they learn is that sumo has a very rigid and strict hierarchy. Wrestlers move up in rank by merit. Age and experience, though these criteria are respected everywhere else in Japan, come second, at the highest level, to winning. Winning, in sumo's top divisions, is all that matters. Those who win go up and those who lose, apart from yokozuna, go down. Even the yokozuna himself, if he loses an unseemly number of times, must retire and never darken the dohyo again. This is the ruthless system that has bred some of the most charming and well-mannered sportsmen in the world, and rookie wrestlers have it forced down the north-west passage of their intellects by the evidence of their daily lives. It fosters among them a kind of camaraderie that makes them fonder of each other than of the outside world, and prompt to close ranks aginst human beings from a more sloppy order.

Those who win are promoted and receive benefits befitting their rank. Rookies dance attendance on them and they are assigned *tsukebito*, or personal servants, whose duty it is to scrub their backs in the bath, help them dress and undress, do their laundry, run their errands, shield them from the rain with umbrellas, and cool their brows in summer with huge paper fans. A high-ranking wrestler may have seven or eight of these young batmen running about at his beck and call. The sekitori stretches out his arm and makes the Japanese beckoning gesture, which is to open and shut his fingers repeatedly against his down-turned palm, and the underling must race towards him, not walk. When he gets there he must bow very nicely and scuttle off to do his master's bidding. The batboys used to be known as *fundoshi katsugi* or loincloth carriers because one of their tasks is to fetch and hump the lacquered wickerwork trunks containing the sekitori's marvellous aprons and belts.

The system is very fair because any underling, given sufficient talent to begin with, can achieve the same privileges by work and winning. He too can make his way up the ranking system to a better life. In the mean time he is nothing and no one. At the end of every training session in the stable, all the novices squat on their haunches with their eyes closed and their mouths shut, meditating. A not uncommon text hanging from the wall in a scroll is *mu* or nothingness. Each gym has a little Shinto shrine in one alcove, called the *kamidana*. It is hung with paper zigzags (*gohei*) and sacred shimenawa rope, just like the belt of the yokozuna. A young rikishi must contemplate these things, and what they ultimately mean. Before he begins his training each day he must clap his hands and bow to the shrine, and he must do this again after he has been covered in dirt and bruises and red weals from his sumo practice. It is a struggle very hard for a modern Westerner to understand although Jesuit monks captured the spirit when they recited the prayer of St Ignatius Loyala: 'Teach us, heavenly Father, to give and not to count the cost, to fight and not to heed the wounds, to toil and not to seek for rest, to labour and not to ask for any reward, save that of knowing we do Thy will.' When Westerners marvel at the impeccable courtesy of sumo wrestlers on the dohyo, winning and losing with equal humility, they are seeing the products of an ancient finishing school.

The juniors' day begins at dawn, or before dawn in winter: 3.30 a.m. is not unknown. They wake on the communal sleeping floor, roll up their individual *futon* mattresses and duvets and then get washed and off to sumo school (where they are trained *en masse*) or into their *mawashi* or

fighting belts. The lowest ranks wear dark blue or black, which changes to white for a senior wrestler's training, and coloured satins to adorn him in the ring. (The fact that one or two great rikishi, like Chiyonofuji, still choose to wear a black mawashi on the dohyo may not be without significance.) In winter the rookies stamp their feet and puff steam as they perform their ablutions. There is no heating whatever at night in the stable. Flush toilets are the only refinement. Even in the depths of winter underlings are permitted to wear only a loose cotton *yukata* or kimono outdoors. You have to be a senior to merit a *haori* (jacket) over the top which, together with the voluminous pleated culottes or *hakama*, make up the regulation outfit of the higher ranks. They may wear casual Western dress for golf or in the privacy of their own homes, and seniors often have special extra-large tracksuits made for winter comfort about the heya, a thought which crosses many a rookie's mind as he rushes near naked to the practice area. There is no porridge or hot drink to keep him warm either. Breakfast is not permitted; the exercises are simply too strenuous.

Between 5 and 6 a.m. new recruits not assigned to attend sumo school in the Kokugikan Stadium are downstairs limbering up on the pounded clay – covered with a layer of moist sand to prevent abrasions. Their feet are always bare, with at most a sock to cover bandages. All shoes and sandals are left at the stable entrance (this is standard practice in all Japanese homes), and even visitors must obey this heya rule. This is sacred ground, and the Japanese have a strange and wonderful relationship with the soil beneath their feet. Old Kabuki theatres were originally constructed on burial sites, to enable spirits to creep up the actor's legs and inspire his perform-ance, and here in the heya when the senior wrestlers arrive, they will throw salt to purify the surface.

Formal practice begins when the oyakata appears, shinai in hand. The bamboo stick is whacked against the boys' bare flesh, leaving a bright red mark. Seniors (sekitori) are still in bed, either at home if they are married or can afford to 'live out', or upstairs in their private rooms. They show up at around 8 o'clock, whereupon juniors are immediately seen scurrying about with their mawashi and kimono, helping them to dress and fetching a bamboo ladle with a long handle for those who want to rinse out their mouths with water. By now the place is beginning to liven up, with a small spectators' platform on the side of the practice area gradually filling with press people, fans, neighbours and even the odd TV crew, all in their stockinged feet, having left their shoes at the entrance.

The seniors look formidably larger than the newer recruits, and the top wrestlers in a stable may also wield the shinai, making them a fairly fearsome sight. They begin 'helping' the new boys by shouting, man-handling and walloping them cheerfully to make them more determined. The rookies are whacked for insufficient effort, insufficient courage in meeting a challenge, insufficient grasp of instructions and sometimes for no reason at all, except to get them going with more vim. Practice – called *keiko* or *-geiko* – is made up of two basic parts: exercises and contact rehearsal. The first the wrestlers do on their own; the second they practise with another junior, or with a wrestler of higher rank.

Most of the exercises are painful to a degree. (One, the *matawari*, is positive torture.) Everyone is expected to do about a hundred shiko, or high stamps, a day, as well as squats and frog-walks to strengthen the hips and knees. Then there is the teppo pole, which has to be rhythmically smacked with the hands or shoulders, exhaling on impact. But these are small beer compared with the horrifying matawari, or thigh split. This exercise looks physically impossible but hardened rikishi practise it routinely without apparent discomfort, and this is how it is done. The trainee sits on the clay with his legs spreadeagled at either side of his body. The legs must stick out in a straight line for the full benefit. This in itself is rather painful, but the real enjoyment comes when the trainee is required to duck his head and chest down until it touches the clay before him. As nature never intended the human form to persecute itself in this way, a helpful senior, burly and boisterous, comes from behind and presses the new recruit on the back of the neck, forcing his spine forward to the accompaniment of moans and whimperings from the trainee, who firmly believes he is dying. A few doses of this and the rookie's other aches and pains pale into insignificance.

Contact practice takes various forms. *Moshiai-geiko* is knock-out sparring (elimination, though concussion is always a possibility). The winners go on to fresh challenges and therefore get more practice, becoming more proficient. If a low-ranker beats a sekitori, he must fight him again and again until the senior gets the better of him. In *butsukari-geiko*, a senior stands in the middle of the ring and meets a rushing junior full-tilt trying to push him backwards. The junior may perform with all the more verve after being lambasted with the bamboo cane from behind, and it is not unknown for the youngster to be spat upon or have salt thrown in his mouth if he is not fulfilling his promise. The more promise you have, the more you will be driven to bring it out, as this is considered a kindness. If the rookie falls over by his own momentum, he must avoid trying to break his fall with his hands. The plunge off the dohyo during tournaments, falling two feet, often backwards and at speed, must be second nature to the wrestler if he is not to tense up under pressure, and all rikishi must fall and tumble like acrobats, letting themselves go to avoid injury. Finally, *sanban-geiko* is a long series of bouts against the same opponent to train the mind against a variety of assaults. The whole session, which lasts until about 10.30 a.m., is followed by winding-down exercises, callisthenics, weight-training and, last of all, the meditative squat with hands on knees and the eyes closed. This is the only relaxation the rookies get, as they have many a chore in front of them.

The seniors now look forward to a nice hot bath, followed by a midday meal of wrestlers' stew – the main meal of the day. The juniors hurry about their appointed tasks, some helping with the cooking, some scrubbing a senior's enormous back in the *ofuro* (giant bath), some running errands or cleaning shoes. The sekitori, steaming from their baths, are served at table in order of rank, sitting by seniority. They sit round a huge pot of *chanko-nabe*, the sumo stew of vegetables, fish, meat or poultry, and *tofu* (bean curd) accompanied by tasty side-dishes and bowls of white rice, all of which the underlings have been preparing and chopping in between their other labours. The stable chefs are usually middle-rankers who have acquired a taste for heya life and a few privileges but who are not bent on becoming champions and therefore have time for the culinary arts. Some, after their retirement, open restaurants specializing in sumo stews. But the real drudgery – shopping, chopping, cleaning,

Enazakura at the chanko pot: The Cherry likes cooking.

washing up and serving at table – is done by the rookies, who have themselves been up the longest with nothing past their lips except the occasional mouthful of sand. When their turn finally comes at the pot, their dregs are tepid and their rice is cold, but this doesn't stop them heroically forcing down four or five bowls of it so as to build up extra weight – weight they may one day throw around like their superiors, now snoozing upstairs in after-dinner bliss. It is now high noon at the stable, and the rookies, after a quick shower, have to look sharp for other duties.

In the afternoons, apprentices in their first six months return from sumo school at Kokugikan Stadium, where they have been through the same toils and practice. Here they also learn calligraphy, reading, sumo history, poetry recital, domestic science for their heya chores, physiology, sports medicine, and the background and thinking behind their sacred sport. They learn to sing lustily, as well, especially *jinku*, or sumo songs. At the stable, juniors get busy helping the seniors dress for any celebrity appearances and appointments arranged for them. The youngsters clean and wash, do the laundry (of which there are huge quantities), help with mailings (for example, to their senior wrestlers' fan clubs), braid and starch *sagari* (the strange belt fringes worn by their superiors in the ring), and stack piles of blank cards by ink pads ready for sekitori to make palm prints (which are afterwards autographed with a flourish of the calligraphy brush and given to fans and sponsors).

In their spare time, such as it is, they may live it up by going to a *pachinko* (pinball) parlour and blowing their pocket money, or to the local McDonald's, or the *snakku* (snack bar) round the corner for noodles or a hot dog. Wrestlers of all ranks who stay at the heya occupy themselves with card games like *hanafuda*, or Mah-Jong, or comics (Japanese adults love the equivalents of *Beano* and *Dandy*), or else they do jigsaws (Konishiki enjoys these), or watch television or videos, or listen to music on a personal stereo, or play an instrument (the guitar is popular). Rikishi also enjoy golf, fishing and baseball – the last often improvised with an adhesive roll in place of a ball. Most of their hobbies are far from exotic, with perhaps discos (like the Roppongi in Tokyo) being the most jet-set. The wrestlers are slightly encumbered in their mastery of modern dance by having to wear traditional dress, sandals and topknots, but they are all very light on their feet. By about 9 p.m. the juniors are curfewed, and too exhausted in any case to do much other than unroll their mattresses on the floor and lie staring into the darkness, wondering no doubt what life is all about. This is their daily routine on all except Sundays and the five days after each basho, when the stable is simply ticking over and requiring ordinary housework.

The seniors lead a different, much more publicly accountable existence in the afternoons. Their unusual size and hairstyles single them out for attention in the streets, and fans, who believe they own all sports personalities they happen to find lurking about in daily life, are apt to come at them from all sides. The problem is compounded by the numerous duties and obligations sumo wrestlers bear towards the people of Japan. They are national heroes, with national responsibilities. Even their appearance is very strictly controlled. Before they go out, they must go through the rites of their distinctive sumo coiffure. In a corner of the stable's ground floor, kneeling on a straw *tatami* mat, is the heya hairdresser or *tokoyama*, with his combs and tongs and oily *bintsuke* wax for setting the *chonmage* (topknot) and *o-icho-mage* (formal style) in place. The older wrestlers' sleek black shoulder-length hair must be combed and oiled into the basic topknot, doubling it forward and tying it securely with rolled paper string. For official engagements and appearances on the basho dohyo, the style is more elaborate. The ends of the ponytail are fanned out with boxwood combs or tongs to form a crescent on top of the head, resembling the sacred gingko leaf. The rest of the hair is teased out in a ridge above the ears and across the back of the neck, rather like a German helmet. Traditionally a small patch is shaved on the crown to achieve the correct shape, though some modern rikishi appear to have avoided this tonsure. The whole hairdo, which is camellia-scented from the oils and quite beautiful, is a badge of the rikishi going back many hundreds of years when variants of the chonmage were worn by all Japanese men. It is a symbol of sumo's very ancient origins and betokens dignity.

If there is a tournament on, the wrestlers repair to Kokugikan Stadium if they are in Tokyo (or elsewhere for the three regional basho), where the seniors spend a long time sitting in the *shitaku beya* (dressing room) having bandages put on, or having acupuncture, or staring into space preparing their minds for their forthcoming bouts. The room is very quiet. On senshuraku, after the fifteenth and final day of the basho, there will be loud and healthy partying, but for now there is only obedient silence. During regional tournaments the wrestlers lodge in a temple, reminding them, in case they need any reminding, that they are not like other sportsmen and that there is more to sumo than the physical battle.

If there is no tournament, sekitori either go home or do public relations work for their sponsors, or for charity. They show up at shrines and stores, being polite to everyone and receiving cash and other gifts. They visit schools, telling children to behave themselves, and do other public-spirited tasks, like encouraging people to help prevent crime, fires or drug addiction. Sumo wrestlers, to the Japanese, stand for tradition, authority and self-restraint, and in an age when politicians are increasingly associated with immoral goings-on, the public view Chiyonofuji and his colleagues with a special respect. In the evening a top wrestler can expect to be wined and dined by his sponsors or rich businessmen bathing in his reflected glory. Rikishi consume enormous amounts of alcohol without any noticeable loss of control: they drink bowls of beer with their midday meal, and whisky and saké by the litre without so much as slurring their speech. Medical research might discover the alcohol seeps into their mammoth dimensions in some way as yet unknown. In any case, it would be very shameful for their stable if they were to get drunk and disorderly. They travel by car or taxi to avoid being lionized in the streets, and by 11 o'clock are usually fast asleep, either at home or at the heya. They have another heavy day ahead tomorrow.

A British rikishi

All things considered, the life of a rikishi may not sound everyone's cup of saké, but there is at least one courageous young man from Britain who was prepared to take it on. Nathan Strange is a former photographic print worker from Herne Bay in Essex (his dad was studio director). At 17 he took the mind-boggling step of going out to

Japan and joining the Azumazeki stable of Jesse Takamiyama, who specializes in 'bringing on' foreign rikishi like himself. Nathan fell in love with sumo when he saw it on television, and joined the British Sumo Association, formed by judo 7th dan Syd Hoare – a man who speaks and writes Japanese and who has lived and worked in Japan for many years, learning the martial arts. Nathan spent nine months picking up the basic techniques, though Syd estimated it would take him five years to gain sufficient stature to weather the blows and throws of the Big Game.

At the time Nathan weighed just 102 kilograms, which is a slight disadvantage to a lad of 6 ft 5 in. When he became a stable rookie, the combination of hard training and chanko-nabe ('disgusting' as he calls it) caused his weight to head down instead of up. He only survived by snacking on pizzas and hamburgers whenever he could, and doing weight lifting in the evenings in his spare time. In the end he could do 50 push-ups instead of 10, and 200 sit-ups instead of 100. But he was certainly put through the mill. At one point he found 47 cuts and bruises on himself, some of them infected. His *ani-deshi* (older brother wrestlers) were very severe on him, at one point making him do 20-minute non-stop butsukari-geiko. You grow up fast in a sumo stable, and Nathan responded in the only way known to get the big boys off his back – by winning. Despite hands trembling with nerves he fought through his *Maezumo* preliminaries and got onto the bottom of the banzuke in tiny writing as Hidenokuni Hajime ('England's First') for the November 1989 basho. He had a broken nose from training and during his first bout he coolly observed blood running down his opponent's back. It was from his 'hooter', so Nathan thought he'd better go for broke! He got his first win under his belt, survived some smashing attacks to his face, rallied from 1–2 down and ended the tournament kachi-koshi, with 7–5.

He celebrated by going out to a disco with triumphant yusho-winner Konishiki and Azumazeki Oyakata. The sight of 6 ft 5 in beanpole Nathan, the 35½-stone Dump Truck and the almost equally rotund Jesse on a dance floor would be enough to boggle most minds, but they ended up drinking tequila till all hours, Nathan's thoughts drifting towards pizza parlours and how many pizzas could be purchased with his £350 prize money in the coming weeks.

Nathan had a regulation topknot by now, and a lot of fan mail coming in, following his early triumphs and appearances on television. But he found that his bashings increased after the basho, as his older stable-mates were keen to prevent the fame going to his head. He tried not to make any long-term plans as he knew the going would get tougher from here, and he has finally decided to call it a day and return to England. He was on the verge of promotion to Jonidan, and he'd really like to have been able to survive long enough to get onto the 1991 Japan Festival tour of Britain. He had shown remarkable technical skill, and no matter how nervous he was before he fought, his mind cleared on the dohyo. He had at least one Zen experience. Amid the torture of training in the heat, he took a bite from a water melon and for an instant knew what true happiness was. Let us hope others will follow in Nathan's footsteps, and that we may one day see the first-ever European sumotori with a moro-zashi on a yokozuna!

SCHEDULES AND SALARIES

A sumo wrestler's career is generally brief and busy. Most retire soon after their 30th birthday, or before if they are badly injured or unlikely to make the grade. But during their short lives as active sumotori, they pack a lot in. Each year there are six official 15-day basho. Tickets go on sale six weeks beforehand and prices range from £4 to over £40, traditionally sold through a system of *chaya* or tea shops. The best seats go to VIPs and regular patrons, and senshuraku, the final day, is always a sell-out. The tournaments once used to be held in temple precincts, and until fairly recently there were four, based on the seasons. Now they are as follows:

Hatsu basho (New Year basho)	January
Haru basho (Spring basho)	March
Natsu basho (Summer basho)	May
Nagoya basho	July
Aki basho (Autumn basho)	September
Kyushu basho	November

Channel 4's coverage has so far been confined to the September tournament each year. This basho, like those in January and May, is held in the Kokugikan Stadium in Ryogoku, Tokyo. The Haru tournament is in Osaka. The Nagoya and Kyushu events were added to the schedule in the 1950s, the latter being staged in Fukuoka.

But these official basho (*honbasho*) are not all. Dotted between them are provincial excursions and foreign tours, with the sumo personnel loaded onto special trains, coaches and planes, and stopping off around Japan and overseas. These tours, during which the entire sumo circus stays at inns, hotels or in private homes, are known as *jungyo*. They vary in length, include unofficial basho on the itinerary, and involve the lower-rankers in a lot of extra work, frantically setting up temporary dressing rooms and lugging gear from trucks. It's not uncommon, on one of the special sumo tour trains, to find juniors comatose on the floor, having had to sacrifice their seats to make more room for large sekitori bottoms, and exhausted from their day-long labours.

Jungyo are organized by the Japan Sumo Association (which works under the auspices of the Ministry of Education) and the Sumo Kyokai does not expect to make any money out of them. They are intended to build grass-roots support and show off Japan's national sport in outlying districts. Foreign goodwill tours began with the famous US excursion by Hitachiyama and fellow-sumotori in 1907–8, which went on into Europe. The great Taiho headed a tour to Russia in 1965, and China was visited in 1973 to celebrate the normalization of relations between China and Japan. Europe enjoyed another visit in 1986, during which Chiyonofuji performed his dohyo-iri in Paris City Hall, and the whole charabanc is coming to Britain as part of the Japan Festival in 1991 for a tour which will take in the Royal Albert Hall in October (details of this *Koen* from the Festival organizers on 071 603 5148).

Salaries

There have been several strikes by sumo wrestlers, some of them very dramatic and most of them having to do with pay and conditions. As professional sportsmen sumotori put up with an awful lot, accepting disciplines and conditions that Western athletes would laugh at. But because their financial standing has been precarious they have sometimes felt obliged to speak out. In 1932, half the top division cut off their topknots, resigned from the Association, and set up a rival sumo body to look after their interests. Since 1957 the sekitori (First and Second Divisions) have received a regular monthly salary plus other benefits. But the system is extremely complicated and even some of the wrestlers themselves aren't sure what they are supposed to be getting at any one time. And whilst Chiyonofuji may be a millionaire (salting away more than 800 million yen as a yokozuna), those at the other end of the ladder are very much living from hand to mouth. Overall, for all the golden grandeur of their martial art, sumo wrestlers aren't nearly as well off as their equivalent stars in Western sports. They rely heavily on patronage rather than hardboiled wheeler-dealing agents for their living, and they suffer accordingly. On the other hand, who would want them to change into modern mercenaries?

Sumo wrestlers refer to their money as *okome*, which means 'rice', rather in the same way that Westerners refer to 'bread'. Their pay is made up of a monthly salary (sekitori only), a monthly allowance (sekitori again), a tournament allowance, a travelling allowance, bonuses on wins (called *hoshokin*), banzuke promotion fees (for high-rankers), tsuna stipends (for yokozuna only), cash prize money, sponsors' prizes, retirement benefit (sekitori only), severance pay (according to rank) and finally – and crucially – money from patrons and support groups or *koenkai*. For the big names, they may add up to a sizeable sum since their patrons include prominent business-men and politicians. For the low-rankers though, there isn't such lucrative adulation, and to meet their big expenses many have to rely on their home-town supporters, to whom they are local heroes.

Sekitori, the 'haves' of sumo, get a monthly income ranging from about Y488,000 in Juryo to over Y1,087,000 for a yokozuna. The tournament allowance is on a sliding scale according to rank: a Makushita man could expect about £400 from this source; a lower-ranker much less. Prize money is rather complicated, and depends on the sponsorship of individual bouts, with companies'

banners paraded round the dohyo by yobidashi to show that they are involved in the cash pool. Cash prizes like this are called *ken-sho*. An individual bout might command as little as £80; a tourna-ment prize around £10,000 or upwards. Yusho prizes are augmented by sponsors' gifts, some of them worth a good deal more than the prize money. Firms involved include PanAm, Coca Cola and Toyota, and their names are listed in a special catalogue presented to the winner. There are all kinds of assorted trophies and special awards. For lower-rankers upsetting yokozuna and ozeki there is the Shukun-sho for Outstanding Performance, and this carries a one million yen prize-tag. Similar awards for Fighting Spirit (Kanto-sho) and for Technical Skill (Gino-sho) carry the same amount, though these special awards are not always presented.

The bonus system is perhaps the most curious and complicated method of payment anywhere in sport, but it is painstakingly fair and acts as a major incentive to winning. When a wrestler appears for the first time on the banzuke, his name is credited with the princely sum of three yen. He doesn't actually see this money, but he can look forward to it if and when he reaches Juryo, the Second Division. Each time the youngster produces a winning record, his 'credits' increase, until at last, when he breaks into Juryo, they are suddenly backdated, and multiplied by 1,500 as well, and all of this money now material-izes. The better a fighter gets, the more his aggregate improves. Winning a Kinboshi or Gold Star for giant-killing a yokozuna, or better still, winning a yusho, causes the amount to go up pleasingly by leaps and bounds, until at the end of a really successful career, the bonus money after every basho is very handsome indeed. The great Taiho in the 1960s was receiving nearly 1½ million yen in bonuses alone.

At the other end of the scale, those who fail to win their majorities find they fare rather miserably on bonuses and in every other sphere as well. Failing to make sekitori, they miss out on most of the special payments and allowances, and when they retire, crestfallen, to try their hand at some-thing else, their severance pay is derisory. The secret, in sumo, is to succeed.

Every aspect of the sport is controlled by the Japan Sumo Association, and what happens to a wrestler when he retires depends very largely on

Retirement poses no threat to Takamisugi: he has a second career already.

whether he has been able to afford to buy stock in this organization. The stock, or *toshiyori kabu*, comprises 107 shares, two of them non-transferable and belonging to Taiho Oyakata and Kitanoumi Oyakata, and each of the remaining 105 carrying hereditary names which are adopted by the purchaser (who will have had at least three names already during his sumo career).

To qualify as a *toshi yori* or elder able to buy one of the shares, a retiring wrestler must have fought at least one tournament in Makunouchi, or 20 consecutively in Juryo, and be able to afford the going rate of around half a million pounds. It is possible to rent a share, pending the retirement of its present owner (elders must retire at 65). The money is paid over to the outgoing elder or his heirs. A stockholder is entitled to run his own stable, at least in theory. In practice, there are only

39 such heya, and proliferation has been discouraged, as well as being mind-bogglingly expensive. What usually happens is that a new stockholder will take up a post training in someone else's heya, though there is no guarantee that he will not one day leave, set up his own stable, and take some of his favourite wrestlers with him. All elders, whether stable masters or not, are entitled to be addressed as 'Oyakata'. They are sumo VIPs.

Wrestlers who have not been successful enough, or adored by sufficient patrons, to have salted away toshiyori kabu-type savings can look forward to a slimmer time altogether (and most do indeed shed a few stones when their fighting days are over). One thing stable life prepares a fellow for, apart from grappling, is cooking, and most sumotori know more about the culinary arts and buying fresh vegetables than the average housewife. When they retire, many gravitate towards the catering industry, and quite a few open or work in restaurants specializing in chanko, or sumo hotpot. Others trade on their lovely tenor and baritone voices and their popularity with the ladies and become successful recording stars. Konishiki, Kotogaume, Asahifuji and Takamisugi all have excellent prospects at this, should they choose to leave sumo behind them and follow in the footsteps of former Yokozuna Kitanofuji, alias Kokonoe Oyakata, who made a few chartbusters in his day before becoming a Grand Champion. The Sumo Association has cracked down on wrestlers' recording contracts during their fighting careers, but there is nothing to stop them warbling when they retire.

One of the other possibilities one might suggest is politics. Chiyonofuji recently became the first sumo wrestler ever to be honoured with the People's Award, for earning 'the respect and affection of the nation's people' and for 'giving society hope'. One of the dignitaries keen to present this award to Chiyo was Prime Minister Toshiki Kaifu, and to judge by recent upheavals in Japanese politics, The Wolf might make a better fist of the top job than some recent incumbents.

The danpatsu-shiki

Sumo wrestlers are generally, throughout their careers, models of self-control and courtesy. On or off the dohyo they behave with dignity and decorum, never showing off, never losing their temper, never drunk or disorderly, never giving vent to their emotions about winning or losing, even though their whole lives depend on their results. But when it comes to saying goodbye to sumo, and going through this heartbreaking farewell in public, even these extremely self-possessed gentlemen give way to their feelings and cry openly, mopping their eyes with big hankies.

All retiring wrestlers have to endure the sad ceremony known as *danpatsu-shiki*, the ritual of haircutting. For those who never made the exalted ranks of the sekitori, the ceremony is usually rather private, with only their stable-mates and friends and their own fans present for the occasion. But successful men of the top two divisions can expect their distressing goodbye to sumo to be very public indeed, because it takes place on the dohyo in front of 12,000 people at the Kokugikan and will be recorded for posterity by the camera banks as well.

During the week after a Tokyo tournament, the retiring star is presented to various dignitaries throughout the day, and then ushered to a chair on the ring beneath the television lights. Beside him in full ceremonial finery is a gyoji with a pair of long brass scissors on a tray, and now begins a seemingly endless procession of people he has known – rather like 'This is Your Life' only more prolonged – all of whom file up one by one on to the dohyo and snip a small lock of his hair (for which privilege they have paid into a benefit kitty for their hero). For some prominent sumotori, like Ozeki Asashio who retired in September 1989, there may be as many as 400 people solemnly stepping up to cut a few strands, and the big man is invariably reduced to tears.

The last cut, which removes the topknot altogether, is made by the wrestler's own stable-master, who holds the black object aloft to tremendous cheers. The shorn star then goes off to the dressing room to be professionally barbered, while his fellow-wrestlers raise money for him, performing far-from-serious exhibition bouts and party turns. The climax comes when the retiring hero, smartly turned out in Western suit and tie, returns to thank all his friends and supporters, and ask for their indulgence in his new life. Partying goes on till all hours, but nothing can alter the fact that this is a very sad occasion, and that in the middle of all the merrymaking is a man who has lost the thing he loves. A topknot, symbolic of the sumo calling, is always lovingly stored in a case, either at home or at the stable, and few ex-sumotori can look at this memento without feeling a little twinge inside.

ZEN IN THE ART OF MACHISMO MAINTENANCE

As you may have noticed, there is more to sumo than meets the eye. Much of its unseen side has to do with Shinto, Japan's ancient religion which celebrates life and extols purification. In every stable there is a small Shinto shrine, complete with shimenawa or sacred white rope, and both oyakata and rikishi bow to it dutifully. But sumo partakes of a force as well as a faith, and if the faith is certainly Shinto, the force is probably Zen.

Sumo is a martial art, arguably the oldest of all martial arts. Its exponents are Samurai; specifically they are 'strong Samurai' or rikishi. When sumo was adopted by the warrior class in the twelfth century, it went through a process of change. The Shogunate elevated sumo from the popular entertainment that it had become, and from the divination ritual that it had always been, and turned it into a spiritual contest or *shiai*. Warrior wrestlers who belonged to a warlord's household were permitted to carry two swords (a yokozuna's Samurai sword is still part of his dohyo-iri). The methods used by such 'strong Samurai' were rather different from the bloodless and courteous grappling we see today. They took part in lethal hand-to-hand combat, and if either their strength or their spirit failed them, they died. A huge strong man cut down by the sword is just as dead as a deceased fellow of five foot two who couldn't knock the skin off his rice pudding.

There are records of rikishi going into battle with weapons, including oak logs and tree trunks.

Their techniques included pinning holds prior to administering the *coup de grâce*, and many were undoubtedly killed executing these manoeuvres. In the thick of such fighting they were entering a world where even Shinto could not help them, since Shinto does not concern itself with death and considers death an impure state. What fortified the Samurai in this emergency was Zen, and the warriors steeped themselves in a Zen way of life which came to be known as bushido, 'the way of the warlord's knight.' 'Zen' derived originally from the sanskrit word *dhyana*, or 'meditation', but it is not a religion as we understand the term, and has no rigid articles of faith. The warriors embraced it because it taught them how to face ultimate reality, and death, without turning a hair.

The Samurai sword which is borne into the ring by the yokozuna's *tachi mochi* is a sacred symbol in Japanese thought. The sword cuts between life and death and decides a man's fate in an instant. It is believed to bear a soul, and to transmit vital energy, and no Japanese treats it with disrespect. Every day, every rikishi is reminded of this sacred symbol as he practises at the stable, because in the oyakata's hand is the *shinai*, made of four polished bamboo blades bound together with thongs. The shinai is no mere stick for administering punishment. In *kendo* ('the way of the sword') it is used for fighting. It bears the spirit of the sword, and always symbolizes the dividing line

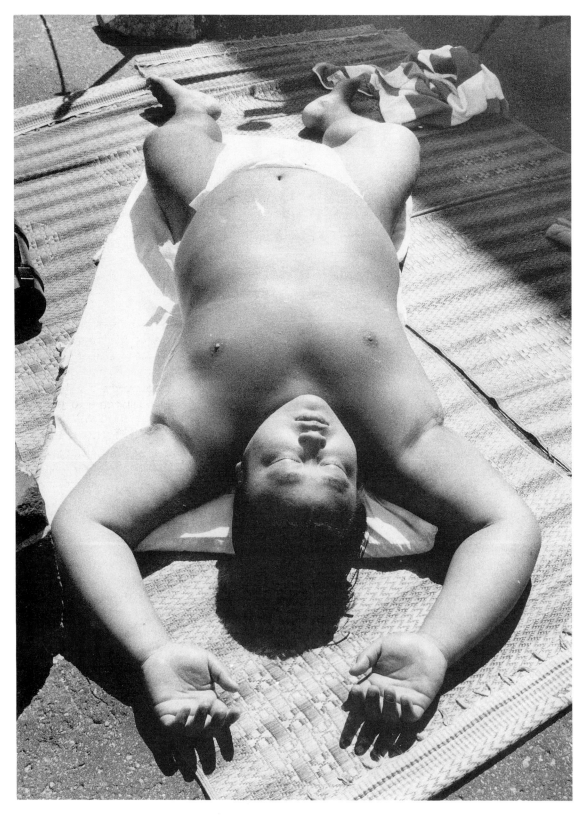

Mastering the unseen – an exhausting business.

between life and death.

Sumo practice, or *keiko*, is not simply training for strength, or mastery of technique. Of course these are important: a man may lift weights, and improve his techniques, and become quite brilliant at them, and beat many opponents. But without training for his spirit and his heart, he will simply grow big, win bouts, and then go the way of all flesh. He will never become a great champion, because without a strong spirit he will beat himself, and he will fail at his personal barriers. He will succumb to fear and tension, and not be able to make use of all the strength and techniques that he has learned. He will simply be another sportsman, like Western sportsmen: one who gets nervous, and unaccountably 'chokes' when he is faced with his ultimate challenge. Keiko (from *kei*, 'go beyond', and *ko*, 'forebears') is designed to strengthen his spirit by teaching him to extend himself. As Chiyonofuji explained to Channel 4 viewers, 'The essence is to use more than your full strength in the dohyo… In practice you must concentrate on the mental aspects too' (pointing with his fingers at his middle). Chiyo says that some people practise but can't reproduce it on the dohyo, 'which makes you wonder what they're practising for'.

Keiko includes arduous and extremely painful exercises, repeated *ad nauseam*, to push each apprentice beyond what he thinks he can do. In breaking through his physical limits, he learns that there is more to fighting than strength or size. When a man sees a snake on the floor, he may jump onto a table without knowing how he got there. A woman who finds her child trapped under a car may summon the strength to lift the bumper and get him out. A lunatic may have 'the strength of ten men'. Inner resources remain hidden until something occurs to bring them out, and keiko is designed to bring them out. The very hardship of a rikishi's stable life is part of this process. When a person is totally exhausted, he learns to deliver a blow to save his life. This state is called *kirikaeshi*, which is also the name of a sumo technique and a kendo basic training method.

The three elements of a sumotori's training are jointly expressed as *shin-gi-tai*. The first, and by far the most important, is *shin* or *kokoro*, which sums up what Westerners mean by 'heart', 'character', 'spirit' or 'soul'. Shin refers to the heavenly or spiritual realm. The second element is *gi*, which means craft or technique. Gi refers to the earthly or worldly realm. The third quality is *tai*, which means body. Tai refers to man himself, and the human realm. A wrestler must train for all three – for spirit, for skill and for physical strength. Modern-minded sumotori are apt to get a bit carried away with the importance of the second two. Increasingly, they are interested in perfecting their physical skills, and building their muscles by weight-training. It is possible to get by in sumo by learning it in terms of holds and throws, and this is called *sumo-jutsu*. But when the more traditional rikishi get together to talk about their work, they use the word *sumo-do*, adding the Chinese suffix for 'way' or 'path'. This is a reference to the precepts of the unseen. They are saying, sumo is a way of life (like bushido, judo, and kendo), and not just a sport.

As the very foundation of a great yokozuna, shin has been emphasized in Channel 4 interviews by wrestlers and elders alike. Sadogatake Oyakata says that technique and physique can be developed naturally by a fighter, but that 'If he can't think properly, he will come to nothing'. Oshima Oyakata agrees: 'Even if you're strong, you must have the right spirit,' and Kokonoe Oyakata attributes Chiyonofuji's success to his having 'four times the spirit' of other wrestlers, despite his small physique. Chiyo himself, asked if shin was the most important element, agreed: 'Yes, it is the spirit', he said, and added it was vital not just in sumo, but 'in everything I suppose'. His stable boss believes that he himself was not a great yokozuna because though he had physique and technique, he was deficient in shin, or spirit.

The sumotori must educate himself to deal with the invisible: the space between himself and his opponent, the rhythm of the fight, the blow or hold designed to destroy him as it enters the mind of his attacker. This, we may assume, is why, at the end of every keiko session, the rikishi squat on their haunches with their eyes closed. They are familiarizing themselves with the dimension of the unseen. The shikiri itself, according to some sources, evolved from the time when sumo was practised as a Zen warrior skill. Likewise the bow ceremony. Likewise the use of the gyoji's gumbai, the war fan, to signal the release of the fighters at the tachi-ai.

Anyone who underestimates this side of sumo

is presumably apt to see it as another brutal clash between strong men, like boxing or American football. It would be a great pity if Westerners were to view sumo like this, and even more of a pity if young Western-influenced rikishi forgot the tradition they have inherited, and began to think of sumo as a quest for physical force. Arguably the greatest sumotori who ever lived, Futabayama, came as a shock to those who had never seen him, and who expected him to be built like the side of a house. Wakanohana, being introduced, was pole-axed, and could not believe his eyes. Futabayama, he said, was not much bigger than the average man. Wakanohana knew from that moment that sumo was not about body, but about spirit.

In the days when masterless Samurai or *ronin* travelled from place to place seeking challengers, their survival, as well as their livelihood, depended on their completeness as martial artists. They were a little like gun-slingers, wandering round Japan in search of the faster draw, the ultimate opponent. In a way, the rivals themselves were irrelevant; a means to an end. The Samurai needed to expose himself to danger in order to encounter his inner powers, and the greater the challenge, and the stiller his mind, the greater was this encounter. It was a spiritual quest, with ultimate reality at stake. Facing a potentially deadly situation with a quiet mind, the Samurai found himself truly free, truly unstoppable. With long and arduous mental and physical training, he found that he could go beyond the normally recognized human limits. He could excel his own personal strength and speed, and no man could stand against him by mere strength and speed either.

What happens on the dohyo today may not appear to Western eyes very dangerous. Indeed, sumo wrestlers often look and fall like huge babies, and hardly appear to hurt themselves. But that is because Westerners see only the physical battle, and not the spiritual war. We can spot that a wrestler wins by this or that technique, but we do not understand that the outcome may already have been decided; that it is merely a recapitulation of an earlier fight, when the wrestlers looked into each other's minds in the shikiri naoshi, or paused in one energized breath before the tachiai. We may note that the referee has signalled the start of the bout with a war fan and think this

rather quaint, but then our minds are apt to stray towards a particular hold on the belt, or who is larger than whom. And we miss the point of the spectacle altogether. But if we cannot 'read' sumo as a Japanese audience can, we can at least try to show proper respect for the realm of the unseen. The following are a few provocative ideas on this spiritual side of sumo. Despite extensive literature on Zen in the art of everything from archery to motor-cycle maintenance, not much has been written about this aspect of this particular martial art, at least not in the West. Yet sumo is, of all martial arts, surely the most steeped in ancient mysteries and shin, so here are some suggestions on what we might call 'Zen in the Art of Machismo Maintenance'!

The dohyo

Nothing to do with boxing rings, the dohyo is a spiritual battleground, and comes as close to symbolizing this as can be arranged. The four pillars which once stood in place of today's four great hanging tassels were based on the *I Ching*, the Book of Changes. The circle is intended to mean the *t'ai chi*, the Realm of the Absolute. The entrances from the *hanamichi* represent *yin* and *yang*, negative and positive, passive and active, feminine and masculine. The four great tassels, and the four pillars they replaced, represent the four seasons. The clay of the dohyo represents the earth. Together with the four tassels or pillars, it invokes the five elements and the five virtues of Confucianism. The dohyo was once surrounded by large rice bales, intended to signify the five grains of life (rice, barley, millet, beans and wheat), and so on. Every care has been taken to ensure that the dohyo is preserved as a sacred place, a symbolic arena which must never be defiled. Seen from above, it is said to resemble a Buddhist meditative symbol depicting the universe.

The code of the unseen

Sumo is a martial art, and, in so far as it resembles other martial arts, it belongs to the warrior code, bushido. According to this code, the opponent, and beating the opponent, are only a means to an end. The real goal is to encounter reality by putting one's self at risk and confronting the void.

During the shikiri naoshi, the fighters look into each other's hearts. The eye is the window of the soul, and rikishi practise eye contact as they practise other skills. To see an opponent properly is to sense what he will do.

Before the fighters are released by the gyoji, they must reach the point of greatest energy yet remain at the point of greatest stillness. When their breathing and their looks are synchronized, they can be let go like a bowstring, and will meet at the precise midpoint of the space between them. This is the tachi-ai, meaning to rise and meet.

The fighter at the tachi-ai must, if he is like the Samurai warrior, leave behind all that he has learned, all that he knows, and all that he thinks or believes, all that he wishes or desires or wants, and enter the void. Mitoizumi: 'If you think too much, your tachi-ai becomes awkward and your wrestling suffers'. Hokutenyu: 'If I kept thinking of my opponent's next move, I wouldn't be able to wrestle'. Akinoshima: 'After the tachi-ai, I think of nothing at all'.

The interval between any two combatants, according to Japanese thought, is called *ma* (time and space). Ma is a force field, and he who enters this field has already entered the battle. *Ma-ai* is the strategy of this battle.

The Samurai's mind must be pure and serene. He must face any attack from whatever quarter with implacable serenity (*zanshin*) and an empty heart (*mushin*). He must not 'mind' victory or defeat, or think about anything at all. If he thinks, he will be beaten.

The force of the universe, *ki*, resides in the centre of all things. The centre of a martial artist is his belly, *hara*. The conduit through which the force flows is the *tanden*, two centimetres below his navel. This is not the same thing as the centre of gravity, but a source of vital energy – traditionally the 'field of cinnabar' is said to resonate from here. Before you laugh, consider the Western meaning of the word 'gut' (as in gut-reaction) and 'guts' (as in courage).

Learning to tap the universal force requires exercise and meditation. Ki also means 'breath', and one of the exercises a martial artist learns is in controlled, calm breathing. Breathing in this special way, from the centre of the abdomen, 'inspires' a fighter with ki. When students are practising this exercise, they experience a pleasant warmth and tingling which tells them that they are doing it correctly.

Any martial artist must practise holding his mind empty and still. When the mind is absolutely still, a fighter will find that ki springs out and defends him in whatever way is necessary. The still mind can sense an attack, and movements invisible to the naked eye. This power to sense an attack in repose is called *genshin*.

The perfect manoeuvre is the one which is made by ki, without any conscious decision to attempt it. This is not the same thing as an 'instinctive' move, for instincts are not ki. The instinct for self-preservation is a form of fear, and must be overcome.

A martial artist cannot consciously command or control ki. The moment he turns his mind on it, it disappears. He cannot take credit for the moves it executes, or the bouts it wins. This would be like a concert pianist, having performed in the grip of great music, saying, 'My word, I played that well!' Ki, like inspiration, comes to those who have given up such vanity. It is nothing to get excited about, but a natural event.

Though a fighter cannot control ki, he can focus himself so as to make a perfect channel for it. In doing so, he may even deliver ki in a particular direction. The fighter who can bring ki to bear like this is said to have *kokyu* – he is spiritually focused. *Kokyu nage* is throwing an opponent by channelling ki.

The martial artist must be focused, but he must not fix his mind on any point, idea or object. If he does, he becomes its prisoner, and a fighter must be free.

A martial artist must give up worrying about himself. *Muga-mushin* means obliterating the self from the mind. How a sumo wrestler looks, feels or fares in front of the television cameras is of no consequence. He must fight to encounter reality. If he commits himself to this fight, he will probably become a great sumo star with big fan clubs. If on the other hand he fights to become a great sumo star, he may well chop chanko veg. for the rest of his career.

Any spiritual fighter must not be concerned about hurting himself, or saving himself from injury. If he is, this will cause tension, and tension serves no purpose. If anything, it will make him vulnerable to injury.

The fighter must commit himself totally to the fight. He must not hold back or check the power flowing through him, even if it puts him in danger. *Sutemi* is the art of sacrifice. It refers to the Samurai's self-abandonment at the moment of attack.

A fighter who reduces sumo to *sumo-jutsu* — blows and holds — reduces it to a sport like other sports. In time, Westerners will emerge who are better at blows and holds than he is.

Finally, in a winning score or *kachi-koshi*, the magic figure of 8 stands for 'circle' in Shinto tradition. In attaining the circle, a fighter attains his goal, even though the circle may having nothing in it.

The goal is always ultimately the void, from which 'nothing' all things flow.

SUMO GLOSSARY

abise-taoshi the chest lunge
banzuke ranking list
basho tournament
beya stable
butsukari-geiko pushing practice
chanko wrestlers' hotpot
chonmage informal topknot hairdo
danpatsu-shiki topknot removal ceremony
deshi apprentice
dohyo clay ring
dohyo-iri ring-entering ceremony
enka traditional Japanese singing
gaijin foreigner
gingko leaf leaf of sacred tree
Gino-sho prize for Technical Skill
gyoji referee
hakama divided skirt
hansoku foul
haori Japanese overcoat
hataki-komi the dodge and slap-down
heya stable (same as beya)
hidari-yotsu mutual double hold position with left hand inside on the belt
hiki-otoshi the front pull-down
hikkake the arm grab pull-down
ichimon family of stables
Jonidan Fifth Division
Jonokuchi Sixth Division
jungyo tour
Juryo Second Division
kachi-koshi winning majority (8–7 or better)
kadoban liable for demotion
kanroku dignity
Kanto-sho Fighting Spirit prize
katasu kashi the arm-lock force down
keiko (or -geiko) training
kesho-mawashi ceremonial apron
keta-guri the trip and pull
kimarite techniques
Kinboshi Gold 'yokozuna-beating' Star
kokoro spirit, mind, heart
komusubi Junior Champion, 2nd grade
kote-nage the forearm throw
kubi-nage the neck throw
kyokai association
maegashira top division senior

make-koshi majority of losses over wins (7–8 or worse)
Makunouchi First Division
Maku-uchi First Division
Makushita Third Division
matawari sumo splits
matta false start
mawashi fighting belt
migi-yotsu mutual double hold with right hand inside on the belt
moro-zashi both hands inside on the belt
moshiai-geiko knock-out sparring
nodowa (-zeme) throat thrust
o-icho-mage ceremonial hairdo
okuri-dashi the push-out from behind
okuri-taoshi the push out and down from behind
oshi pushing
oshi-dashi the push-out
oshi-taoshi the push-down
oshi-zumo pushing techniques
oyakata elder (title of stable boss)
ozeki 2nd-highest rank or 'Great Barrier'
rensho bout-winning streak
rikishi wrestler, 'Strong Samurai'
sagari fringe of tassels
sanban-geiko training with one opponent
Sandanme Fourth Division
sanyaku collective term for top 3 ranks below Grand Champion
sekitori wrestler in either First or Second Division
sekiwake Junior Champion proper
senshuraku last day of tournament
shikiri naoshi pre-fight staring and squatting preliminaries
shiko 'strong leg' stamp
shikona fighting name
shimpan judge
shin heart, spirit
shitate dashi nage pulling inner arm throw
shitate-nage the inner arm throw
Shukun-sho Outstanding Performance prize
soto-gake the outer leg trip
sukui nage the scoop throw
Sumo Kyokai Sumo Association
sumotori wrestler
tachi-ai the jump-off

Tennoshihai Emperor's Cup
teppo pole pole in training area used for slapping and pushing exercises
tsukebito personal servant
tsuki thrusting
tsuki-dashi the thrust-out
tsuki-otoshi the side twist-down
tsuki-taoshi the thrust-down
tsuna Grand Champion's ceremonial rope belt
tsuppari slapping attack
tsuri-dashi the lift-out
tsuri-otoshi the lift and wrench down
uchi-gake the inner leg trip

utchari the backward pivot throw
uwate dashi nage the pulling outer arm throw
uwate-nage the outer arm throw
yobidashi announcer
yokozuna Grand Champion
yori-kiri the force-out
yori taoshi the force out and down
yotsu-zumo belt sumo
yumitori-shiki bow ceremony
yusho tournament win
zensho-yusho perfect-scoring tournament win (15–0)

FURTHER READING

Japan, Strategy of the Unseen, Michel Random, Crucible, 1987

Rikishi, The Men of Sumo, Joel Sackett and Wes Benson, Weatherhill, New York and Tokyo, 1986

Sumo, Andy Adams and Clyde Newton, Hamlyn Publishing Group, 1989

Sumo, Lyall Watson, a Channel 4 Book, Sidgwick and Jackson, 1988

Sumo, From Rite to Sport, P.L. Cuyler, Weatherhill, New York and Tokyo, 1979

Sumo, The Sport and the Tradition, J.A. Sargeant, Charles E. Tuttle Co, USA and Japan, 1959

Sumo World (magazine) published by Andy Adams (*see* Introduction)

Takamiyama, The World of Sumo, Jesse Kuhaulua, Kodansha International, USA (Hawaii) and Japan, 1973

PICTURE CREDITS

Black and white

Colorific: 83. Colorsport: 103, 126. Frank Spooner Pictures: 128. *Great Sumo Wrestling**: 26, 80, 98, 99, 102, 112, 115, 117, 118, 142, 149, 152. K.K. Kyodo News Service, Tokyo: 16, 21, 46, 52, 58, 70, 75, 88, 93, 100, 107, 124. Keyphotos, Tokyo: 12-13, 36, 66, 105, 108, 110, 114, 120, 122, 129.

The prints on pages 23 and 134 are reproduced by kind permission of Malcolm Dennes.

Colour section

Allsport: 3, 6, 7, 9, 14. *Great Sumo Wrestling**: 1, 4, 5, 8, 10, 11. Impact Photos: 2. Keyphotos, Tokyo: 12, 13.

*Published monthly by Yomiuri Shimbun, Tokyo.